IMPERIAL LEGACIES

*The British Empire
Around the World*

Jeremy Black

New York • London

First American edition published in 2019 by Encounter Books, an activity of Encounter for Culture and Education, Inc., a nonprofit, tax exempt corporation. Encounter Books website address: www.encounterbooks.com

Manufactured in the United States and printed on acid-free paper. The paper used in this publication meets the minimum requirements of ANSI/NISO Z39.48–1992 (R 1997) (*Permanence of Paper*).

FIRST AMERICAN EDITION

LIBRARY OF CONGRESS CATALOGING-IN-PUBLICATION DATA
Names: Black, Jeremy, 1955– author.
Title: Imperial legacies : the British Empire around the world / By Jeremy Black.
Description: New York : Encounter Books, [2019] | Includes bibliographical references and index.
Identifiers: LCCN 2018043853 (print) | LCCN 2018044783 (ebook) | ISBN 9781641770392 (ebook) | ISBN 9781641770385 (hardcover : alk. paper)
Subjects: LCSH: Great Britain—Colonies—History. | United States—Foreign relations. | Liberty.
Classification: LCC DA16 (ebook) | LCC DA16 .B587 2019 (print) | DDC 909/.0971241–dc23
LC record available at https://lccn.loc.gov/2018043853

For
Stephanie Speakman

CONTENTS

PREFACE

The United States can see its present and future reflected through the mirror of the treatment of the British Empire. This is Britain, but also the United States in its "culture wars"; "culture wars" that can be seen more clearly in the mirror of Britain. Much of the hysteria that greets the word "imperialism" relates to the United States, even if the ostensible target is Britain.

Mealtimes, "institutional racism," and "historical amnesia of British colonialism" were all there in London on January 27, 2018, when a group of fourteen led by SOAS (School of African and Oriental Studies) students protested in the Blighty UK Café in Finsbury Park, chanting, "we have nothing to lose but our chains." They demanded that Chris Evans, the owner, "apologise to the local community" for commemorating Winston Churchill instead of presenting him as a racist who perpetuated the injustices of the empire. The café offers a breakfast entitled the Winston and features décor depicting model Spitfires and a mock-up of an air raid shelter. A change of décor and menu was demanded. The SOAS Students' Union, in a statement, declared that the café "exercises a concerted historical amnesia of British colonialism, which is offensive to those who continue to experience institutional racism." Earlier, a large mural of Churchill had been repeatedly defaced.

The phlegmatic Evans remarked, "If you cannot celebrate Britain and great Britons you are just erasing history and if you cannot celebrate Churchill, you cannot celebrate anyone."[1] This was especially so, given that in 2002, Churchill was voted as the "Greatest Briton" in a large-scale BBC poll. Subsequently, in March 2018, some of those involved took part in a violent blockade of the main SOAS building, their statement protesting at "the white-supremacist hetero-patriarchal capitalist order" of university life.

Meanwhile, in February 2018, the controversy was over Birmingham Museum and Art Gallery's exhibition "The Past is Now," in which information boards claimed that "the relationship between European colonialism, industrial production and capitalism is unique in its brutality." The key Birmingham politician of the Victorian period, Joseph Chamberlain, an exponent of a stronger British Empire who became secretary of state for the Colonies (1895–1903), was described as "still revered despite his aggressive and racist imperial policy." One board attacked Britain's "hasty" departure from India in 1947 for "trauma and misogyny," and a second board offers another partisan context: "Capitalism is a system that prioritises the interests of the individuals and their companies at the expense of the majority." Janine Eason, the director of engagement, said that it was "not possible" for a museum to present a "neutral voice, particularly for something as multifaceted as stories relating to the British Empire," and, instead, that the exhibition was both a way to serve the multicultural population of Birmingham and was intended "to provoke." Of course, real provocation would have been to offer a different account, one that was more grounded in historical awareness, or, even more, two or more accounts.

Each month, another controversy emerged. In July 2018, the portrait of Edward Colston, an eighteenth-century slave trader and philanthropist, that has long hung in the office of the lord mayor of Bristol, was removed on the instructions of Cleo Lake, the current mayor, a Green counselor, and member of the group Countering Colston, who stated that she "simply couldn't stand" being in the same room. Lake added, "Many of the issues today such as Afriphobia, racism and inequality stem from this episode of history where people of African descent were dehumanised to justify enslaving them." This is a somewhat problematic view that does not really address the more widespread prevalence of coerced labor, including slavery, not at least within Africa. In a remark with which, Americans well-up on "statue wars" will be familiar, she remarked, "Having it on the parlour wall, in my view, sent mixed messages about the city council's values today."

The same month, Satyapal Singh, the Indian minister for higher education, denounced evolution as the legacy of British colonial rule in the shape of an education system reinforcing an imperialist mentality.

Instead, he announced that he would offer a new Hindu theory on the origin of species.

It is difficult to see imperial amnesia in the contention of recent years over the history of the British Empire. Indeed, empire is an aspect of the culture wars: sometimes ridiculous, sometimes bitter, and sometimes both, in Britain and elsewhere, of recent years. It is also an aspect of the problematic nature to many commentators, across the world, of national history and national identity. This is not some obscure issue, but, rather, one that is crucial to the nature of public history and, as such, indicative of a highly significant attitude of these sometimes-ridiculous culture wars. The issue is relevant in Britain, its former empire, and elsewhere. As both a former colony and the successor to this position, the United States is a major part of the equation, mostly because critics frequently decry the United States for allegedly taking part in what are termed "imperialist wars."

The British Empire was not only for long the largest in the world, but also is not lost in the mists of time, so its reputation is most contentious. Indeed, both empire and reputation play a key role in the foundation account of many states, as well as in the subsequent history of a large number. This book considers this imperial legacy from the British perspective, and from those elsewhere. The topic is scarcely one that is free from contention.[2] Indeed part of the 2017–18 controversy over freedom of expression in universities—in other words, the freedom to think outside the authorized box, particularly in Britain but also elsewhere, including in the United States, related to the treatment of imperialism.

I do not imagine that all will treat my thesis sympathetically; indeed, I am certain it will not be treated as such. It is always difficult to get the balance, for example, in criticizing British imperial violence while also drawing attention to the unethical violence of pre- and postcolonial governments and societies. Indians call this approach "whataboutery," and it can be problematic if it lessens the shock felt. Indeed, ethical citizens and scholars should criticize, and support the criticism of, injustice; but everywhere. That, of course, does not mean restricting their criticism to Britain and the United States, nor to their imperialism.

I hope that those who disagree with my assessment will benefit from having read an alternative account to that of those who support their views. This book is not the first I have written on the British Empire, but there has been rethinking on my part, notably with reference to the controversies of the present. As I cannot expect that previous works will have been read, some arguments have been refreshed.

In preparing this work, I profited from opportunities to visit Antigua, Australia, Barbados, Belize, Brunei, the Cayman Isles, Canada, Fiji, Gibraltar, Hong Kong, India, Ireland, Jamaica, Malaysia, Malta, New Zealand, St. Lucia, Singapore, Sri Lanka, Tonga, and the United States in recent years. An invitation from the Japan Institute of International Affairs to speak in Tokyo in 2017 at a conference on how best to present Asian history proved especially helpful, as did another to a McDonald Centre Colloquium in Oxford in 2018 on "A Case for Colonialism?" I have benefited greatly from the comments of Pradeep Barua, Nigel Biggar, Steve Bodger, George Boyce, Nandini Chatterjee, Philip Cunliffe, Jacques Frémeaux, Hao Gao, Bill Gibson, Bruce Gilley, Angus Hawkins, Erik Jensen, Max King, Geoffrey Plank, Duncan Proudfoot, George Robb, William Robinson, Tirthanker Roy, and Keith Windschuttle on an earlier draft. None are responsible for any errors that remain. It is a great pleasure to dedicate this book to Stephanie Speakman, a thoughtful and considerate friend whose company I have long enjoyed, and, in making this dedication, also to honor other East Coast friends.

I

INTRODUCTION

Empire reflects power, its existence, and its use. Each, in itself, is morally neutral, but they all are criticized bitterly in the modern world and employed in order to decry Britain's past and the United States' present. Between 1750 and 1900, Britain became the foremost power in the world, both territorially and economically. An intellectual powerhouse, Britain also became a model political system for much of the world, as the United States would eventually do in the twentieth century. These changes were interrelated. Territorial expansion provided Britain and the United States with raw materials, markets, and employment, and, combined with evangelical Protestantism and national self-confidence, encouraged a sense in Britain and the United States as being at the cutting edge of civilization, with the last presented in Western and Westernizing terms. Indeed, empire was in part supported and defended on the grounds that it provided opportunities for the advance of civilization. This was seen not least by ending what were regarded as uncivilized, as well as unchristian, practices, such as widow burning and ritual banditry in India, and slavery and piracy across the world. In turn, these practices, and their presentation, helped to define British views of civilization. Moreover, as a different, but contributory, point, British exceptionalism was to be the godparent of its American successor, just as the two world systems succeeded one another with some, often much, uneasiness, but also in alliance at crucial points.

The relationship between the reputation of the British Empire and that of American power has become a close one.

To treat these contemporary attitudes to empire (like also the social conditions then, or the treatment of women) as if Britain, and later the United States, could have been abstracted from the age, and should be judged accordingly, is unhelpful and ahistorical. Such a treatment is not a case of historical amnesia, but rather of amnesia about history and the process of change through time; or at least, and the distinction is important, the latter as approached in a scholarly, rather than polemical, fashion. Moreover, within the constraints of the attitudes and technologies of the nineteenth century, Britain was more liberal, culturally, economically, socially, and politically, than the other major European powers, just as the United States was to be in the twentieth century. Britain offered powerful support to the struggles for independence in Latin America and Greece, from Spanish and Turkish rule, respectively. Causes such as Greek independence and, later on, the Italian *Risorgimento* were genuinely popular in the nineteenth century, as was that of support for the Northern (Union), anti-slavery side in the American Civil War (1861–65).

In addition, as will be discussed in chapter 8, the British, although earlier the most active of the slave traders, were instrumental in ending the slave trade and slavery. This was despite the severe economic damage thereby done to the British colonies in the West Indies. Indeed, the Act for the Abolition of the Slave Trade (1807) reflected the strength of the moral strand in British public life. This strand drew greatly on the world of public discussion in Britain that reached into every hamlet, through the press and public collections and meetings. For example, anti-slavery literature was prolific and struck evangelical, providential, and humanitarian notes, as well as those focused on economics, just as opposition to the slave trade had done.[1] Similarly, despite massive disruption in the shape of a destructive, as well as unpredictable, civil war, the U.S. Union states forced through the abolition of slavery in the United States, which hit the Southern economy hard.

The balance and character of moral concerns and engagement in the past may appear flawed through the perspective of hindsight, indeed very flawed (as ours of course also will be), but such concerns and engagement were strong. Furthermore, those who deploy hindsight might be better served directing their energy toward urgent present abuses, which include a continued slave trade and slavery; and both in Britain and elsewhere. A consideration of the past can lend urgency and energy to debate about the present, and valuably so, but applying hindsight is also far easier than correcting present abuses.

Blaming imperial rule, however, served, and to this day serves, a variety of cultural, intellectual, and political strategies at a number of levels. Domestically, aside from the "culture wars" and identity struggles, which, always vibrant, appear to be becoming far more active and potent, it is in part a strategy designed to create a new public identity. This is not least by integrating, or rather, *claiming* to integrate, immigrant communities as an aspect of a rejection of a past that could also be used to stigmatize an alternative present. This is a process that can serve various public (political) purposes, both overt and covert.

At the global level, criticism of empire serves a similar purpose. It is used repeatedly in order to try to ease political relations between one-time imperial powers and colonies, notably by appealing to public opinion in the latter, thus seeking to ground relations in a wider support.

Apologizing at the expense of the past costs little in modern Western culture. Indeed, as a result, it can appear glib, a diversion, and an abdication of any commitment both to lasting values and to serious debate, as well as helpful, or, at least, expedient. Perception of the process is very varied and, to a degree, important in its evaluation. Alongside more positive accounts, it can be an aspect of the "virtue signaling" of conspicuous morality. This signaling is a process that is highly important to individual and political assertion, and notably so given the emphasis on feelings as a way to validate attitudes and to justify policies: "I feel," rather than "I think."

The cult of the victim is also pertinent, and not least to the discussion of empire and imperial legacy. While working on the last section of this book, I relaxed by reading *A Place of Hiding* by Elizabeth George, an American novelist who has written extensively about Britain, where she lives part of the year. A passage that struck me comes from the end: "'I think she found injustice in places where other people simply found life,' Deborah told him. 'And she couldn't manage to get past the thought of that injustice: what had happened.'"[2] This describes the culprit, who essentially stages the murder in order to frame someone else, a classic instance of the over-the-top anger transferring, as well as denying, responsibility that appears all too common in the topic under discussion.

Presentism is an inevitable aspect of historical understanding, be it popular, governmental, or scholarly, for it is the concerns of the present that help explain why topics are undertaken and how they are perceived. And so also for the empire. Presentism explains the focus on the subject, as well as the standard way in which it is treated; the two being closely linked.

In a sense, indeed, the style and tone of attention have been transformed, and from one problematic perspective to another. There was a culture of imperialism in which the fact and process of imperial rule (or rather of Western imperial rule, for, conspicuously, there was generally not Western praise for that by non-Western powers, such as China and the Ottoman Turks) was believed and proclaimed to be valuable. This value, it was argued, was the case both for the imperialists and for those who experienced their attention. Each supposedly benefited from character building, albeit of a very different form. Moreover, the teleology expressed in the language of imperialism fed into the imperialists' belief that it had a normative and necessary character and, as such, took a key role in historical development.

To a considerable extent, the treatment of Ireland (see chapter 4), notably the seizure of land, and the quest for profit, as well as security, helped set the pattern for English imperialism in the seventeenth century, particularly in the West Indies and North America. There was a clear sense, with England (from 1707, Britain) as of other empires, of superiority to lesser societies and of the value, both to England and in world-historical terms, of bringing them under control and, through the plantation system of establishing settlers, of using the land in a more fruitful fashion. Indeed, imperialism was an aspect of "progressive" analyses and narratives, not only of national betterment, but also of those of civilization as a whole. The would-be victors, and especially so when they had won, of course, defined the latter. There was a clear attempt to present Western civilization as not only superior to other civilizations, but also as defining the allegedly de-civilized nature of these civilizations. Thomas Jefferson's view of the necessary and inevitable future for Native Americans, a choice between assimilation as "civilized republicans and good Americans" or being driven into remote fastnesses, reflected similar values.[3]

The extent to which imperialism could be presented and defended as a progressive agenda, however misleadingly, underlines the degree to which justifications for it were not solely offered in terms of national and sectional self-interest. Instead, this agenda was seen as late as the 1950s, with the efforts then by Britain to bring economic growth to colonies and to "prepare" them for independence within the context of the (newish) Commonwealth. Less positively, Soviet totalitarianism, which proved to last longer, was defended on developmental grounds.

Looking to the past, these ideas are generally underrated, if not neglected, today, but they were of significance at the time. Indeed, the effort involved in imperialism was often considerable, not least in thwarting and fighting other imperial powers, both European and non-European. The justification of this effort drew on the specifics of winning this competition, but also on more general alleged benefits for Britain and for those who were ruled. Again, comparing Britain with the United States is instructive: it was believed, and not necessarily without reason, that it would be better if territory was ruled by the Americans, rather than by Spaniards, Mexicans, Britons, or Native Americans.

At the same time, it is incorrect to think of one single type of imperialism, and therefore one sole rationale for it. Indeed, part of the problem with the modern debate over imperialism, and an aspect of the way in which empire can be, indeed frequently is, stereotyped, is that there is frequently just such a simplistic approach to the concept of empire, which is presented, in past or present, as "good" or "bad," "progressive" or "negative," and usually the latter of each, respectively.

In practice, however, imperialism ranged, and still ranges, widely. This point is underlined by an understanding of the extent to which it did not necessarily entail territorial rule. The assumptions, goals, and forms, bound up in concepts such as "informal empire" and "soft power," concepts applied to both Britain and the United States, underline the extent to which there was a gradient of presence involved. This gradient was linked not just to the response in the areas affected but also to very different goals; and it is unhelpful if critiques are read from one to another as if there were few "essential" contrasts between different types of imperialism.

Their empire was presented by British commentators, or at least most of them, until there was a significant shift of perspective in the mid-twentieth century, as the apogee of the historical process. This process was supposedly founded on the ancient civilizations of the Middle East and the Mediterranean, which were described as the "cradles of civilization," and also looking back to the Holy Land, the two overlapping. This linkage implied a powerful theme of continuity, indeed another version of the medieval *translatio imperii* in which the transfer of rule kept the dream and example of Classical Rome alive.

The linkage was also part of a diffusionist model of cultural history, with Classical Rome and modern Britain each shaping their world, and to positive purposes. This was an approach that was to be adopted much later by American commentators in order to describe themselves. In an 1862 essay on colonies published in the *Rambler*, a Catholic monthly, Sir John Acton (1834–1902), then a Liberal MP, later, as Lord Acton, a prominent historian, presented colonialization as a necessary prelude to the spread of Christian civilization: "We may assume (as part of the divine economy which appears in the whole history of religion) that the conquest of the world by the Christian powers is the preliminary step to its conversion." As a child, I was taught history at school in a process that twice began with the Classical world, albeit a world of the Middle East and Europe, starting with ancient Egypt and Mesopotamia, but totally excluding India and China.

In turn, and notably in recent decades, has come a strong hostility to imperialism as a process that supposedly distorted the imperialists and the "imperialized," and, in particular, exposed the latter to the toxicity of imperial rule. Conquest alone was not bad enough. Being imperial subjects was presented as bad, if not worse. The clear-cut rejection of imperial rule that influences the presentation of the past can also lead to a misleading division between "collaborators" and "resisters." This is a division that totally fails to grasp the contingencies, compromises, and nuances of the past, not least the way in which people then understood their position and adapted to it.[4]

Each of these approaches is, to a degree, highly questionable and ahistorical, but is also rooted in its time. The move from one approach to the other raises questions about historical method and the conceptual tools available for discussing the past and our relationship with it. The assumption that it is essentially the past that constructed myths, or, rather, in which myths were constructed, is all too convenient. Instead, just as past views and practices attract valuable critical scrutiny, so the same should be the case for the situation today, as we will, in turn, face what E. P. Thompson, with reason, termed the "enormous condescension of posterity."[5]

Moreover, there are dangers in misrepresenting and misunderstanding past attitudes. In presenting people, both the colonizers and those colonized, the British (and Americans) themselves, as the victims of imperialism, they are robbed of agency and instrumentalized. In addition, when criticizing those who applauded, aided, and accepted imperialism, from the British (and American) working classes to colonial inhabitants, the charge of false consciousness is a concept that is easy, but also too easy, to deploy in this context. This is the case whether assessing the past or the present. The charge offers the reductionism and instrumentalism of those discussed in order to underline the criticism. Doubtless, this also will be the case when the present is considered in the future.

Historians of empire and decolonization, whether in imperial homelands or in former colonies, whether for the British Empire or for all others, and whether or not including the United States, are very much taking part in the process they discuss. The difficulty is not that there are intellectual, literary, and professional strategies propagating partisan, somewhat narrow, often ideological, and frequently angry views, for that is always the case with politics, and frequently is the case with history, notably with national history, public history, and the history of memory. The difficulty, instead, is that many, maybe most, writers do not accept that that is what they are doing.

Moreover, as a related but different point, writers can and will tend to argue by the assertion of their views, and by the omission or misrepresentation of those of others. Writing in a political and/or theoretical mindset, or "bubble," as most do, can accentuate this approach. This, indeed, is a particular problem with many of the "postcolonial" stereotyping and criticisms of imperial rule and, indeed, American power. They are as inappropriate as the unthinking praise for empire, which is rightly and, more frequently, criticized.

These are far from the sole conceptual, methodological, and historiographical issues involved, indeed frequently at stake. Among the many that are significant are the strong, even insistent, tendencies to focus on the last 150 to 200 years of empire, and certainly so in the case of Britain,

France, and the United States. But this does not apply to the likes of
China, Turkey, Portugal, and Spain. For India, the emphasis is on the
last 170 years, when India was under British rule, and not on earlier periods when India, or at least part of it, was the basis for imperial power,
notably, but not only, under the Mughals, the key dynastic power in
northern India from 1526 to 1857. For India and for other countries, this
chronological focus is at the expense of both a longer time span[6] and of
what can be gained from such a time span and comparative consideration
accordingly. Indeed, imperial history is too significant, too interesting,
and too complex for it to be helpful if it is defined and described simply,
and solely, in terms of such "end-loaded" coverage and analysis; however
convenient, indeed highly convenient, such an approach might appear in
academic or political terms.

There is, moreover, the tendency to focus on a linear narrative, notably, but not only, of success or failure,[7] and on a teleology accordingly.
The rise and fall of empires has become a narrative that adds epic interest
and moral notes to the cyclical patterns beloved by so many writers. This
cycle is particularly observed in the treatment of the British Empire and
the ("would-be") treatment of the United States, even if the process can
be subliminal (for writer and readers) as much as it can be explicit.

Separate to such narratives, the bitter identity politics of empire and
even more "ex-empire" lead to claims and assertions about collective
memories, amnesia, and forgetfulness.[8] These often-angry politics, encourage the deployment of empire, especially the British Empire, as a
case study for modern intellectual concerns, notably, but not only, about
race and gender; this is a process that is repeated with the United States.
In turn, these concerns become the way for many to study and present
empire, especially the United States. All interesting (or wearily predict-
able), and certainly for many, causes for commitment to, or about, the
subject, but scarcely a rounded account.

So also with the focus on the impact of globalization as a dominant
approach. Globalization is employed as a setting for the discussion of
a range of cultural and identity topics, particularly those focused on
race and migration. In contrast to a concentration on these topics, con-
ventional scholarly parameters and aspects of imperial activity, such as
military and high political ones, let alone their constitutional and legal
counterparts, long the standard themes in the imperial homelands, have

been discarded or dramatically rewritten. That is not an inevitable consequence of globalization, which, as an approach to world political history, can lead to a focus on imperial systems and networks. Nevertheless, if so, the more general approach is a criticism of these and notably so if linked to the imperial state. Globalization, as a topic, approach, and mentality, has offered a means and a cause for historiographical controversy over purpose and value in history, in particular with debates over the value of Western expansion, the British Empire, American history, and liberal economics.

These debates were, and are, frequently directly linked to engagement with modern-world politics. They certainly have proved a way, for both supporters and critics, to contest the American role.[9] However, leaving aside the frequent criticisms of the United States when it does not intervene abroad, there is scant sign that this approach will adapt comparably to the growing place and rising ambition of China. Indeed, much of the Western critique of imperialism now appears dated, even at times inconsequential, as a result; which is, at once, a comment on the critique, as well as on the broader engagement—past, present, and even future—with global history. In this context, it is instructive to watch *Wolf Warrior 2* (2017), a hit Chinese film in which China appears as the salvation of Africa with its intervention, against sadistic European mercenaries and dangerous African rebels, fronted by Leng Feng, a special forces agent (Wolf Warrior), and backed by a strong Chinese fleet. At present (February 2018), the film is China's second highest-earning film ever.

The film chimes with the approach taken by President Xi Jinping in March 2018 in closing the Chinese National Congress, when he promised to make China more assertive and promised that "Every inch of our great nation's territory cannot and absolutely will not be ceded from China." Xi argued that China was on the side of history and promised to make it a great global power by 2050. So much for Taiwanese hopes for continued independence, or for those in Tibet and Xinjiang who might want de-colonialization. This approach also served to criticize past European and Japanese imperial activities toward China.

A focus on China underlines the way in which criticism of the West, while often justified in modern terms (and frequently criticized in those of the time), can lead to a serious failure to engage with other imperialisms, past, present, or future. This is readily apparent when considering present hostility to the United States, which, in a highly unsettling fashion, is often greater than that toward Russia, China, Iran, or Turkey. In this context, however, there is no sign that the particularly hostile character of the treatment of Western imperialism, and notably of the British Empire, will cease.

This treatment can be reconceptualized by looking at the important distinction between Western empires, notably that of Britain, and those in the seventeenth to nineteenth centuries of the Ottomans, Safavids, Mughals, and Manchu. With all its faults, the British Empire, like, subsequently, the American state, arose in the context of modernity and the Enlightenment as broadly conceived: they came with promises of the rule of law, participatory governance, freedom, autonomy, and individualism, to at least some of their members. Moreover, these ideas subsequently spread in their area of power, as with the abolition of slavery and the spread of democracy.

This point undercuts the notion that the British Empire can be automatically incorporated into a world history in which empire is the default setting for large-scale political structures over time. Thus, British imperial history and, even more, the post-1945 American world order of democracy and free-market capitalism, do look different to that of, say, the Mughals. The facts and aspirations of modernity as a break in the pattern of human history need to be taken into account when we consider Western imperial history. Empires look bad from within modernity because they are in tension with some of its overarching goals. Conversely, modern critics of the British Empire are apt to forget that criticism of empire as such (rather than solely Western imperialism) is only readily possible from within the perspective of Western modernity. It is that perspective that highlights the totalitarian nature of modern empires or quasi-empires, such as Russia. Indeed, the Western tradition, in large part thanks to the values developed in theory and practice in Britain and the United States, provided a perspective on liberties and governance in which it was—and is—possible to make relative judgments on empires and, more broadly, to discern an historical development that is comparable with individual freedoms.

2

COMPETING HISTORIES

The Greeks are a western force on an eastern shore demanding justice and retribution, and I think that resonates particularly strongly with a modern audience. We can all think of images we've seen from this century and the last which remind us of the fall of Troy. I wanted to tell the other side because we know the Greek story so well.[1]

D avid Farr, the scriptwriter of the 2018 blockbuster BBC/Netflix series *Troy: Fall of a City*, was very much singing from the standard hymn sheet in his linking of the past and present critique of Western policy and call for a retelling of history from the perspective of a supposedly ignored underdog. Not exactly the way to introduce a balanced or accurate commentary on an obscure, historical episode — the siege of Troy. Instead, in this case, as in many others, history is deployed, or rather, *created*, to serve a modern narrative.

A highly critical and somewhat ahistorical account of empire and, more particularly, the British Empire, prevails in political discussion; education, higher education in particular; colonial and postcolonial literature; and the media. This account reflects the marked transformation of British political culture over the last century, and, more particularly, the last sixty years. This account also reflects the extent to which the overthrowing, or at least the end, of British rule is important to the foundation accounts of so many states, ranging from the United States to India, Ireland to Israel. This situation has become more marked over the last eighty years as, with time, far more states became independent from Britain and defined their national histories accordingly.

Yet in Britain, and in former colonies, there is sometimes a failure to appreciate the extent to which Britain generally was not the conqueror of native peoples ruling themselves in a democratic fashion, but, instead, overcame other imperial systems, and that the latter themselves rested on conquests. So with the tendency to underplay the major differences between the values of the United States and those of its opponents, such as during the two world wars, the Korean War, the Vietnam War, and the Gulf War.

There is also a misleading tendency to blame British imperial rule for many of today's pressures and problems in former colonies. In practice, while being ruled by an imperial power often had unfortunate long-term consequences, these pressures and problems stem, largely or completely, from other causes, notably population increase, modernization, and globalization. A failure to think in terms of a nation can also be a problem, one that encourages sectarian politics and large-scale corruption, and that leads to a situation in which institutions are wrecked by the consequences of patrimonial power systems. There is a tendency to blame this situation on the consequences of British rule and/or American dominance, which, while understandable, is usually far less than an adequate, let alone complete, account.

As a separate point, that does not somehow vindicate British imperialism, but that should be borne in mind, Britain, as an imperial power, engaged in Europe and elsewhere with rival powers, the contours and purposes of whose imperial rule was often harsher, indeed far harsher, than that of Britain. This was particularly true of Britain's leading role, or rather that of the British Empire, in opposition to the genocidal tyranny of Nazi Germany. In addition, its enemy in World War I, Wilhelmine Germany, earlier in the 1900s, followed policies in East and South West Africa that were far harsher than those of Britain, as were those of the Congo when King Leopold II of Belgium ruled it. Moreover, the brutality used by the Italians in the 1920s and 1930s to suppress resistance in Libya and to conquer Ethiopia, and that of the Japanese in Korea and, even more, in China, were far worse than that seen with the British Empire in the same period, or possibly any period.

Italy, having invaded Libya in 1911, finally subdued it between 1928 and 1932, employing great brutality against civilians, of whom over fifty thousand were probably killed. This process was driven forward in order to establish that Benito Mussolini, Italy's Fascist dictator, was more effective than earlier liberal Italian governments had been. Wells were blocked, flocks were slaughtered, and the population was forcibly and harshly resettled.

Moreover, much savagery, including the large-scale use of poison gas (in breach of the 1925 Geneva Gas Protocol), was employed in the Italian conquest of Ethiopia in 1935 and 1936. Again, Mussolini wished to demonstrate that he had greater effectiveness than his predecessors, who had failed in Ethiopia in 1896. Once established, Italian rule in Ethiopia proved to be extremely harsh, thanks mostly to racism, as was the general imperial pattern. The resulting resistance movement was met with savage and very murderous repression,[2] in large part because the Italians could not afford to suffer defeat because of its implications for the Fascist notion of superior and inferior races. At the same time, most of the troops garrisoning Ethiopia came from other African colonies, and they could be very harsh: Eritreans had a history of bitter conflict with Ethiopia, while Libyan troops considered themselves white Arabs closer to Italians than to black Ethiopians.

The war with Ethiopia was accompanied by a mobilization of Italian opinion, which was coordinated by a propaganda ministry established in 1935. This ministry sponsored favorable accounts, hindered unfavorable ones, and sought to manage the flow of information. The war was also used to make the Fascist system seem necessary and superior, and to legitimize both Mussolini and militarization. The serious financial drain of the conflict was ignored. Support for a citizen soldiery became central to Fascism as a political religion. British imperialism did not share these characteristics.

This comparative approach faces conceptual and methodological issues when being used to discuss the British Empire, as all comparisons encounter specific and contextual problems. Nevertheless, the comparative approach is significant for the discussion of that empire in terms of its values, as also, for example, when contrasting the United States with the Japanese and Soviet empires.

So with the willingness in Britain to criticize and investigate abuses by imperial agencies, including the army, a process repeatedly seen, notably with the parliamentary attack in the 1780s on Warren Hastings' administration of India, and continuing into twentieth-century investigations of imperial practices, such as the harsh response to the Mau Mau Uprising in Kenya. By modern standards, the criticism and investigation were doubtlessly insufficient, but that, possibly, was not necessarily the case in then contemporary terms. Ironically, although difficult to measure, corruption, recently and currently, in multiple postimperial states such as India, Kenya, Malawi, and Malta, is far greater than in the days of empire. Critics often blame this situation on the consequences of imperialism, but that is convenient more than it is convincing.

Comparative judgments in the matter of imperial (or any other) rule may strike others as immoral and absurd: any "unfair" rule and arbitrary killing is indeed reprehensible, and there was plenty in the British case. At the same time, however, issues of scale and intention are highly significant, as they are when considering politics and governance as a whole. Linked to this, assessment requires contextualization, as with the contrasting of America's "Indian Wars" with Hitler's *Ostkrieg* against the conflict with Soviet Union between 1941 and 1945.[3]

However, the general tendency is not to make contextual judgments, but rather to present the past in order to satisfy current mores, and this approach leads to a harsh portrayal of empire, and specifically of the British Empire. In contrast, the appropriate contextualization is generally absent, and this is an aspect of the so-called imperial amnesia that deserves attention and requires debate. It requires more work than the reflex references to "forgetting" and "amnesia"[4] on the part of past imperial powers, but is not the worse for that. Empire is no longer seen as a community, however unbalanced, nor is it usual, other than in critical terms, to present the British Empire as the precursor of the Commonwealth, which, in practice, it was.

Although both formal and informal empires still exist, imperialism, as a norm and a value system, has passed into history, or, at least, explicitly so. As such, and as a direct consequence, the controversies about goals and identities that were there from the outset, and were often highly significant to policy and experience, have been reset, reinterpreted, or ignored, and all in a totally new context. Moreover, they have been replaced by other norms and values about goals, character, and consequences. This process is an aspect of a wider rejection of the imperial legacy.

In part, this rejection is a matter of hostility to Britain, other imperial powers, imperialism, and its real and supposed consequences. Linked to this opposition to the fact, memory, and legacy of imperial rule was, and is, in Britain and in former colonies, an aspect of asserting, defining, contesting, and maintaining a new identity; that process varied in its character, depending in part on circumstances, but also on much more, notably political and intellectual strategies. So also with the critique of American power, especially in Latin America.

This definition of a new identity is presented as a throwing-off of the imperial yoke, as it indeed was, and is, and also of the new nationalism.[5] The definition was (and is) also in practice an important aspect of the struggle for influence and control among indigenous groups and political movements in postcolonial societies, including Britain.

Thus, the imperial legacy became, and continues to be, a significant aspect of "culture wars" around the world, "wars" that exist within, as well as between, countries. In India, for example, the widespread process of renaming, in which Bombay became Mumbai in 1995 (and Madras Chennai in 1996), owed something to local assertiveness and something to the Hindu nationalism of the BJP (Bharatiya Janata Party). While directed against the British, renaming was also seen in opposition to earlier rule by Muslim empires, notably, but not only, the Lodis and, even more, the Mughals.[6]

Britain, of course, had also been responsible for renaming when it was an imperial power and, earlier, had also experienced the process itself. Each constituted a form of end, not of history,[7] but of a stage of history. Thus, as Sir Henry Chauncy began his *Historical Antiquities of Hertfordshire* (1700):

> When the Saxons had subdued the Britons and made themselves masters of this land, they endeavoured to extinguish the religion, laws, and language of the ancient inhabitants; therefore destroyed all marks of Antiquity that nothing might remain which could discover to the people of future ages that any other but themselves were the first inhabitants of this country; they gave new names to all towns, villages and other places.[8]

Opposition to Britain and to Muslims was crucial to the BJP approach to history, and remains so, on which more will be seen in chapter 4. More generally, the idea of statehood and political legitimacy was presented in India and elsewhere as resting on an historical continuity that had allegedly been ruptured by British conquest and rule, a practice more generally seen with criticism of empires. A negative account of British imperialism was necessary not only to give additional meaning to the process of national liberation, but also in order to provide a stronger logic for nation, country, and state, and, more particularly, to identify the last with the first two. Political parties prominent in the gaining of independence, or who could be presented in that light, benefited greatly, but also had a strong particular interest in decrying imperialism, or at least in decrying being subjected to what was presented as British imperialism. In Britain, this approach can be seen with the Scottish National Party, and its role accordingly is more generally instructive, not least the tendentious and politically convenient histories of Scotland and Britain that it offers.

In contrast, the extent to which the territorial scope, and thus ethnic composition, of many states were the work of British conquerors and negotiators, and therefore relatively recent, created problems for the presentation of both the past and the present. There was a more complex relationship than that of rejection and blame. Operating within difficult domestic and international constraints, postcolonial states and societies employed British territorialization, British concepts of identity and political authority, British governing practice, and, often, American notions of democracy as well. This process was crucial to the understandable paradox of postcolonial nationalism; not so much that independence movements pledged to preserve freedom but then frequently acted to limit it, but rather that these movements claimed to reject the imperial state, but in practice sought to take it over and maintain its power. Continuity was particularly the case with the retention of imperial frontiers and therefore of the peoples thereby included and/or divided.

Conflicts were linked to this process, although the tensions they expressed frequently preceded the period of British rule. The brutal suppression of Biafran separatism within Nigeria, in a civil war (1967–70) in which maybe one million died, many by a famine caused by blockade, and the repression of peoples such as the Karens in Myanmar, were key instances. So, differently, was the treatment of the particular views of Turkish Cypriots. The war launched in Sri Lanka in 1983 by the Tamil Tigers (the Liberation Tigers of Tamil Eelam), a war in which the army, which reflected the Sinhalese majority, finally prevailed in 2009 with many Tamil casualties, was very bloody.

At the same time, the issues of territory and other continuities, and the problems created, or allegedly created, became a way to blame British rule, as if frontiers were responsible for strife. Moreover, Britain and the United States were assailed for the "type of domestic neo-colonialism" that prevailed, now at the hands of established local leaderships.[9] "Neo-colonialism," of course, is scarcely a value-free description. The transfer of blame to the British Empire and/or to the United States was all too typical of a postcolonial failure to accept responsibility, a process also seen in debate within Britain and the United States.

The creation of a new national history, the post-independence rethinking of the colonial period, and the need to "place" the latter in a hostile light have led to an emphasis on resistance to colonial rule, for example, by the Maroons of Jamaica in the eighteenth century, and also the "Indian Rebellion," the renaming of the "Indian Mutiny." However, this emphasis tended to involve a misleading treatment of much resistance in terms of later, nationalistic, anti-colonialism. An instructive instance is provided with the presentation of the Moroccan siege of English-held Tangier in 1680, in terms of postcolonial politics of resistance.[10] That scarcely describes a situation in which Islamic anti-Christian feeling was more to the fore; Morocco was itself an empire with a history from the early 1590s of violent expansionism south across the Sahara into the Niger Valley, and its prime challenges came from Ottoman power based in neighboring Algiers and from Spain and Portugal; and not from England, later Britain, which, had obtained Tangier as a royal dowry.

The standard popular account of empire, both in former colonies and in imperial heartlands, can underplay the emergence of local colonial elites that cooperated with British imperial rule and greatly benefited from it, while also helping define and determine its local impact. This was a practice more generally true of empires, and indeed of American dominance, and one that greatly aided the introduction, imposition, spread, and sustaining of British imperial rule and that of other empires.[11] These elites, from time to time, also helped preside over the postcolonial aftermath; and part of the subsequent history of empires, as of the United States from the 1780s to the 1860s, revolves around struggles not just between these elites and their challengers, but also within both groups. The latter point serves as a reminder of the problem posed by discussing politics in terms of the legacies of empire. In India, there is continuing tension within the Hindu middle class regarding the elite, some of whom were educated in Britain, that looked to Congress, and a different group that turned to the BJP.

Consideration of the colonial period was, and is, politically problematic, as it poses a major question against the success of postcolonial governments in improving living standards, maintaining stability and the rule of law, limiting corruption, or simply maintaining water supplies. Although difficult to define, let alone measure, corruption appears to have gotten worse since imperial rule ended in many countries. Corruption is linked not only to private profit, but also to the efforts of the post-independence state to advance particular interests, notably religious, ethnic, and regional ones, which in itself can be a parallel to the very different cases of private and public slavery. These issues remain pertinent, which helps explain why it is so necessary for so many to "trash" empire, again, a situation shared by the United States.

Imperial governments could pursue reform and ultimately incite opposition. In the case of India (as elsewhere), British imperial reforming intentions could be provocative or, at least, unwelcome. The British meant taxation to be fairer and uncorrupted, which entailed removing corrupt tax collectors. They had indeed been corrupt, but taxpayers could do deals with them, and end up both paying a bribe and paying fewer taxes than under the new system. This contributed to the longer-term reasons for the "Mutiny" between 1857 and 1859, as *sepoys* (native soldiers serving for the British) had homes and families who resented the new taxation, however just or well intentioned it might have been. In the 1760s, the British quest to share the burden of imperial defense caused the 1765 Stamp Act crisis in the North American colonies.

In countering the problems of the past (and the present), it is politically valuable to advance the nationalist cry of independence and self-determination. Precisely because, during and after de-colonization, it was not clear how "peoples" were to be defined; there was an emphasis, instead, on the allegedly national character of states and proto-states. However, modern concepts of nationality have generally been employed misleadingly to interpret the polities and politics of the past. Indeed, in contrast, alongside considerable and long-standing migration across what have since been constructed as national borders, there was a willingness, in what were really "composite states" (to employ a later term) to seek support where it could be found. Such willingness was shown by at least some of the people as much as by the imperial government. In practice, this process eased imperial penetration by providing the cooperation and compromise that in part constituted imperialism, as well as other systems of rule.

Like other empires, the British Empire relied heavily on cooperation, and was quite prepared to acknowledge this, albeit not usually to an extent that matches current sensitivities. For example, in 1815, in Ceylon (Sri Lanka), George III (then confined for health reasons in Windsor Castle) replaced Sri Vikrama Rajasimha, the highly unpopular and brutal last king of Kandy, as a result of a convention with the Kandyan chiefs, as well as of the British conquest of Kandy that year. Cooperation, there and elsewhere, was significant both during conquest, and even more during subsequent rule.

Cooperation within empire was not on the basis of equality; it was actually far from it, but such a basis was unusual for any governance. Furthermore, however attractive, the modern criterion of equality is not a terribly helpful one when considering values prior to the twentieth century. Instead, the key equality was generally that of the fact of being a subject or, alternatively, a citizen.

Moreover, the terms of cooperation (or indeed coercion) and the nature of networks were rarely those in which imperialists and subjects formed coherent blocs, however much such a view is offered today. Instead, alongside hostility, opposition and conflict,[12] there was inter-marriage, intermixing, compromise, co-existence, and the process of negotiation that is sometimes referred to as the "middle-ground."[13] This situation, its causes, course, and consequences, were often particularly pronounced in borderlands, which included "inner frontiers" within both empires and other states. The range of the "middle-ground" was vast, from interracial personal relationships[14] to business, government, and military service.

Cooperation was a relationship that was very much subject to amnesia after imperial rule, with the amnesia essentially on the part of the newly independent, as with the treatment of Loyalists in the United States. This amnesia was a part of the collapsing of all aspects of imperialism, indeed all facets of international politics, including military conquest, geopolitical rivalry, national expansion, the consolidation of control, and subsequent political, social, economic, and cultural arrangements, into a somehow monolithic trans-historic imperialism.

"Amnesia," however, is a term that is not only employed selectively, but has also been "weaponized" as a term of criticism. This is notably (but not only) in Britain today as an aspect of the rhetorical dimension of controversy. This dimension can challenge the entire process of discussion and debate. In practice, the character of imperialism is open to debate; debate rather than automatic justification or criticism. This is debate on overlapping categories and complex and shifting situations that do not, in practice, readily match modern polemical engagement.

True across the range of British colonies, this point is also pertinent for those in which there was an insurrection and where there has been particular controversy. For example, critics sometimes underplay the extent to which the Mau Mau Uprising in Kenya in the 1950s and early 1960s involved murderous attacks on other Africans, who indeed made up the bulk of the victims. British reliance on African police and troops was also significant.[15] Such a level of complexity is lost when counter-insurgency operations are referred to simply in terms of "the British."

A similar point is relevant, for example, of the killing of demonstrators at Amritsar in Punjab in 1919, on which see chapter 4. This observation is not made in order to extenuate the appalling action, and Brigadier-General Reginald Dyer clearly had the commanding responsibility. He regarded force as a key constituent of control: "I considered that this is the least amount of firing which would produce the necessary moral and widespread effect it was my duty to produce." In causing great controversy at the time in Britain as well as India, the events in Amritsar marked a major transition in the character and tone of the British Empire.[16] They deserve consideration, however, at least in part, as with more recent Indian military activity in Amritsar, in terms of the security situation of the time and the related complexities of counter-insurgency,[17] as in chapter 4.

You may think that reasonable or unreasonable, "complicit" or extenuating, but to give you a flavor of much of the discussion, an anonymous reader's report for Oxford University Press New York on a text some years ago in which I had made that remark described it as akin to justification of "the Nazi regime."[18] The academic in question clearly treated issues of intentionality, scale and, persistence as naught, but also reflected a total lack of judgment in tone as well as content. The more common comparison, also totally inappropriate, is of modern Israel and Nazi Germany. Both comparisons ironically serve to minimize the seriousness of the Holocaust, which is clearly not intended, but, nevertheless, very much the case.

It is readily apparent that in counter-insurgency operations, notably in Malaya, Cyprus, Aden, and Kenya, British soldiers displayed frequent brutality, which was often condoned by their officers and accepted as a way to end the crisis.[19] At the same time, questions of policy, scale, and intentionality continue to recur, and certainly the comparison above is seriously flawed, in other words, wrong. Coercion definitely played a key role in counter-insurgency policy and practice. Collective punishment, large-scale detentions—with a peak in December 1954 of 71,346 people detained in Kenya—and the movement of people (i.e., mass eviction) relied ultimately on the availability of overwhelming and coercive force, and on the central role of the army, for which minimum force meant minimum necessary force, but only as it defined it. Following guilty verdicts, 1,090 Kenyans were hanged. Public executions were employed as exemplary force, as a form of intimidation, and as an aspect of a multifaceted propaganda war.[20]

The possibility of different policies was shown in Kenya in the summer of 1953 with an emphasis on amnesties and a growing willingness to punish brutality, or, at least, conspicuous brutality. Similarly, in Malaya, there was a shift in policy from a defensive, counter-terror strategy in 1948 and 1949, to a less vigorous, proactive stance in which persuasion played a role.[21] The latter was more successful, but possibly the former, directed against a brutal opponent, was first necessary, and possibly not.

More broadly, although the British compared themselves favorably to the French, there were parallels between British and French conduct. Although the emphasis for both was on managed decolonization or orderly transfers of power, the reality was often a mixture of harsh resistance to change and the rushed abandonment of power. For every instance of violence avoided by the British and the French, there were examples of conflict chosen, even positively embraced. These choices were made in the light of lessons drawn from other places and other empires. Prosaic terminology, notably that of law and order, was intended, or at least served, to depoliticize anti-colonial rebellion and make the resultant repression, often with large-scale incarceration, appear limited and excusable.[22] In practice, the repression was certainly more limited than counter-insurgency policies in several former colonies. In Portuguese Africa, a far more persistent effort was made to retain imperial control.

The British imperial authorities sought to improve their ability to cope with opposition, whatever form it took. For example, concern with subversive ideas encouraged British intelligence organizations and operations that relied heavily on the cooperation of supportive imperial subjects, without whom these operations were in a very weak position. These organizations and operations reflected the fear that colonial populations were readily manipulated, as well as the range, and ambiguities and nuances, involved in the term "cooperation," and the related concerns to which the latter gave rise.[23] In colonies such as India and Jamaica, administrators and officers had for a long time been concerned regarding how best to control populous territories with very small forces. The military strength available was regarded as the crucial support of a moral authority on which rule and control rested. This was an attitude that helped lead some in Britain and among the British in India to support Dyer's harsh and bloody response.

Alongside force, confidence was a key element in power. In 1904, the director of military operations in the British War Office warned:

The fact cannot be too plainly stated that throughout Egypt and the Sudan, and throughout the great protectorates of Uganda and British East Africa [Kenya], our whole position depends entirely on prestige. We are governing with a mere handful of white officials vast populations alien to us in race, language and religion, and for the most part but little superior in civilisation to savages. Except for the small, and from a military point of view inadequate, British force in Egypt, the authority of these officials is supported only by troops recruited from the subject races, whose obedience to their officers rests on no other basis than a belief in the invincibility of the British government and confidence in its promises. If that belief and confidence be once shaken the foundations of all British authority between Cairo and Mombasa [on the Kenyan coast] will be undermined, and at any moment a storm of mutiny and insurrection will sweep us into the sea.

This view captured a sense of precariousness in the face of insurgency and the reliance of empire on a confidence in power.

Military success certainly fostered and secured cooperation, and notably so in wartime. These factors were not unrelated. Thus, in June 1940, General Archibald Wavell, Commander of British Forces in the Middle East, wrote from the British Middle East Headquarters as such:

> The internal security problem in Egypt, in Palestine, and in Iran, and elsewhere occupy a very great deal of the attention and time of the Middle East Staff. An improvement in propaganda may help the situation, but only military successes or evidence of strength and determination will really do it.[24]

Many of the works that are published on empire are certainly very politically committed, as are their presentation. This establishes norms within which further works are written, presented, published, and considered. I offer a few examples, selected in order to display the range of books at issue, including the degree to which criticism can come from differing points on the political spectrum. The text, backcover, and catalog copy of Richard Gott's *Britain's Empire. Resistance, Repression and Revolt* (2011) were happy to rank the leaders of the empire alongside Hitler. Moreover:

> This revelatory history punctures the widely held belief that the British Empire was an imaginative and civilising enterprise. Instead, *Britain's Empire* reveals a history of systemic repression and almost perpetual violence, showing how British rule was imposed as a military operation and maintained as a military dictatorship. For colonised peoples, the experience was a horrific one, of slavery, famine, battle and extermination. Yet, as Richard Gott shows, the empire's oppressed peoples did not go quietly into this good night. Wherever Britain tried to plant its flag, it met with opposition. From Ireland to India, from the American colonies to Australia, Gott traces the rebellions and resistance of subject peoples whose all-but-forgotten stories are excluded from traditional accounts of empire. He shows too, how the British Empire provide a blueprint for the annihilation of peoples in twentieth-century Europe, and argues that its leaders

must rank alongside the dictators of the twentieth century as authors of crimes against humanity on an infamous scale.

Ironically, Gott's book has on the book cover, and in the catalog of the publisher, Verso, which claims to "challenge the apologists of Empire and Capital," illustrations relating to the British conflict with Tipu, Sultan of Mysore in southern India (r. 1782–99). A long-standing symbol of resistance to imperialism, who was killed when the British successfully stormed his capital, Seringapatam, in 1799, Tipu and his father, Haidar Ali, a soldier of fortune who seized control of Mysore in 1761, were also (like earlier the Mughals) Muslim imperialists whose brutal expansion was a cause of great instability in Southern India, where they killed large numbers of citizens and were often harsh to non-Muslims. They were certainly scant advertisement for the place and prosperity of India before the Raj. Gott, however, was as little interested in contextualizing British or Western imperialism in terms of a wider pattern of such rule, across history and the world, as in discussing the "middle-ground" of empire.

Less strident and much more thoughtful in 2011, was *Ghosts of Empire: Britain's Legacies in the Modern World*, from the Conservative MP Kwasi Kwarteng. His book argued that the empire was poorly run (which is also true of much postcolonial government and, in many respects, of modern Britain), and that the consequences are still apparent today. Kwarteng's focus on Iraq, Nigeria, Myanmar, Sudan, and Kashmir, however, produced a somewhat limited view, as British rule in all of them was short-lived, and notably so in Iraq. None of Kwarteng's choices were settler colonies, yet, despite the treatment of the indigenous populations, Australia and Canada have both become highly successful countries, and can be seen as a vindication of the hopes of imperialists while accepting all the caveats that stem from an understanding of the prejudices of the latter. The United States is also worthy of consideration as a former settler colony. Ghana, a relative success story, does not attract attention in the book, nor Hong Kong, whose population had higher standards of liberty than those in Mainland China, nor Singapore.

The question "Which empire?" was one from the outset, with differing views on the desirability and significance of particular models of imperial rule and directions of imperial expansion. This diversity and debate has continued to the modern era. For example, the idea of the

"Anglosphere" was significant from the late nineteenth century until the mid-twentieth century, and then again, in some political circles on the right today.[25] In turn, the idea has attracted critics.

In 2012, a major academic work, published by a prominent academic publisher, *Macaulay and Son: Architects of Imperial Britain*, by Catherine Hall, Professor of History at University College, London, added to the potent litany of criticism of empire. Hall wrote that she became an historian of Britain and empire in order to explain the legacies of colonialism for the British and that she started work on Thomas Macaulay in the wake of the "War on Terror," or, rather, the "Global War on Terrorism." Pressing on to observe that she was opposed to the 2003 Gulf War, Hall noted that she was:

> horrified by the claim that the West had the right to assume such positions of moral certitude, apparently with no memory of past "civilising missions," key aspects of some phases of European colonialisms. This was the return of the . . . assumption that Britain, despite its loss of empire, could use force and legislate for those others who were stuck in barbaric times, who needed white knights to rescue them. Moral rectitude was masking new geo-political claims. Britain's shameful history in Iraq, and subsequently in Afghanistan, seemed to be entirely forgotten. The discourse of liberal humanitarian intervention under the sign of gender equality was deployed unproblematically. Yet this was a reconfiguration of the arguments made by nineteenth-century imperialists – including both Macaulays – for an empire of virtue and civilisation.[26]

Hall then offered a brief intellectual autobiography, commenting that her formation as a historian was at the highpoint of radical social history in the 1960s, and noting how she had then moved on to argue that "racial thinking underpinned white English identities."[27] Hall argued that Britain, thanks in part to empire and imperial manhood, became "a nation founded on gender, class and ethnic inclusions and exclusions,"[28] an incomplete and problematic formulation. As with many other books on empire, this is not some theme offered in the introduction and then discarded in favor of a less-committed scholarship. Instead, this thesis is presented throughout. For example, Thomas Macaulay is depicted, like Charles Dickens, as hating slavery, but as feeling "only contempt for Africans and their defenders," which Hall saw as an aspect of a more wide-ranging "space of difference, the gap between imperial men and their colonised others."[29] Indeed, there has been much discussion of the racist character of past policy, and notably so in Africa.[30]

As with much discussion of British imperialism, especially by the public, there was a failure by Hall to consider that of other powers of the time, whether it be Western or non-Western. Linked to this lack of adequate contextualization, there is also a sense of "So what?" Is it surprising that Whig intellectuals, whether or not presented as apologists, offered a view of the world in which they associated their values and interest with progress and civilization? Ironically, but all too typically, and again understandably, Hall displayed the same tendency, identifying values with her own concept of progress, and providing a valuation, more especially criticism, of the past accordingly. So also with commentators who hold other values.

This raises the bigger question of how best, in the contexts of modern British and modern American history, to discuss imperialism. Clearly it would be helpful to see authors debate their own interpretations. Personal commitment, however, does not excuse any fondness for argument both by assertion and without adequate qualification or sufficient caveats. More generally, how is empire to be presented in a way that does more than make sense of it largely in terms of modern values?

And so on, and for prominent and commercially successful works, rather than academic works, as in Shashi Tharoor's *Inglorious Empire: What the British Did to India* (2017).[31] Tharoor is an eloquent and ambitious Congress politician who is a keen populist and a bitter critic of Churchill. Ironically, one assumes he did not consider that the cover employed for his book was in part a frequently reproduced painting by Henry Martens (1790–1868), *The 62nd Regiment on the second day of Ferozeshah*. This British victory over the Sikhs in 1845, a key episode in the First Anglo-Sikh War (1845–46), was, in practice, the victory of one empire expanding over another. Moreover, the Sikhs had cooperated with the British in the complex power politics focused on Afghanistan: the Durrani empire of Afghanistan had put much pressure on the Sikhs, with religion as well as politics playing a key role. British rule is simply explained by Tharoor as "a totally amoral, rapacious, imperialist machine bent on the subjugation of Indians for the purpose of profit" (p. 222). His account of the economic consequences of British rule, however, is deeply flawed,[32] as is much of the book.

More perceptive criticisms of British control of India are available than those by Tharoor.[33] At the same time, these and other criticisms should be considered alongside the achievements of this control. These were varied. There was what was achieved. For example, there was the success of the penny post, which helped to end the tyranny of distance and was subject to scant censorship.[34] Postal services, however, also helped support British imperial transport links, notably the extension of regular steamer routes by P. and O. There is also what was avoided: in India, from 1911 to 1937, there was none of the highly destructive civil warfare seen in China in this period.

The "Woes of Capitalism" are to the fore in much of the work on imperialism, not the woes experienced by capitalism but the woes it imposes. This can be seen, for example, in Erika Rappaport's *A Thirst for Empire: How Tea Shaped the Modern World* (2017), an account of the relationships between tea drinking, the British Empire, and capitalism, from the seventeenth century and, more especially, the nineteenth century, to the decline of tea drinking in Britain as empire went by. Particular attention is devoted by Rappaport to the role of advertising and lobbying in spreading and sustaining the drinking of Indian tea from the 1880s, and in associating it within an ideological framework in which tea was contrasted with alcohol, for both men and women, and was linked with an Evangelical manliness and an appropriate femininity. There is stress in much of such work on power, control, manipulation, and the creation of false consciousness in which advertising is joined to imperialism, in order to explain baleful consequences.[35]

Capitalism is seen not as a way to link demand and supply, to cut costs, to offer a range of products, or to provide employment; but, instead, it is presented as a negative force. I recall Tony Wedgwood Benn, lucid stalwart of the British radical Left, saying at a public meeting I attended that commercial television made Socialism impossible in Britain, a remark that dates the process to the mid-1950s, just before the British "bolt from empire." Such simplistic, mono-dimensional assumptions are typical of much of the work on the political economy of imperialism. Of course, there is also a tendency to downplay other considerations, such as strategic fear or need, both of which are themselves constructions, but it is much easier to attribute policy to a quest for cotton, gold, iron, or, more recently, as with the United States and the Gulf Wars, oil. In the case of tea, it would be instructive to add in French and other consumption patterns, and the extent to which British consumption of, for example, American grain or Danish bacon, was certainly not necessarily limited to imperial relationships. Moreover, advertising was as much a reflex mode of an urbanizing society as the product of a proactive manipulation.

Nor, despite the energy and attention devoted to it, was the Rhodes Must Fall (RMF) movement one of great edification. In 2015, the movement succeeded in having a statue at the University of Cape Town, one dedicated to Cecil Rhodes, removed. This movement was presented as a contest about a lack of transformation in South Africa following the end of apartheid and as a testimony to the question or polemic, whose history is told and whose is swept under the carpet.[36] The "decolonization of education" was a theme, including the limited number of black professors.

The campaign against Rhodes had a following elsewhere in South Africa, where it extended to criticism of Gandhi's undoubtedly racist views on Africans and led to a concomitant call to remove his statues. Rhodes was also a target in Oxford, where, in 2015, led by a South African Rhodes scholar, students pressed for a statue of Rhodes to be removed from Oriel College, which he had attended and to which he had left a large bequest. The students also called for the university to show greater racial sensitivity and be "decolonized," in part by a greater understanding of the university's role in colonialism, a process that could only have had one conclusion. The confused notion that the university required "decolonization," an approach also adopted in the Untied States, is highly problematic. A term adopted more widely to describe fashionable attitudes clearly places added opprobrium on colonialization. This is anti-colonialism unmoored in the scholarly world. Separately, in 2018, SOAS established a "working group" on decolonization, its head, Baroness Amos, announcing: "We are looking at how to decolonise knowledge and in particular decolonise our literature and pedagogy."[37] In my own university, Exeter, anonymous flysheets appeared in 2018 on the noticeboards of some academics and elsewhere, declaring, "Say No To Racism, Sexism, Classism, Bullying And Corruption Within the UK University System." This catchall denunciation contributed absolutely nothing to the level or content of discussion.

In the event, Oriel College, allegedly torn between political correct-
ness and the wishes of alumni, a key source of finance, as well as continuity, decided that the statue would remain. In Oxford this decision led
to suggestions that a copy of the statue be produced on which students
could write graffiti, providing a classic instance of the extent to which
students are encouraged to be unaccountable, a process in which many
academics share.

The controversy rolled on and broadened out. Nigel Biggar, former
chaplain of Oriel and the Regius Professor of Theology, sought to offer a
balanced view on Rhodes, presenting him as an imperialist, not a racist.[38]
In January 2016, Biggar opposed the RMF movement in a debate at the
Oxford Union.[39] The "Ethics and Empire" project launched in July 2017
by the McDonald Centre for Theology, Ethics and Public Life, of which
Biggar was Director, led to fresh disputes. In the conflict of 2017–18, disagreement, often heated, between academics followed Biggar's attempt
to defend aspects of empire.

The same thing happened with Bruce Gilley's controversial article "The Case for Colonialism," published in *Third World Quarterly* in
September 2017.[40] Half of the editorial board resigned following the
publication of the article, while academics, writing to the *Times Higher
Education*, declared that it should not have been published, as it constituted "historical revisionism for what is a crime against humanity."[41]
Subsequently, Gilley's article was formally "withdrawn" after what were
described as "serious and credible threats of personal violence" received
by the journal editor.

These controversies showed how contentious the subject remained,
how strident the critics of empire are, and how the overwhelming theme
is that of criticism. Indeed, it can be difficult for those seeking to offer
a different view to get their works published, a situation to which I can
attest. There is scant attempt by critics to explain why empires arose.
There is almost a zeal to suggest that Britain was as bad as the most murderous regimes in history, as with references to "Britain's *gulag*" when
discussing the response to the Mau Mau (there is no valid comparison),
or when comparing the treatment of detainees in the Boer War, the far
more deadly and serious Bengal famine, and much else, with the actions
of the Germans in World War II (again, no valid comparisons). Individ-
ually, these criticisms largely rest on emotion and hyperbole instead of

informed knowledge, but that does not prevent the comparisons from being credited by at least some.

Moreover, these criticisms progressively gain more airtime. This can be seen, for example, in the call, in 2017 by Afua Hirsch, in an article in the *Guardian*, for Nelson's Column to be pulled down. She described Nelson "without hesitation" as "a white supremacist" because he spoke in favor of slavery. Hirsch, who pressed for Britain to face its role in the slave trade and attitudes linked to its empire building, backed the RMF movement vigorously.[42] In a BBC program on May 29, 2018, "The Battle for Britain's Heroes," Hirsch returned to the attack on Nelson and presented Churchill as a nasty racist whose racism was key to his slowness to respond to the Bengal famine (see chapter 4). This did not really address the point that Churchill was a vigorous exponent of the bombing of Germany and that the Germans, like the Italians who were also bombed, were white. Other contributors offered a range of views, from Neil Mac-Gregor's depiction of Britain as a country in denial—"If you don't ask the right questions about how we behaved in the past, we're not going to get it right for the future"—to Simon Jenkins' "vilifying the past is a silly thing to do... it clouds the debate with anger."

Taking offense in this fashion has become endemic in Britain, the United States, and more generally. Anita Dent, a friend, complained to me in 2017 that wearing a green tie meant that I supported Hamas. Never aware of that, I pointed out that it could more readily be taken to imply support for Irish nationalism, but that, in fact, I was wearing it because I liked the tie which had been given to me by another friend, and without any political intention. Indeed, I did not know that green was the color of Hamas. I clearly lack sensitivity as I go on wearing it. Doubtless, I now have to add that, as is the case, I abhor Hamas.

Relativism plays a major role in the critique, as does an emphasis on feeling, not thought. Particular hostility is directed at the British Empire. There is far less anger if, for example, suggestions are made that continued Habsburg rule would have been better for the Balkans than twentieth-century nationalism; not that that is a realistic suggestion nor one that sufficiently notes the problems caused by the low-caliber nature of Habsburg leadership in its closing decades.

Separately, making contrite apologies about imperial rule is presented, in Britain and elsewhere, as a key aspect of coming to terms with the past, and facilitating a postcolonial future in which the strains of multi-culturalism can be confronted.[43] In practice, this is a very unclear process. Intellectually, coming to terms can be bogus and often ahistorical, as in the discussion of human rights and, separately, the alleged transference of responsibilities across the generations.[44] There are also different views on the past, both in the former colonies and in the metropole, differences that are swept aside or, at the very least, misrepresented. More seriously, the process can also lead to the reiteration of grievances and the entrenchment of anger, such that it harms attempts to address serious issues of identity, cohesion, equity, and social purpose in the present day.

Looked at differently, rather than focusing on an agreed narrative with the concomitant politicizing, including anger and apologies, attempts to engage with diverse understandings of imperial history provide an opportunity, instead, to return us to the complexities of the past; although they do not dispense with the anger. These complexities include those of metropole, officials, settlers, and the public, as well as those who experienced imperialism, and that whether the accent was, and is, on exploitation or cooperation. Public memorialization that can offer more than one view may appear confusing. Yet, that itself is not only the stuff of politics, past, and present, but also valuably captures the extent to which the assessment of empire, as of the past as a whole, was, and should be, inherently varied, multifaceted, and multi-focused.

3

WHY EMPIRE?

On my wall the colours of the maps are running
From Africa the winds they talk of changes coming.
. . .
In the islands where I grew up
Nothing seems the same
It's just the patterns that remain,
An empty shell.
          —"On The Border," Al Stewart, 1976.

In Britain, the United States, and even beyond, empire appears to be totally redundant. Empire also seems utterly undesirable from the perspective of a modern account of development focused on self-determination, democracy, and human rights, as well, separately, as with reference to the identity politics so prevalent in parts of Western opinion today. Human rights are understood as absolute and, in a collective, as well as an individual, fashion. Moreover, this collective character for many is clearly expressed in, and through, self-determination and democracy. In addition, during the 1950s and 1960s, anti-imperialists appropriated the language of human rights to advance their central demands of self-determination and racial equality, and even to redefine human rights according to anti-imperialist principles.

As a consequence of the emphasis on self-determination, imperialism appears as an undesirable other, intrusion, and interference. Moreover, it is more specifically argued, decisions affecting colonies were taken by the metropolitan power, regularly for its domestic political and economic reasons, or for causes, notably strategic ones, quite unrelated to the colony and its people. The perception, an understandable one, remains that the colony existed for the benefit of the colonizer—providing raw materials, markets, bases, jobs, and, not least, prestige, and also for the benefit of those who cooperated with them.

Linked to this, imperialism is seen, both openly and subliminally, as a stage in the past that had, and has, to be overcome in order to reach the present, and/or a desired future. The Hegelian-Marxist tradition of analysis in terms of thesis and antithesis ensures that this theme of overcoming imperialism is presented as necessarily involving strife and struggle. More specifically, imperialism is depicted as adding to the oppression of capitalism. Imperialism is regarded not only as ending self-determination by ensuring foreign rule, but it is also presented as compromising internal liberties (either explicitly or implicitly), and as creating a false superiority/inferiority between "equal" peoples, and thus as blocking equality, democracy, and appropriate development. This list of faults, which is far from exhaustive, indicates the many criticisms made, and the way in which, in this criticism, they support each other and merge into each other, thus becoming more potent in doing so.

Separately, but closely related to this, imperialism serves for many critics as an equivalent to, or surrogate for, capitalism. Indeed, appropriation is a key term for critics of imperial rule. For many, imperialism and capitalism are equivalent terms. While convenient as a way for some to blame the United States and Britain, the approach is also misleading, as can be seen with both imperialism and capitalism today, and was also far from necessarily the case in the past. Capitalists, however defined, did not always want to bear the protection costs of conquering, controlling, and protecting territorial possessions.

If the bankers and businessmen of empire are treated as undesirable, then missionaries, explorers, generals, and rulers will be treated the same way. British imperialism is judged accordingly, and is also affected by the wash from criticism of other empires,[1] although less so for much of the British public as knowledge of this criticism is frequently limited. So also for the Americans.

Empire is also frequently attacked as part of present-day polemics, as in the statement: "Scratch a Brexiteer and you're likely to find an imperial nostalgist," a claim made in the *Times Literary Supplement*[2] that ignores the range of emotions, assumptions, and reasons involved in Brexit (and Remain). Empire thus becomes a value-laden, totemic term employed as a noun and an adjective (imperial), rather like appeasement.

The allegedly undesirable character of imperialism is taken further as a result of the origin accounts of many states, governments, political movements, social and cultural tendencies, families, and individuals. They frequently present themselves, and assert their past and legitimacy, in terms of the resistance to, and overthrow of, alien imperial control. "Alien" and "imperial" are seen as conditions of each other, which means that cooperation with imperial rule is disparaged, if not worse, being frequently treated as treasonable. The necessity of overthrow becomes an explanation of past, present, and future, an explanation that is at both teleological and self-serving.

A dimension of gender is added by arguing that imperialism is quintessentially a form of aggressive masculinity, and notably one that ravishes the colonized, which was a claim made about the British government by American colonists in the 1770s. Thus, sexual violence, or at least control, a highly negative image and practice, becomes part of the equation.[3] This is not a terribly helpful explanation, however, as sexual violence and gender oppression can be seen not only in imperial systems, but also in all aspects of rule and control, not that that lessens their unacceptable nature. The polygamy of Islamic societies rests on socio-economic power and status. Although slave owners could practice a form of polygamy, it was (and is not) matched in the British case as far as the public ideology was concerned. In the United States, Utah was only permitted to join the Union after polygamy was banned.

There was certainly a potent image of empire as masculine or, rather, pertaining to values generally regarded as masculine, such as fortitude. That presentation, however, did not exclude an explicit role for women (not least in displaying fortitude), alongside the reality of their partly unacknowledged activities as wives, mothers, and workers, all of which contributed greatly to imperial activity and the imperial presence. The Victoria League, which was the leading voluntarist movement in this sphere, supported female emigration to the empire and served to underline the role of empire as a place of domesticity, family, and home virtues, as well as the masculine assertion more prominently discussed and celebrated. Female emigration was regarded as the best way to ensure that the empire became a site and source of the British nation's expansion. It therefore addressed long-standing concerns about population loss through emigration and about deracination through the consequences of men being abroad as a result of imperial activity.

At the same time, women also emigrated for a wide range of other

reasons, just as men did. Women went overseas as Christian missionaries, to explore, to enhance their economic opportunities, to engage in
scientific research, to escape the rigors of British domesticity, and to find
husbands. Others emigrated as members of families and communities
with the mission of replicating British domesticity in the empire.

The origin accounts of many states indicate the prominence of empire in world history, a prominence increasingly present in the scholarly
literature.[4] These accounts include not only states that emerged from
the British Empire and its fall, but also those that were created from
other empires. The decline of the Spanish empire in the early nineteenth
century in the shape of the loss of its mainland American possessions
was the key episode across much of the Americas; and that of the Soviet
Union between 1989 and 1991 was central for much of Eurasia from the
River Elbe in Germany, for part of its course the frontier between West
(democratic) and East (Communist) Germany, to the borders of China.
The expansionism, from 1792, of Revolutionary and, even more, Napoleonic France led to the end of imperial rule, for example by Austria in
Belgium and Lombardy, but also caused the creation of a dynamic and
expansionist French empire. The latter was overthrown in 1813–1814 as
a consequence both of foreign invasion by Russia and of what came to
be seen, in another national "origin account," as the War of German
Liberation.

In part, however, the latter was a rationalization of Prussian expansionism, and notably so at the expense of Napoleon's German allies,
especially Bavaria and, even more, Saxony, rather as the *Risorgimento*, or
unification of Italy, was intertwined with Piedmontese expansion. This
sets a precedent for considering more recent situations, including wars
of decolonization that tended to benefit particular tribal groups, as in
Angola.

There is also a continuing nature to the situation in the creation of
new opportunities for anti-imperial discussion. This can be seen with
the opposition to Pakistani rule in East Pakistan, which was overthrown
in 1971, creating Bangladesh, and with that to Serbian policy and power
between 1995 and 1999, first in Bosnia and then in Kosovo.

The interaction of control and proto-nationalism is also seen, more
controversially, in current, or very recent, attempts to overthrow unwelcome rule, for example persistent separatist tensions within India and
Indonesia. The Kashmir imbroglio, which is significant to the process of

identification in Salman Rushdie's novel *Midnight's Children*,[5] becomes, in one light, an opposition to Indian imperialism, one made more acute by the religious division involved: the Kashmiri separatists are Muslim. Moreover, Indian policy in Sri Lanka and toward Sikkim, Bhutan, and Nepal can also be treated as imperialist. In Nepal, where India symbolically took over from Britain the former embassy, the Indians were, and are, regularly criticized for intervening in the imperious character of the Raj. Pakistani commentators have long regarded Indian influence in Afghanistan as imperialist and this was encouraged during the Cold War by the Soviet alignment with India. With India, echoes can be seen of expansionist Mughal policy in Afghanistan and the Himalayas in the seventeenth century. Indian competition with China appears as a new and more urgent imperialist "Great Game," one redolent of the competition between Britain and Russia in the nineteenth century in which the Afghans and others were incidental.

India taking over British geopolitical interests, for example, opposition to China in the Himalayas, was the British hope and intention when considering Indian independence in the mid-twentieth century. Possibly a small part of the anger expressed in India about British imperialism comes from a consciousness of following British examples. We may, indeed, be in a postcolonial world, but we are certainly not in a postimperial one. Moreover, settlement colonies are apparent in some parts of the world, as with the growing presence of the Han Chinese in Tibet.

Indian power politics is still very active today, as in January 2018, when India reached an agreement with the Seychelles to establish a military base there. In February, moreover, again with regard to the Indian Ocean, Indian strategic hawks pressed for the overthrow of the undemocratic government of the Maldives, which has aligned with China. The threat of Indian action led to Chinese talk of a response. For India, there is an apparent need to respond to China, as with concern in 2018 about increasing Chinese influence in Nepal, influence which reflected the strength of nationalist, anti-Indian views there. India is also anxious about the major expansion of the scale and range of Chinese naval powers, one creating an imperial "race" for naval bases in the Indian Ocean. With India and China, there are echoes of relations in the nineteenth century between Britain and both France and Russia.

To critics, Indonesia, moreover, is regarded as succeeding to the imperialist position and policies of the Dutch East Indies, a colony put together by imperial conquest, and a state that owes its genesis to this. Opposition to Indonesia, notably in Achin (Atceh) in Sumatra, and Papua New Guinea, can be presented as anti-imperialist and in the first case looks back to long-standing opposition, first to Portugal and later to Dutch expansion. Furthermore, the Indonesian seizure of the Portuguese colony of East Timor in 1975 against the wishes of the local population was an imperialist step and was defended with force and intimidation. The departure of Indonesian forces can be seen in terms of decolonization. Ironically, it owed much to pressure from Australia, another state created by colonialism and a heir to British imperial activity in the Southwest Pacific.

This imperialist process has a long history that greatly affects present attitudes and claims, and in both general ways and more specifically across a wide range. For example, in 2007, Ethiopia submitted a formal restriction claim for the restoration of what was taken by a British military expedition in 1868. However, some of this treasure had itself been seized by Ethiopia, a major imperial power in the late nineteenth century, from elsewhere in Africa, which underlines the problems involved with the very reasonable issue of restitution.

The language of imperialism might change, and that was certainly true of India and Indonesia. However, the reality remains, and this can represent a major qualification to the standard critique of British imperialism. This imperialism was frequently part of a sequence, one that has continued subsequently. So also with China in Tibet and Xinjiang, earlier positions re-established by conquest by the Manchu dynasty and maintained by force, notably in the shape of garrison-colonies. Indeed, the Chinese conquest of Tibet in 1950 repeated the conquests of the eighteenth century, while a conquest of Taiwan, if it were to occur, would repeat the conquest of the late seventeenth century. Possibly it is a sense of impotence in confronting this situation that partly accounts for Indian criticism of Britain: it is far easier to complain about Britain in the past than to address the issue of China today and how to respond. There is also a passive-aggressive character to the critique.

The United States presents the possible ambivalence of references to imperialism in a particularly clear fashion. Repeated mention, outside as well as within the United States, of the Declaration of Independence in 1776, and of the related liberation from an allegedly overbearing British

empire, underlines the extent to which anti-imperialism is a central feature in the ideology, both American and global, domestic and international, of the last quarter-millennium.[6] "Patriots" presented opposition to
George III of Britain and to the Westminster Parliament as anti-imperial,
as well as advancing freedom.

Thereafter, alongside significant anglophiles, notably during the
Gilded Era of the late nineteenth century, the United States adopted that
history and took that approach as a key theme in attitudes toward the
outside world. This anti-imperial stance was seen in President Woodrow
Wilson's support for national self-determination at the close of World War
I, notably in Eastern Europe and China. It was also present in President
Franklin Delano Roosevelt's anti-imperial attitudes during the World War
II, such as opposition to any return of British rule to Hong Kong after the
war brought to a close the Japanese occupation begun with conquest in
December 1941. Oliver Stanley, the Colonial Secretary, pertinently replied
to Roosevelt in January 1945 by drawing attention to American gains
in the Mexican–American War, which had occurred in the 1840s, a few
years after that of Hong Kong by the British. Roosevelt also criticized the
British stance over India. Anti-imperial attitudes were seen in American
policy at the time of the Suez Crisis of 1956, which became a fundamental
defeat for the British Empire, as it led to a crucial loss of confidence.

This process of continuing American hostility to empire, notably to
that of Britain, was encouraged by the extent to which many immigrants
to the United States fled imperial rule elsewhere, or could be presented
as doing so. This was the case with Jews leaving Russia, both under the
Romanov dynasty and under the Communists. The Irish diaspora in the
United States is instructive in this light. The devastating Irish Famine
that occurred between 1845 and 1852 and the resulting large-scale emigration (also to England and Scotland) attract lasting attention, and thus
characterize the Irish experience of the British Empire in a very hostile
light. In contrast, the representation of Ireland and, eventually, of Irish
Catholic voters in the Westminster Parliament tends to be ignored, as
does the large Irish presence in the British army and the number of "Irish
Americans" descended from Protestants. This is possibly because many
of these people went into agriculture and the South, while the Catholics concentrated in major cities, notably Boston and New York, where
they became politically influential. In practice, the majority of emigrants

who left the British Isles in the nineteenth century came from England, but English Americans do not act as a lobby, and their contribution to American life tends to be seriously undervalued.[7]

American hostility to imperial rule was seen in the rejection of European intervention in the Americas, notably with the Monroe Doctrine of 1823 and the criticism of Emperor Maximilian, the French-backed Austrian ruler of Mexico, in the 1860s. Opposition to the maintenance of the European empires after 1945 was also apparent. Despite being NATO allies, the Americans proved unwilling to back the French presence in Algeria, which was seen in France as a part of metropolitan France and not as a colony, or to support the Portuguese position in Goa, which was forcibly seized by India in 1961. Arguably, Thatcher's personality was a key factor in preventing the Americans from providing Argentina with diplomatic support in 1982 during the Falklands War. Americans, nevertheless, continued to regard imperialism as anachronistic. Attitudes within Britain, the colonies, and elsewhere to the British Empire were greatly affected by this context of American hostility and, in turn, affected policies toward other imperial powers.

As with India, Indonesia, and China, it is an irony unappreciated by most Americans and resented by many of them that the United States was itself to be regarded as an imperial power. It certainly took an imperialist course in North America in the nineteenth century at the expense of Native Americans, Spain, and Mexico, and in attempts to conquer Canada and later to limit its expansion.[8] Subsequently, the American imperialist course was to be discerned and resented in Central and South America, the Caribbean, the Pacific, and more generally after 1945. Indeed, opposition to American imperialism became a standard theme during the Cold War. It was very much employed during the Vietnam War.

Seeking to find parallels and precursors for the recent and current American position, commentators, both American and non-American, have long looked at earlier imperial periods, and notably so in the 1990s and early 2000s, although the tendency continues to be present to this day. A common theme, and one generally offered in a highly critical manner, or, at least, to challenge ideas of American exceptionalism, was of modern America as an empire.[9] That approach influenced readings of the British Empire. Those who disliked American policy and decried it as imperialist were able to treat Britain as an example of the wrongs of imperialism, indeed as a precursor of American imperialism. The comparison was not generally intended as favorable, although those who favored the idea of an Anglosphere were more positive. Indeed, this book is therefore, for many, implicitly or explicitly, about America's reputation as much as Britain's.

There were, of course, important differences between the British and American "empires." Outside North America, the Pacific, and the Caribbean, "informal" empire fitted the American trajectory more so than that of Britain. Yet, these were major exceptions, and in many areas, such as South America, the emphasis for both Britain and the United States was on "informal" empire. Moreover, differences between British and American imperialism tended to be downplayed when the emphasis was on criticism.

Ironically, none of this criticism was new, not for the United States, China, nor India. From the outset, states that had an anti-imperial slant in their foundation accounts or public history were frequently to be regarded, then or subsequently, and with reason, as empires themselves. In Antiquity, the Greeks developed a lasting rhetoric of anti-imperialism in depicting Persian rule, one that was to be repeated as part of the Classical tradition taught in schools to the later imperial leaders of Britain. As experienced by Greek cities in Asia Minor (Turkey), and as threatened for the rest of Greece with the Persian invasions of 490 and, even more, between 480 and 479 BCE, this rule could be presented as both despotic and barbarian, with each apparently demonstrating the other. As foreign, it could be presented as barbarian and foreign. The major cultural legacy of Greece in the West ensured that this set of beliefs was to be important subsequently to critical discussions about imperialism.

However, the distinctions drawn between good and bad rulers within Greece provided a way to explain why, depending on that circumstance, rule by an individual could be both undesirable, and thus imperializing, and desirable, and therefore appropriate; although the Greeks tended to regard monarchical rule as tyrannical. As such, discussion of imperial rule overlapped with that about "tyrants" in the Greek city-states. Ascribing barbarian and foreign characteristics to imperial rule complicated, and to this day complicates, the discussion of such practices within the Greek world. Having created an anti-imperial language, the Greeks then faced difficulties in using it effectively against other Greeks. Yet Athens and other leading city-states, notably its rival Sparta, were to be regarded as imperial powers, with Athens employing a form of "informal empire" to direct the Delian League, sometimes very brutally so with the "informal" becoming forcefully "formal."

The view that colonies are dangerous to the health of democracy goes back to the Classical world, and, more specifically, the argument that imperial strivings harm the chances for an egalitarian social order in the metropole.[10] That is a long-standing rhetorical position for which the evidence is scanty.

Separately, and again helping to "locate" British and American imperialism, Athens and Rome, as their alleged forbears, have recently been criticized for their imperial policies and for denigrating other cultures. Thus, in the "out of Africa" debate, an alleged modern Western failure to appreciate the strengths of African culture, more specifically, the alleged failure adequately to acknowledge the African character of Ancient Egypt, and its influence on Greece and the Western tradition, was traced to Classical influences as well as to Western racism. Criticizing Athens and Rome becomes part of a pattern of trashing the Western legacy, a pattern that locates, and is located by, the critiques of British and American imperialism. In the case of the "out of Africa" debate, this is highly problematic and, as generally discussed, a product of tendentious modern anti-Western views.[11]

Some of the Classical Greeks, most prominently Demosthenes (c. 383–322 BCE) in his *Philippics*, developed anti-imperial language against the expansionist menace of Philip of Macedon (r. 359–336 BCE). Demosthenes, however, was unsuccessful other than with posterity, which is the fate of many critics of imperialism and possibly increases their bitterness. The critics tend to be those who do not adapt and many are exiles.

The Greeks were absorbed, a word meaning "conquest," notably between 352 and 338 BCE, for some, and cooperation for others, within the Macedonian world, in the form of the League of Corinth, a league under Philip, established in 337 BCE. The Greeks then found themselves part, and swiftly, only a very minor part of a widespread Macedonian empire.

Philip's son, Alexander the Great (r. 336–323 BCE), overthrew the Persian empire and conquered from the Aegean Sea and Egypt to Afghanistan and India. If his empire lacked cohesion and fell apart after his early death, the Hellenistic successor empires in turn were far-flung, especially that of the Seleucids in Southwest Asia. Moreover, alongside cooperation with local elites, they faced anti-imperial opposition, notably with the eventually successful Maccabean Revolt in Israel (167–160 BCE), a revolt against the Seleucids and against Hellenistic influence in Jewish life.

The latter provided a prime instance of the subsequent use of opposition to the empires of Antiquity in order to vindicate later assertions of national independence. Thus, modern Israel looks back to the Maccabees and even more to the self-sacrificing resistance at Masada to the conquering imperial forces of Rome in CE 72–73, not least because these instances provided a more assertive and forceful account than an origin for Israel in terms of the Holocaust. The latter lacked the armed resistance, as well as the location in Israel, that Israeli commentators thought necessary.

The Israeli tradition, one that has been influential more widely, notably in the United States, is strongly anti-imperial. The opposition to the Seleucids and Romans was important to Jewish culture, and was given greater relevance and resonance by a critical account of British imperial rule and, subsequently, by the depiction of Muslim opponents as imperialists, notably in the case of Iran. Egypt, which Israel fought in 1948 to 1949, and in 1956, 1967, and 1973, certainly acted as an imperial power, seeking to expand control or influence not only against Israel, but also in Libya, Sudan, Syria, and Yemen, deploying its forces to support several of these goals. That attracted less criticism than that directed against Israel.

Opposition to Rome repeatedly proved a rallying symbol for later nationalists, who, ironically, were usually dependent for their information on the writers of Classical Rome, such as Tacitus in the case of Caledonia (Scotland). Successful resistance to the Roman Empire, especially the victory of Arminius over Varus and his three legions in 9 CE, probably in the Teutonburger Wald, was echoed by German commentators, seeking an exemplary history, at the time of the Reformation, notably Martin Luther. In a different context, this process occurred again in the late nineteenth century. This was particularly so after the formation of the Second German Empire, when Arminius was celebrated under his German name Hermann, most dramatically with the completion of a massive statue of Arminius near Detmold. In turn, Germany rapidly became a major imperial power itself.

So also with the Dutch. Opposition to Classical Rome was deployed at the time of the successful Dutch Revolt against Philip II of Spain in the late sixteenth century. This continued to be a pattern. In 1660, the Amsterdam city authorities commissioned Rembrandt to paint the *Conspiracy of Claudius Civilis*, a large canvas, for the new town hall which itself was an impressive statement of the city's significance. Civilis had led resistance to the Romans in 69 CE. Aside from conquering the Catholic "Generality Lands" to the south in the early seventeenth century, the Dutch also rapidly became a major imperial power, and on a global scale: from the Caribbean, via West Africa and South Asia, to the East Indies.

So, moreover, with England/Britain. At the height of its imperial power, Britain, in 1898, erected Thomas Thornycroft's dramatic sculpture of Boudicca by Westminster Bridge in London, close to the Houses of Parliament. As ruler of the Iceni, a tribe in what was to be named, after the Angles, successful later invaders, East Anglia, she had rebelled in 60–61 CE against the brutality of Roman imperial rule, and could be presented as a heroic failure.[12] The sculpture underlined the ability of empire to incorporate a variety of historical episodes, and in a frequently inconsistent fashion. The British were keen to draw on the example of Rome, and did so in iconography and literature, as with James, Viscount Bryce's *The Ancient Roman Empire and the British Empire in India* (1914).[13]

Yet, opposition to Rome could appear heroic, as in the depiction of leading opponents, notably Caractacus and Boudicca, each of whom was depicted as brave failures. Moreover, as an instructive guide to the fate of statues, there has been no pressure to remove that of Boudicca. The British presented, and to a degree continue to present, their history in terms of successful opposition to the imperial projects of others, notably Philip II at the time of the Spanish Armada in 1588, Louis XIV of France, Napoleon, and Germany in both world wars. Alfred was incorporated as both the opponent of Viking invaders and the originator of the English state.[14] This was scarcely the complete list of heroes resisting imperial expansion. Edward Bulwer-Lytton (1803–1873) produced an epic poem, *King Arthur* (1848–1849), as well as the novel *Harold, the Last of the Saxon Kings* (1848). He went on to become secretary of state for the Colonies (1858–1859), taking an active role in the development of British Columbia as "a second England on the shores of the Pacific," and his son became Viceroy of India. Charles Kingsley offered, in his novel *Hereward the Wake* (1866), an inspiring account of resistance to the Norman Conquest. He was then Regius Professor of Modern History at Cambridge. In the depiction of opposition to Germany in 1940, the stress was, and currently is, often on Britain alone, whereas in practice, it was very much supported by the empire.

Given the background of Athens, the Dutch, Britain, America, and Germany, each in turn deploying anti-imperial accounts while also becoming major imperial powers, it is not surprising today that China, India, Indonesia, or other powers can be seen in terms of the same equation. Moreover, critics of Western imperialism would profit from this understanding of their location.

Today, however, the parallel is denied. Indeed, it can be instructive to hear Indians denounce British imperialism and then defend their own conduct in Kashmir; and their Chinese counterparts do the same over Tibet. This is no more than the pattern seen in the past with the United States. Empire is wrong, so India, China, the United States et al. cannot be imperial, not least because they reject the idea. This is an approach that is historically questionable, and that follows that adopted by, and toward, the Soviet Union by its apologists, both Soviet and foreign, a process continued to this day with respect to Russia. Stalin was presented as seeking a defensive barrier for the Soviet Union and/or seeking to expand the sphere for revolution, and his apologists, a group currently led by President Vladimir Putin, thereby excused his imperialism. Similarly, Islamic commentators are apt to ignore the degree of "inchoate imperialism" in modern Islamic geopolitics, a geopolitics that seeks to justify expansion into one-time Islamic areas, such as Andalusia and Israel,[15] irrespective of the views of the inhabitants.

Historical ironies can be readily multiplied. As part of a litany of victimhood and grievance, Scottish nationalists make much of the alleged subjugation of Scotland in an English-run Britain, and scrutinize their history accordingly. This, ironically, leads to a serious failure to appreciate the history of independent Scotland. Divisions in the latter extended to resistance to the state-building that was based on the Central Belt. In particular, Galloway, Moray, the Highlands, and the Isles, were all, for long, only partly incorporated in the Scottish state and nation. This incorporation was in part achieved by violence, and it is instructive that that is covered in "amnesia," unlike the victory over the Jacobites by the government forces in the battle of Culloden in 1746. The large number of Scots in the army fighting for George II (more than that in the Jacobite army) is generally neglected. The struggle was one not only between dynasties (Hanoverians and Stuarts), but also a contest within Scotland between Presbyterians and Episcopalians, Lowlanders and Highlanders, and not a putative "Scottish nation" against the English one.

The negotiations that helped Scotland expand and acquire the Orkneys and the Shetlands are also generally covered in "amnesia," unlike the Act of Union, which receives continuing attention by Scottish nationalist commentators. The Act of Union is frequently, and misleadingly, attributed to bribery, and there is a widespread failure to understand why influential Scots sought and supported Union. Many (though not all) Scots underplay the central role the Scots subsequently played in British empire building. The selective nature of the political weaponization of history is readily apparent in the case of Scotland. That is also true of England and Britain of course, but far less stridently so.

In the past, the imperial question was generally handled differently. The focus was on a contrast between good empire and bad empire, a contrast that was central to political thought and rhetoric. This contrast drew on the long-standing difference between the existential empires of God and the Devil, a core theme in Saint Augustine's *City of God* (412–427 CE), which was for long, indeed, after the Bible, the fundamental text for medieval Christian thought, and more generally on the role of religion and justice in imperial purposes and ideologies.

Colonial administrators and others also saw this contrast in discussion. Thus, the British debate about India prior to World War I was really a debate about the accountability, competency, and standards of the administration; and not about Indian fitness for self-government. Prior to that war, very few major British politicians thought the latter a realistic prospect within any meaningful timetable. The contrast between "good empire" and "bad empire" has only been automatically replaced by an equation of "empire" and "bad" over the last century, with that equation then read back into history and employed to shape it.

It is not necessary to turn back to the might of the Classical Romans, or to consider current accounts of the replacement of British rule, to find accounts of the defiance of empires at key moments of national formation. The Middle Ages provides many instances. Scots could refer to the war of independence from England between the 1290s and the 1320s, while Flemings and Swiss pointed to glorious victories over the French and the Austrians respectively. William Tell, a probably legendary figure, became the key individual in accounts of the latter and gave Swiss history an anti-imperial character. In turn, the later, strong imperial position of the Habsburgs provided this account with greater resonance.

Subsequently, Habsburg support for the Catholic, or Counter-Reformation, especially in the Thirty Years' War (1618–48), ensured that Czech and German Protestants, and their foreign allies, notably Gustavus Adolphus of Sweden, presented religious liberty in terms of opposition, not only to the imperial religious pretensions of the Papacy, but also to the imperial assumptions of the Habsburg Holy Roman Emperors. British commentators very much shared in this presentation, and accounts of the Thirty Years' War tended to present the Czechs as if they were British. American accounts also supported the Protestants.

For the early modern period, the Spanish empire of Philip II (r. 1556–1598), the first empire on which, thanks to the establishment of positions in the Philippines from 1565, the sun literally never set, became the basis for accounts of Dutch and English independence. The defeat of the apparently overwhelming Spanish Armada in 1588 provided a key and much-celebrated episode in English history and commemoration, as well as substantiating beliefs in a providential dispensation for England. The Americans inherited this approach via the English colonists.

Confidence in divine support was to prove an important bridge between belief in national destiny and confidence in imperial purpose. The religious dimension in imperial history is always important. Churchill presented the struggle with Hitler in religious terms, or at least in religious language, telling the House of Commons on September 3, 1939, that a war with Germany was "in defence of all that is most sacred to man." More generally, attitudes toward Christian trusteeship were significant, in Britain, the United States, and elsewhere, in encouraging support, first and foremost, for imperial rule and then for decolonization.

The religious dimension was separately significant in that imperial rule meant that over other faiths, which created serious issues for both, and notably for those who had never had to confront another religion, or to confront one in a position of equality. The British came to rule over Catholics, Copts, Muslims, Hindus, Buddhists, Sikhs, Jews, and those from a range of other religions, including animists.

Despite the view widely propagated, the choice generally, both his-torically and to a degree today, was not between empire and non-empire. This view is suggested in many public myths, and by writers, both past and present, critical of imperialism. Instead, the choice, generally, was between different empires or, at best, different types of empire. Thus, much of the moralistic discussion of imperialism and imperial legacies is of limited value, although still significant. If, during the American Rev-olutionary War (1776–83), control of East and West Florida, or St. Lucia or Minorca, or the slaving bases in West Africa, such as Gorée, changed hands, it was not a case of the expulsion of imperial powers (which only occurred, during the war, in the Thirteen Colonies of North America), but, rather, of one imperial power replacing another, for France (from 1778), Spain (from 1779), and the Dutch (from 1780), all fought on the American side.

The replacement of one imperial power by another, moreover, would have also happened if the Americans had conquered Canada, as they sought to do between 1775 and 1776 and, with greater effort, between 1812 and 1814. Britain had conquered Canada from France. The Floridas, transferred from Spain to Britain in 1763 at the end of the Seven Years' War, were returned in 1783, and it was from Spain that the United States, using force, was to gain them in the 1810s.

This theme remained important in World War I, with the disposal of German colonies, such as German East Africa, which became British Tanganyika (now, with the addition of Zanzibar, already a British colony, Tanzania). Some German territory was used to expand the British col-onies of Ghana and Nigeria (and to create the French colonies of Togo and Cameroon), while German Southwest Africa (Namibia) went to South Africa. Australia and New Zealand each gained German colonies in the Pacific. The Turkish possessions of Iraq, Palestine, and Transjordan went to Britain.

This transfer process also seemed an option with Italian colonies in World War II, notably Libya, but also Somalia. The United States gained control of Japanese islands in the Pacific. Moreover, imperialism, of a particular form, can be seen in subsequent decolonization, as territories that could have become independent, such as Eritrea, British Somaliland, East Timor, Arab Palestine, the princely states of British India (notably Hyderabad), the Portuguese positions in India, and Arab Palestine (the

West Bank, the Gaza Strip, and the lands seized by Israel), were instead allocated and/or seized in an imperial fashion: by Ethiopia, Somalia, Indonesia, Jordan, India, and (in the case of the last), Jordan, Egypt, and Israel, respectively.

This aspect of imperial history is not ignored, but it is badly underplayed when the merits of imperialism are discussed. In practice, for much of history, the particular identity of the ruling power was contentious and subject to conflict, whereas the fact of imperial rule was not. Thus, in Khorusan (northeast Persia) and western Afghanistan, which were repeatedly contested by the Safavids, Uzbeks, and Mughals in the sixteenth and seventeenth centuries, the question was "Which empire?" and not "Whether empire?" A similar point can be made about Spanish success in between 1519 and 1521 in winning large-scale local support in Mesoamerica (Mexico) against Aztec rule, one empire replacing another. The harshness of Aztec rule helps explain why Hernán Cortés, the Spanish leader, won support, which is a point that tends to be underrated by critics of Spanish expansion and its methods. Britain can be fitted into this account, notably with its expansion in the eighteenth and nineteenth centuries in South Asia into areas ruled by empires or, in some cases, such as Mysore and the Maratha Confederation, proto-empires. In what became northeast India, the choice in areas such as Manipur in the early nineteenth century appeared to be British or Burmese expansionism. In northern Malaya, the choice was British, Burmese, or Thai expansionism, and the threat from the latter two led to the British presence being "welcomed" into Penang in 1786. However, in another light, the East India Company broke the agreement to help the Sultan of Kedah against Thai attack.

In opposition to imperialism, there was not necessarily any clear understanding of statehood, national identity, or frontiers. Indeed, all three tend to be exaggerated and read back by modern commentators seeking a long-term identity for present-day entities, and, thus in part, trying to validate them. Ethnogenesis played, and plays, a major role in this process, as with Sikh separatists from India pressing for Khalistan, an independent Sikh state. The widespread popular assumption, nevertheless, today is empire or non-empire, with the two presented in Manichean terms as polar opposites. On a long-standing process, binary thinking indeed is part of contemporary posture politics. In this context, non-imperialism takes on its meaning as opposed to imperialization, or, at least, to Western imperialism. In part, this situation pertains because the emotional, intellectual and political commitment to anti-imperialism, specifically inherent self-determination, is so great. There is a belief in the self-determination of all peoples and the independent sovereignty of all states. There is also a misleading tendency to apply this belief historically. However, avoiding imperialist behavior did not seem an option to major powers, no more than pacifism was.

These are not only points valid to the treatment of the non-West region by the West. It can also be seen within the West. For example, in Italy, the nationalist discourse and national myth entails the idea of "lost centuries" of foreign rule before Italian unification was achieved in the nineteenth century with the Risorgimento. These lost centuries are popularly approached as if there was a clear Italian alternative, which, however, was not a view offered at the time with any plausibility. Instead, the alternative to rule, direct or indirect, by Spain in the sixteenth and seventeenth centuries, was, frequently, that of an alignment with France. There was no Italian nation-state in prototype or prospect. Nevertheless, a perception of Italy existed abroad, as was, moreover, the case with Germany, which also was divided into many territories. Within Italy, there was a shared identity that was commonly accepted, or at least by those who were a bit literate. At the same time, the Risorgimento in 1860 and 1861, to a degree, represented the conquest of southern by northern Italy, was resented and resisted in the 1860s accordingly, and is still, in this light, an element in Italian public culture and politics. A similar process occurred in many countries as part of decolonization and has affected postcolonial politics.

With imperialism often competitive, in practice if not in theory, there was a determination on the part of imperial powers to prevent the rise of rivals. Imperial competition meant that areas outside imperial control could thus appear as a source of vulnerability, and one that had to be secured by the extension of imperial control, such as with the competition between Ottomans and Safavids for control of the Caucasus from the sixteenth century to the eighteenth century, a competition that Russia increasingly entered and eventually dominated. The Ottomans and Safavids were the ruling dynasties in empires that can be misleadingly described as Turkish and Iranian (earlier Persian), the latter reflecting an anachronistic ethnogenesis that is rooted in modern ideas of national development.

To neighboring empires, the frontiers of non-colonialized areas often represented chaos, threat, and a vacuum that had to be managed. One form of management was to seek to fill the vacuum, albeit often with scant attempt to understand the local situation. This factor helped lead the Romans to invade southern England, as it appeared a way to strengthen their control of Gaul (France). At least, that was the argument employed by Julius Caesar between 55 and 54 BCE in an attempt to justify his continued control of the forces in Gaul.

Moreover, this approach could be frequently seen in the case of the British Empire, for example, with southern Africa, Northeast India, and Burma (Myanmar),[16] or with Sudan once the British were established in Egypt in 1882. In other cases, it was intended that compliant rulers would fill the vacuum, for example, repeatedly in Afghanistan.

Such a functionalist approach to imperialism, however, underplays the values involved, or allegedly involved, in seeking to rule others. These values attract particular attention and opprobrium in the modern world, indeed, possibly disproportionate simplification and attention.

Whether in functional terms or with reference to values, or both, there could be a contrast between empires operating in a highly competitive context, and, on the other hand, those empires that did not face, or acknowledge, comparable imperial powers. The former was the position with Spain and the Ottomans in the Mediterranean in the sixteenth century, or with the Europeans in the late nineteenth century during the "Scramble for Africa." The second was the Chinese position until repeated defeat in the nineteenth century, first by Britain.

That contrast between empires is a realist one, to employ the vocabulary of international relations theory, and this point underlines the extent to which values as the driver of imperialism stemmed, in part, from practicalities, and were, in part, expressed in terms of them. These might be strategic competition, but also commercial issues, notably the frequently competitive drives, for resources and markets. The latter could entail support for particular production systems that might have environmental consequences, distort the economy, and increase inequality. The last, for example, was the case with the British encouragement of cattle ranching in what became Botswana,[17] and of cotton production in Sudan and Uganda. This point overlaps with the investment and other links that were part of informal empire, for example, by British investors in the Cuban sugar industry, still slave-based, in the mid-nineteenth century.

Strategic competition—its rationale, exigencies, compromises, and consequences—does not tend to attract praise today, but it was a frequent factor throughout history and better understood, or at least more clearly articulated in the past. This competition was seen over the last century in what were life-and-death struggles for the Western liberal order (and international system): struggles against Germany and the Soviet Union. In the former case, there were clear instances, on the part of Germany's opponents, of prophylactic imperial interventions, those designed to thwart the possibility that independent states would turn to hostile patrons. This was the case in the British conquest of Iraq in 1941 and in the Anglo-Soviet conquest of Iran later that year. At a time when the British Empire was under great pressure, there was concern about rising German influence in both countries and anxiety about its possible geopolitical consequences. This British imperialism was in large part imperialism directed against other empires.

That was a long-standing British practice as far as Persia/Iran was concerned: in the nineteenth century and the 1900s, the focus of concern had been on the Russian penetration of Persia, albeit with worry about France in the 1800s. In World War I, the concern about Persia focused instead on Turkey and its ally Germany. Thus, on March 21, 1918, the *Times* pressed for British preparations against "a fresh invasion of Persia.... They may move down the Turco-Persian frontier and endeavour to strike at the valuable oilfields of the Anglo-Persian Oil Company. They are quite likely to reach the frontiers of Afghanistan and try to raise the Afghans against us," which would be a threat to British India, as readers, carrying the mental geography of imperialism, would be expected to know. That threat had earlier been deployed to justify action and preparations against Russia, notably during the Crimean War (1854–56).

During World War II, the British plans to plant mines in Norwegian waters in 1940 in order to stop iron ore shipments to Germany, and the establishment of Allied power in the Danish colonies of Iceland and Greenland after the German conquest of Denmark in 1940, can differently be seen in this context of imperial pre-emption. Moreover, French nationalists feared that British imperialism and expansionism played a role in interventions against Vichy (pro-German) rule between 1940 to

1942, notably, successfully, in Syria (1941), Lebanon (1941), and Madagascar (1942), and, unsuccessfully, at Dakar (1940).

It is unsurprising that World War II plays a continuing and major role in the discussion of imperialism, for it represented a highpoint of imperial unity for Britain and a vindication of the empire. As the crisis of that war also served as a justification for action against nationalists who sought decolonization, and some of whom allied with, or otherwise assisted, Nazi Germany, Fascist Italy, and/or Imperial Japan, so, subsequently, the misleading comparison of the British Empire with Nazi Germany and/ or Imperial Japan serves an important role in the anti-imperial narrative. Indeed, trashing the British war effort and, more particularly, Churchill (notably by Indian writers) thus becomes a major part of the critique of historical imperialism. This helps explain the mismatch between popular views within Britain, which usually do not take part in such trashing, and those of the critics of imperialism, both British and foreign.

Imperial power, largely indirect, but at times more overt, was also employed during the Cold War. This was done in part to ensure cohesion and prevent the risk of hostile action, as with American intervention in Iran in 1953 and, very differently in type and far more overt, that of the Soviet Union in Hungary in 1956, in Czechoslovakia in 1968, and, far less successfully, in Afghanistan in 1979. Soviet policy in Eastern Europe was definitely imperial. American policy in Central America and the Caribbean was frequently seen by critics as imperial in character, with new ideologies and issues imprinted on old patterns of concern and intervention, as with the American invasions of the Dominican Republic in 1965, Grenada in 1983, and Panama in 1989, and with American pressure on Cuba from the 1960s and on Nicaragua in the 1980s.

The debate about empire, more specifically about its strategic aspects, now in part reflects the extent to which judgments are being advanced after the world wars and the Cold War (and also with reference to earlier periods) that fail to give due weight to the apparent exigencies of the period (e.g., the highly aggressive Soviet interest in a defensive barrier and in aggressive subversion and power-projection), or that approach them simply in a critical fashion. As such, notably with reference to the Cold War and more particularly toward Britain and the United States, there is a new iteration of earlier anti-imperial propaganda. Thus, criticisms of the British Empire, and of American power and policies, made at the time of the world wars and the Cold War, are given a new life. During the Cold War, such propaganda was pushed hard by, and, in the Communist bloc; by, and in, the non-aligned Third World; and by left-wing and liberal circles in the West. The arguments were influential in Britain, the United States, and elsewhere. Indeed, just as British imperialism had a particular political context, so did anti-imperialism. Each, in turn, changed in response both to cultural-ideological trends and to circumstances. So also with their American counterparts.

Moreover, because a national basis for states became a dominant ideological rhetoric, first in the West and then elsewhere, so alternatives appeared inappropriate, wrong and anachronistic, the last notably so in developmental theories of world history. Imperialism was set up as the highly undesirable "other," and its supposed values were presented in a hostile fashion that validated this undesirability.

In practice, although nation-states and nationalism might offer a prospect of democracy and human rights more extensive than those provided by colonial masters, they also had many faults. Ironically, in terms of their rhetoric, many of the newly independent states, such as Egypt, were authoritarian and/or militaristic, a point that underlines the complexity of judging British policy in the Suez Crisis of 1956.[18] Moreover, "the underlying centrality of slavery in the historical relationship between Egypt and the Sudan" was such that anti-colonial nationalism in Egypt was readily compatible with an Egyptian determination to regain power over Sudan,[19] where, if earlier British colonial rule was, to a degree, violent and destabilizing,[20] so also had been that of Egypt.

Other states that can be seen as authoritarian and/or military include Nigeria and Pakistan. Each in effect was a type of empire, in that groups based in one part of the state, the Punjab, for example, ruled more broadly and suppressed opposition, as in Baluchistan in Pakistan and the Ibo-inhabited region in Southeastern Nigeria. Some other former colonies were soon, or eventually, ruled by military figures who had seized power by force, for example, Uganda and Fiji, and/or who used force once in power, as with Zimbabwe.

Ironically given the critique of imperialism, the nationalist stance can appear of scant validity from the historical perspective, notably given the extent to which, across much of the world, there was only a limited sense of national identity for most of history. Moreover, in many areas, particularly, but not only, in cities, there was not ethnic homogeneity, but a variety of ethnic groups. In a major instance of transnationalism, this variety can be seen as contributing greatly to multi-national empires, which, therefore, were more than states simply incorporating areas each of which had coherent national populations. The Ottoman Empire was a good instance of one in which ethnic groups were mixed, not least in Alexandria, Smyrna (Izmir), Salonica, and Constantinople. Such cities contained large numbers of minority groups, notably Armenians, Greeks, Jews, and Kurds. Similarly, there were considerable numbers of Muslims in rural areas in the Balkans, particularly in Kosovo and Albania.[21]

Subsequent problems in these (and other) areas are not so much a legacy of empire, particularly the British Empire, as Jack Straw suggested in 2002, when he was British foreign secretary—"a lot of the problems we are having to deal with now are a consequence of our colonial past" —but, rather, a legacy of the end of empire, both British and other. "Ethnic Cleansing," or, at least, control, is logical from the perspective of ethnically based states, such as Turkey, Serbia, and Myanmar; but not from that of polyglot empires, or not to the same extent. Under the Treaty of Lausanne of 1923, ending the Greek-Turkish conflict following World War I, and marking the replacement of the Ottoman Empire by Turkey, there was a large-scale expulsion of those who, on religious grounds, were judged alien: Greeks and Turks respectively. Similarly, Protestants did not benefit from Irish independence. Instead, aside from suffering intimidation, there was a far longer-lasting discrimination in which their chances of getting jobs declined.[22]

Apology was scarcely restricted to Straw, a prominent Labour politician. In 2011, when visiting Pakistan, David Cameron, a Conservative, then British prime minister, replied when questioned about the Kashmir question: "I don't want to try to insert Britain in some leading role where, as with so many of the world's problems, we are responsible for the issue in the first place."[23] This remark, which clearly looked back to that by Straw, underplayed the extent to which the dispute was, and is, really about sectarian and geopolitical disputes between India and Pakistan, and also arises from politics and sectarianism within them.

Misplaced blame on Britain was also provided in the film *Viceroy's House* (2017), which offered a conspiratorial account of the 1947 Partition. Deeply flawed, the film was defended by Gurinder Chadha, the director, against criticisms of inaccuracy by reference to Narendra Singh Sarila's problematic *The Shadow of the Great Game: The Untold Story of India's Partition* (2006). In response to criticism by Fatima Bhutto, a Pakistani writer, who argued (correctly) that the film disproportionately blames Muslims, Chadha declared that her film celebrated the "freedom struggle." The central claim that Pakistan was created as a result of a British conspiracy initiated by Churchill is deeply flawed (but frequently repeated in India), and was described in the *Guardian* as bringing "fake history" to the screen.[24] That is a frequent process, with freedom of expression readily sliding into the aggressive propagation of rubbish.

From the perspective of many groups, such as Copts and Jews, empires such as those ruled by the Ottomans, Habsburgs, and Britain were frequently more benign than the ethnically based nation-states that succeeded them. The harsh plight of the East African Indians once British rule ended, such as life in Uganda under the military dictator Idi Amin, was a clear example. Not all empires were benign to minority ethnic groups, as the treatment of Jews in the closing decades of Romanov Russia very much indicated, but many were. The British notably sought to end the enslavement of minorities, and can be criticized today by those who seek to enforce a monoglot interpretation of nationhood, like Buddhists in Myanmar and Sri Lanka and Hindu supremacists in India. This point needs to be borne in mind in any debate about imperialism, as does the argument that ethnic variety itself was functionally an advantage for, and of, imperial systems, particularly for their commercial viability.

Today, in an increasingly multicultural world, marked by mass migrations and new intermixing of peoples, the larger and more capacious political unit can, to some, appear more attractive and efficient than the narrower and more exclusive ones, whether one is looking in present-day terms or historically. Empires indeed arouse particular scholarly interest at present because, for all their faults, they are perceived to embody a wealth of experience in the management of difference and diversity. They were necessarily multifaceted and diverse.

This point has become particularly pertinent over the last quarter-century with a shift toward transnationalism as a means of analysis and as a value system, if not ideology, notably in academic circles. Transnationalism presents the present and the future in terms of international communities that are not contained within, or expressed in terms of, national states. Instead, there is an emphasis on universal values and institutions, expressed in, and through, human rights and international courts, as well as on the extent to which communications, culture, trade, and, in particular, migration, are allegedly making national criteria redundant or, at least, less significant. This account is then read back into the past.[25]

At the same time, however much empires were inherently transnational, as well as sometimes multicultural, in practice universal criteria, such as self-determination, democracy, and human rights, undermined the mental world of imperialism. Imperialism, indeed, was inherently based on difference, that between the metropole and the colonies, as well as between particular empires. Yet the root problem for imperialism in the twentieth century was generally nationalist resistance, and not the universal criteria by which imperialism was frequently found wanting. Looked at differently, this resistance drew on such criteria, including democracy and anti-imperialism, and, from the 1920s, Communism, which ruthlessly exploited anti-imperialism while suppressing it in the Soviet Union.

Separately, and paradoxically, the subsequent use of these supposedly universal criteria allegedly offered what was presented by some as a new internationalist imperialism, a "liberal imperialism" in the shape of a consensus of received views that could be directed against those deemed unacceptable, as in the 1990s, the 2000s, and the 2010s. This was a variant of a longer-term process in which ideology, intellectualism, typologies, and language served to offer definitions that asserted imperialism, and created a hierarchy of acceptability irrespective of the actual fact of rule.

Leading in a variety of directions, transnational accounts have a number of consequences for the discussion of imperialism. The transnational world can be presented as resulting in a new type of empire and new forms of imperialism. This was allegedly the case with the new international order devised in the 1940s, with bodies such as the World Bank, the International Monetary Fund, and the United Nations. The order at once offered liberal international values, such as free trade,[26] and reflected what can be seen as an imperial conceptual order on behalf of the United States.[27]

Although they scarcely define or exhaust transnationalism, the United Nations (UN), the North Atlantic Treaty Organization (NATO), and the European Union (EU), all provide instances of this development. Those subject to interventionist actions by these bodies in the 1990s, 2000s and 2010s, for example, Serbia, Iraq, and Sierra Leone, might note their repeated, indeed mandatory, use of civilizational language that was, and is, similar to that of boosters for imperial rule in the nineteenth century. To be justified, the use of force has to be moralized. There is an emphasis on the positive, especially humanitarian, values that intervention can further, and on the negative aspects of the plight of those requiring such intervention.

Nowadays, this is a matter of human rights, rather than the slave trade and slavery, which were the subject of international action in the nineteenth century. The intention, however, is frequently similar, and thus the supporters of imperialism, like the critics, include a wide range of interests and opinions. Looked at differently, in addition to strange bedfellows, there is a rectitude, but also a naivety and self-interest, on the part of many critics of imperialism that match those seen by many supporters.

Alongside the continuance of "old" forms of imperialism, as by Russia in Crimea and the Caucasus, China in Tibet, and India in Kashmir, an emphasis on humanitarian interventionism as a cutting edge of modern transnationalism, and on its supposed values, presents a way to look at the motivation and cartography of the new imperialism. There were significant intermediary steps, notably the League of Nations' mandates after World War I, which brought Britain control over German East Africa (mainland Tanzania), strips of Togo and the Cameroons, Iraq, Palestine, Transjordan, and the Pacific island of Nauru; and the United Nation's trusteeships after World War II: the African mandates, Nauru, and Somaliland. In these cases, established imperial powers, notably Britain, France, and the United States, were linked to supervision by new international agencies, although the Permanent Mandates Commission of the League of Nations in practice supported the continuation of imperial control.[28]

Such an approach to imperialism, its history, and humanitarian interventionism, may appear both ridiculous and offensive in light of the frequently harsh character of late-nineteenth- and early twentieth-century imperialism. However, the idea of the modern period as an age of empire appears more plausible if imperialism is treated not as an essential state, with one particularly true manifestation that was found in a given period, but, instead, as a shifting practice and, moreover, a practice that is far from uniform even for one given period. Such an approach both complicates the understanding of decolonization and displaces attention from the classic age of high imperialism in the late nineteenth century, and from Britain, which, indeed, had a longer and more complex history of imperialism. Such complexity can also be seen in the case of the United States.

This approach, however, risks having imperialism become another term for rule. That terminological looseness, nevertheless, is understandable, as imperialism is harder to determine in practice than it is to define in theory or the empty yet abusive clarity of rhetoric. Indeed, the range of types of rule described and criticized, or described through criticism, as imperial or imperialism is very extensive. It operates as a catchall phrase for the external imposition of power, although external, imposition and power are all subject to varied understandings and usage.

Moreover, however defined, there was a variety of moods and tones in the case of imperialism, its policies, and attitudes, as well as the context, response, and consequences. In particular, the supposed triumphalism of empire was invariably tempered by anxiety, such that empire was a state that had to be endured (albeit on very different terms) by the ruler and the ruled, one in which there was often little to hope for and much to fear. This situation was/is linked to empire always being a work in being, and thus never having equilibrium. This point may be true of all governments, but it is especially so of imperial rule. So also with the limits, domestic and foreign, to empire and imperialism.[29] The British Empire was under growing internal and external strains in the two decades before and after World War I, which was also a period of imperial apogee.

In practice, once imperialism includes economic factors, informal empire, and soft power, all ideas used to describe American imperialism in the twentieth century, there cannot be any close, let alone precise, definition. There were overlaps between the factors involved, as in the 1930s advertisement sporting the Union Jack: "Wherever flies the flag that's braved a thousand years the battle and the breeze, there Beecham's Pills will triumph o'er disease," but also contrasts. Informal empire in particular is a concept that directs attention away from conquest, rule and sovereignty as central to imperialism. Informal empire also provided a way for Britain to inherit elite links from the Portuguese, Dutch, Spanish, and French empires and to tie local elites into a global economy. In turn, notably in Latin America, America inherited these systems and practices.[30] Not least due to opposition from left-wing nationalist movements supported by Communist powers, the process was frequently a difficult one.

If the concept and term "informal empire" can be used in the case of the nineteenth century, it is unclear why it should not also be used for the twenty-first century, both now and in the future. Informal empire can serve, for example, to discuss the spreading economic and military power of China, or the interventionist conduct of Russia and India in neighboring states, or the attempts of Brazil, Nigeria, and South Africa to act as regional powers. Myanmar, Cambodia, Sri Lanka, and Nepal appear as parts of a Chinese informal empire. Similar, and other, aspects of this imperialism can be seen further afield as China establishes control over resources, notably in Africa, for example, such as the oil of Equatorial Guinea, but also elsewhere, such as copper in Afghanistan, and minerals and harbors in Pacific islands such as Vanuatu.

Economic dominance is linked to geopolitical competition. Already powerful in Laos, China competes with Vietnam for influence in Cambodia, while China's already-significant and still-growing strategic role in Myanmar, Pakistan, and Sri Lanka is clearly directed against India. China's growing presence in Micronesia is seen as a challenge to Australia. China's establishment of naval bases, such as Djibouti and Gwalior (in Pakistan), and its growing presence at Hambantota in Sri Lanka become a key instance of power, as in the nineteenth century for Britain. As then, the Indian Ocean, and the routes to it, are particular foci of power-projection and contention.

Chinese policy in Africa can be compared to that of Britain in nineteenth-century Latin America. This comparison can be qualified by reference to the specific circumstances of particular periods and individual imperialisms. Nevertheless, the comparison serves to underline, if not the universality of imperialism, at least the extent to which it is a lasting theme in international assumptions and political organization.

Transnationalism, therefore, can be deployed both to defend imperialism, as a way to organize and protect a multi-ethnic world, and also to provide a basis for condemning imperialism as a form of national imposition on such a world. Again, there is a level of ahistoricism in both approaches. The idea that governance should automatically seek to protect diversity is, in many respects, a modern view. Moreover, the treatment of imperialism as a form of national imposition on other nations is highly problematic for periods prior to the nineteenth century. This treatment can downplay the functional and, indeed, ideological nature, and to a degree normality, of imperialism, both then and in other periods. At any rate, alongside the customary diatribes, there is now a greater willingness than at any time between the 1960s and the 1990s to suggest that empire, however phrased,[31] might not be irredeemably bad,[32] and might even have some lessons to offer. Such an approach appears particularly appropriate if the commonplace, even for many normative, character of empire for much of history is considered.

4

BRITISH RULE AND FOUNDATION ACCOUNTS: INDIA AND IRELAND

Britain did not become an Indian power in order to help the Dalits, whom, drawing on Indian practice, they called the *Untouchables*. However, like others, the Dalits could benefit from British imperialism. Moreover, despite the attempts of postcolonial states to filter out the experience of cooperation with empire, this cooperation can still play a role in present-day commemoration and, therefore, identity, indeed a prominent role. In 1818, at the Battle of Koregaon, the British fought off the far larger forces of the Maratha ruler, Peshwa Baji Rao II. The British army included Dalit soldiers. The names of the East India Company soldiers killed in the battle feature on an obelisk describing "one of the proudest triumphs of the British Army in the East." Twenty-two of the forty-one names are those of Dalits, and they see the obelisk today as an important symbol. From 1927, when the Dalit leader visited the site, the anniversary has become a significant Dalit occasion.[1]

Dalits celebrate the victory as a landmark in their ongoing struggle against the caste-based oppression that seems ever-present in India. In January 2018, Hindu nationalists, who self-consciously look back to the Marathas, and in many respects represent this continuing oppression, raided the Dalit celebrations. This raid led to clashes that included strikes, blockades, and rioting in Mumbai and in several other cities in Maharashtra state in Western India.

Anger at the discrimination and violence suffered by the Dalits is scarcely a marginal situation, nor irrelevant on the world scale, as there are maybe about 200 million Dalits: the 2011 census registers 16.6 percent of the population as members of the Scheduled Castes. The word "Dalit" means "oppressed" in Sanskrit and "broken" in Hindu, and the Dalits are definitely oppressed.[2] The Indian state uses its powers to contain their activism, and Dalit activists, notably the Dalit Panthers' movement founded in 1972, criticize the very social norms and practices of India. Ashok Bharti, head of the National Conference of Dalit Organizations, referred in January 2018 to "an authoritarian regime," adding that: "India is divided...between people who are humiliated and those who humiliate."

This charge echoed earlier Indian complaints about British rule. That comparison is scarcely ironic as it is all too common with postcolonial circumstances. Indeed, a useful "control" on the incessant criticism of British imperial rule is offered by considering these circumstances.

The reputation of the British Empire takes a battering around much of its former sway, but especially so in India and Ireland, which is why they are to the fore here. Although the histories of India and Ireland are different, and the criticisms of imperial rule are far from identical,[3] they share important aspects. Moreover, there were significant connections between Indian and Irish nationalists in London in the late nineteenth century, as with Alfred Webb, an Irish nationalist who was president of the 1894 Indian National Congress.[4] In each case today, there is a tendency to underplay the capacity of empire to integrate interests and, at the same time, of its dependence on cooperation, as well as consent. This integration and cooperation rested on practices and senses of interest that were ideological and political as much as material, and that were seen both from imperialists and from those who experienced empire. India is a key country to consider when discussing the imperial legacy, as it is the most populous former colony in the world, as well as a leading state and country where there is a well-defined critique of British imperialism. Ireland is significant because the numerous and articulate Irish diaspora has greatly affected American views on the subject. Thus, part of this chapter is about the context for American views, a position enhanced by the growing Indian population there.

INDIA

The Cellular Jail, the Indian Bastille, stands as a mute witness to the untold suffering, valiant defiance and undaunted spirit of the fire-brand revolutionaries against the brutalities of the British barbarisms.

The plaque outside the partly preserved Cellular Jail at Port Blair on South Andaman Island in the Bay of Bengal was installed when the jail was visited, "as a mark of respect to the freedom fighters dedicated to the nation," in 1979 by the Indian prime minister, Morarji Desai. Desai (1896–1995) had been a civil servant under the British in Mumbai before, in 1930, becoming a supporter of Gandhi and being imprisoned by the British for civil disobedience. Ironically, Desai was imprisoned anew by the government of Indira Gandhi during her totalitarian "Emergency" of 1975 (to 1977), a period of rule by decree and the imprisonment without trial of about 140,000 opponents. Moreover, the forced mass-sterilization campaign initiative by the Indian government in 1976 scarcely accorded with most views of human rights. This, obviously, however, was not a point worthy of mention when the focus was on the iniquities of the British, nor one that is relevant at the Cellular Jail.

The stance Desai took as Chief Minister of Bombay State in ordering police in 1955 to fire at demonstrators of the *Samyukta Maharashtra Samiti* movement pressing for a Maratha-only state is instructive. Opening fire led to the killing of 105 protestors, including an eleven-year-old child. The episode was reminiscent of Amritsar in 1919, not, however, a comparison conspicuous in memorialization. The Flora Fountain in Mumbai (built in 1864) where the killing took place was renamed in 1960 Hutatma Chowk (Martyrs' Square in Marathi), and a memorial was erected accordingly.

Rather like Taiwan, Tibet, and Xinkiang for China and Manchu conquests, Port Blair itself is only Indian because of India succeeding to the British imperial position in the Andaman Islands and the nearby Nicobar Islands. The islands, never before "Indian" in the sense of being ruled by an Indian power, could have been transferred to Burma, or kept for later independence, like the Maldives and the Seychelles were by Britain. The British overcame opposition in the Andamans by the local indigenous population in the late 1850s.

The Cellular Jail, however, provides Indians with an ability to re-iterate a hostile account of the British Empire. The British from 1858 developed Port Blair as a penal settlement for those who had taken part in the Indian Mutiny, or "Rebellion," or "Uprising," or First War of In-dependence, against British rule and dominance. The choice of term is important, not least because the last term looks toward the struggle for independence from Britain prior to 1947. The concept of successive wars of independence emphasizes the Indian role in obtaining independence, as opposed to stressing the British willingness to cede control and, earlier, to seek to conciliate Indian concerns by granting a considerable degree of autonomy. This tension over words and meaning is important to all historical narratives of decolonization and, more generally, of change.

Port Blair became the site of the Cellular Jail, which was built by Britain between 1896 and 1906 for political detainees deported from mainland India to what seemed a distant destination; although it was far closer and quicker than, for example, British transportation of pris-oners, in the age of sail, to Australia where the first penal settlement was established in 1788. In 1921, following revelations of brutality by prison guards, it was decided to end the transportation of prisoners to Port Blair and to repatriate the political prisoners to mainland Indian jails. However, in turn, overcrowding in mainland jails resulted in a revival of the transportation of non-political prisoners, while political violence in India led to the dispatch of political detainees to the jail. This was contentious, notably because of hunger strikes in 1933 and 1937 against conditions there. As a result of this controversy, political prisoners were returned to mainland India.

In the Cellular Jail, as now presented to visitors, the harsh nature of the prison regime, and thus allegedly of imperial rule by Britain, is demonstrated by both commission and omission. There is a presenta-tion of single cells and the consequent nighttime solitary confinement as abuses designed to break the spirit of prisoners, and not an explanation that these were then advanced practice and likely to lessen the serious risks of the spread of infection. The routine, and sometimes deadly, abuse of prisoners in shared cells by other inmates is itself a serious problem in modern India (and elsewhere), although the well-connected do not tend to go to prison or, indeed, face the risk of conviction. Far from be-ing a matter simply of colonial control, moreover, the Cellular Jail was constructed on lines similar to Pentonville Prison in London, which had been opened in 1842, and was considered state-of-the-art, as it indeed was.

Present-day information for visitors to the Cellular Jail praises the hunger strikers as courting "martyrdom," refers to "brutal and sadistic torture," and describes the work that detainees did as "soul shattering" and "intended to function as a form of torture." This approach scarcely captures the extent to which such work was fairly typical for prison regimes, and in both domestic and imperial contexts. There is a life-sized model of a prisoner being flogged, as well as the remains of the gallows. Displays provide highly emotive comments:

> living hell... today a sacred place... the everlasting flame for achieving freedom... holy fire in memory of freedom fighters who died here... so that future generations could know about the revolutionary freedom movement and appreciate the tremendous cost at which our independence was achieved.

Priyadarshan drove these iniquities home for those who could not travel to Port Blair in a 1996 film. It was a film entitled *Kaalapani* in Malayalam and *Siraichalai* in Tamil. Expounding through history the value of independence, the jail now serves as an account of both a valiant struggle for freedom and the harshness of imperial rule, the latter apparently demonstrating the need for this freedom.

The imperial perspective, understandably, is absent. That some of the cases for which prisoners were imprisoned at Port Blair, for example, the Lahore Conspiracy case of 1915, occurred when Britain was involved in World War I, in which many Indian volunteers fought for the empire, is not brought out. Nor is the point that the murderers of judges generally are not treated as heroes. Moreover, they were being targeted for political reasons, not because it was difficult, if not impossible, to get white juries to convict white killers and rapists of Indian men and women.

Mention of Lahore, which is in Pakistan, underlines the extent to which the prison for British India has been appropriated for modern India, as if that state represents the culmination of pre-1947 nationalism. In practice, Pakistan took a very different nationalist trajectory. However, in most Indian eyes, an independent Pakistan arises from a separatist aberration in this nationalist struggle and/or from malign British politics. More generally, "generations of nationalist intellectuals have lent India's leaders a hand by writing nationalist annals of 'all India,'"[5] approaches that underplay the major success of the Muslim League in the 1945–46 elections, and the extent to which key Congress figures, including Sardar Patel, were ready to back Partition as the solution to Muslim separatism.

Moreover, other Indian perspectives are not considered at the jail. In practice, indeed, Indians disagree about the unity and heroic status of the prisoners. For example, the shock created for the prisoners by losing caste in being sent to prison meant more to some Indians than others, and is not mentioned in the jail. Caste rifts between patriots are not part of the narrative. There was also a tension, again not mentioned, between the prisoners" stance in the 1930s and that of the nonviolent opposition to British rule associated with Gandhi.[6] Conversely, there was also an overlap between the Hindustan Socialist Revolutionary Army and Congress.[7]

Newly independent India did not only look at recent history as part of the process by which anti-imperialism became a way to engage the new concept of the people, and as such to ensure an appropriate social mobilization.[8] There was also a far more critical account of all of India's history under British rule, as well as an attempt to argue that India had a cultural unity that predated British rule—an assertion, however, that is highly flawed. India, as a state covering all of independent India, indeed as a single nation, was in practice a British creation. Mughal control in Southern India in the late seventeenth century was ephemeral, indeed lasted for a shorter period than British rule, and other Indian rulers had not controlled the far south.

The criticism also entailed minimizing the positive features of British rule, including the end of war within India, for the decline of Mughal power from the 1700s had seen a marked increase in domestic conflict. In part, this was a matter of the major expansion of large-scale Maratha raiding, which was very devastating, not least to the important industrial area of Bengal. That is not a point made by those who wish to blame Indian economic performance on British rule. In addition, the attempts by regional rulers, such as the Nizam of Hyderabad and the Nawab of Bengal, to define their position led to serious conflict with other Indian rulers. Moreover, major invasions, from Nadir Shah of Persia between 1739 and 1740 and, and from the 1750s to the 1790s by Afghan forces, were also significant. There were no such invasions in the period of British rule until the unsuccessful Japanese one from Burma in 1944.

The standard criticisms of imperial rule applauded those who opposed it, and ignored the many who cooperated, not least by serving in the large and important army. Thus, aside from arguing that Indian resources were used to help Britain expand its empire, empire was presented in India as a vehicle for British expropriation and exploitation, and as a negative force in the historical continuum that offset earlier Indian advantages and delayed the development of the country. In place of the British emphasis on progress toward modernity under colonial rule, came strident criticism of the latter, as well as more scholarly work that more accurately drew attention to the numerous racist contexts and inflections in British policy.[9]

This approach was linked to a rewriting of episodes in the conflicts of imperial conquest, in particular Indian atrocities which had been discussed by the British in part in justification of their claim to be superior and, therefore, as an apparent excuse to justify imperial rule, a pattern similar to that by which imperial powers more generally expounded and explained their policies. A prominent, and much repeated, instance was the Black Hole of Calcutta, in which Siraj-ud-daula, the nawab of Bengal, had, in 1756, imprisoned, with fatal results, British captives from the East India Company base at Calcutta.[10]

So also with the treatment of British women and children during the "Indian Mutiny" of between 1857 and 1859, especially the massacre at Kanpur ("Cawnpore") of over two hundred people in 1857, the details of which still have the capacity to shock.[11] Now the emphasis has moved, instead, to British atrocities, which were indeed harsh and plentiful, as with the treatment of captured *sepoys* during the Mutiny that has been reinterpreted and renamed as a war of independence. This latter approach entails downplaying the important role of religious sectarianism in the rebellion, a role that did not suit those seeking an acceptable genesis for independence. As mutineers, the *sepoys* were treated in accordance with the military law and conventions of the period. Lieutenant Hugh Pearson wrote to his parents in August 1857: "We took two *sepoy* prisoners the other day and they were blown away from the guns: the stink of fresh flesh was sickening in the extreme, but I have seen so many disgusting sights and so much bloodshed that I have grown quite callous." The recent discovery of the skull of *sepoy* Alum Beg, executed by cannon for murdering a British missionary family, caused much interest in Britain. His skull had been kept in a pub.[12] This invites comparison with General Kitchener destroying the Mahdi's tomb after his capture of Khartoum in 1898, spreading his ashes into the River Nile, and retaining his skull as a potential inkpot.

Other Indians, however, as well as *sepoys*, were also killed by the British army, including civilians strung up on the roadside as retribution for Kanpur. Alongside hostility to the massacres by the rebels, there was criticism in Britain about the brutal, and often arbitrary, nature of the British reprisals. These harsh and frequently indiscriminate reprisals continue to attract hostile attention in India, and understandably so. Less attention is devoted to the many Indians who helped suppress the rebellion.

Twentieth-century Indian history was a matter of contention from the outset, with disagreement over how far, and how best, to present Indian pressure for autonomy and, subsequently, independence. The perception of this pressure, and of the response to it, was an important aspect of the politics of the period and subsequently. This can be clearly seen first by considering the response to the 1919 Amritsar Massacre, in which at least 379 Indians were killed and 1,200 wounded by the army,[13] and then with assessing India's stance during World War II. In 2013, David Cameron, Britain's prime minister, laid a wreath at the Amritsar memorial, bowed his head, stood in silence to pay respect to those who died, and wrote in the book of condolences:

> This was a deeply shameful event in British history, one that Winston Churchill rightly described at the time as "monstrous." We must never forget what happened here, and in remembering we must ensure that the United Kingdom stands up for the right of peaceful protest around the world.

His view saw not only a doubtless heartfelt personal apology, but also the coincidence of convenience so important in politics, in this case for both India and Britain. The occasion testified to Indian accounts of their national struggle. The memorial plaque at Amritsar declares: "This place is saturated with the blood of those Indian patriots who were martyred in a nonviolent struggle to free India from British domination." As such, the massacre is implicitly contrasted with the violence used, notably in the 1980s, by Sikhs seeking independence from India for the Punjab, the very region in which Amritsar is located. Thus, the plaque explicitly excuses the highly militarized nature of the Indian response in storming sacred sites occupied by Sikh militants, especially the 1984 *Hari Mandir* (Golden Temple) raid.

It is instructive that 1919 Amritsar Massacre can push out the reality of Operation Blue Star in 1984. Although, in the latter, the army claimed that five hundred Sikh militants were killed while it lost eighty-three, unofficial casualty figures are far higher, indeed rising to thousands on both sides.[14] In practice, there was not only an attack on the militants in Amritsar, but also the army taking control of the entire Punjab, with fighting at many *gurdwaras*, the employment of tanks against civilians (as in China in 1989), and heavy civilian losses also due to the use of artillery. Planning the operation for a Sikh religious day caused greater civilian casualties, as the shrine was crowded. There were also reliable reports about the shooting dead of militant prisoners and suspects. The army's burning down of the Sikh Reference Library has been seen as an attack on Sikh culture. The Indian state went on to use martial law, troops, police, and paramilitaries to ensure that, in asserting control, about twenty-five thousand people eventually were killed, and, as a result, India was criticized by an Amnesty International report in 1992.

This underlines the point that nation-states are no more necessarily "good" or "bad" than empires, and that their treatment of dissent or alleged dissent can be as harsh or harsher, as the history of Cambodia over the last 150 years clearly shows: French rule versus that by Pol Pot. The latter does not excuse the former, but it provides a context for judgments.

In the hypercritical Indian press, Cameron's remarks in 2013 about 1919 were criticized as too late by some Indian commentators and, separately, as designed to appeal to Sikh voters in Britain. His remarks certainly associated Cameron with Churchill, who had condemned the massacre, and with a goal that presented the modern British government in a benign light, distinguishing it for example from the Iranian government's brutal (and successful) suppression of pro-democracy demonstrators in 2009, a suppression that Britain condemned. Keen also to encourage Indian trade with Britain, Cameron was scarcely going to draw attention to the far larger-scale sectarian massacres, especially in the Punjab, at the time of partition in 1947.

Nor was it relevant to note the continuing extent of sectarian violence in India, as in the state of Gujarat in 2002 in which over one thousand people, mostly Muslims, were slaughtered, with the state government doing little to stop the process. Moreover, in the early 1990s, BJA activists played a role in the destruction of the Babri Masj'id mosque, supposedly built on the birthplace of Lord Rama, the incarnation of a Hindu god. In contrast, the British colonial authorities had successfully kept a lid on this controversy.[15] In 2018, Surendra Singh, a BJP MP, pressed for renaming the Taj Mahal, a Mogul mausoleum, after a Hindu god. Communalization has become more important in Indian politics since the 1980s,[16] rather than simply being due to British rule as argued by some critics of this rule; an argument that is not necessarily flawed through being convenient, but that is of limited accuracy. The same is true of other former colonies, notably Sri Lanka and Nigeria.

Contextualization links 1919 and 1984. In 1919, Britain faced an unprecedented crisis of imperial overstretch, one that was compounded in northwest India both by opposition there and by the proximity of an Afghan war. In 1983–1984, India faced an issue with Sikh opposition. A civil disobedience movement was beginning. Major contrasts with 1919 were that the 1984 operation was ordered by the government, and at the highest level, and that the operation lasted only for several days. Moreover, the casualty rate was far higher in 1984. At the same time, there was a violent separatist group to overcome in 1984, unlike in Amritsar in 1919.

In 1940, Sir Michael O'Dwyer, the lieutenant-governor of the Punjab from 1912 to 1919, who had termed Dyer's role at Amritsar as the "correct action," was murdered at a public meeting in London by Udham Singh, a Sikh living in Britain, who, in turn, was executed. The murderer was treated as a hero by many Indian contemporaries, and has since been seen in the same light, notably by Nehru in 1962. There is a museum dedicated to him in Amritsar, and he has been the subject of films. The day of his death is a public holiday in Punjab. He is also celebrated with a statue in Amritsar.

In turn, in October 1984, in response to Operation Blue Star, the Indian prime minister, Indira Gandhi, was assassinated by two of her Sikh bodyguards, an episode that led to the mob killings of about eight thousand Sikhs, especially in Delhi, and, in 1986, General Arun Shridhar

Vaidya the Chief of Army Staff at the time of Operation Blue Star, was assassinated. Local Congress politicians, none of whom were ever punished, encouraged the 1984 mob killings. The police failed to act, and, unlike in Amritsar in 1984, the army was not sent in to restore order. Some Sikh commentators have made comparisons with the Nazis, but these comments are totally misplaced. However, the episode, which was a massacre, contributes to continued Sikh bitterness and thus the variety of narratives about India that are possible. In London, the official launch of the book that made such a comparison was hosted in the House of Lords by the Network of Sikh Organizations, whose maxim is "Unity is Strength."[17]

As an interesting aside about alleged British culpability that does not attract much attention, there are reports that the British government had provided a SAS officer to advise the Indian military in Amritsar.[18] Given the tendency to advance conspiratorial, even paranoid, accounts of British imperial policy, it is noteworthy that there have been suggestions that Sikh militants were provided with assistance by elements of the Indian secret service in order to serve the political goals of the latter in discrediting moderate Sikhs. An Indian journalist friend investigating the matter was killed in an unexplained road accident.

More clearly, the Sikhs are scarcely alone: the Indian government from 2005 has used great brutality against the Naxalite insurgency, a Maoist movement in east-central India, notably by encouraging paramilitaries, an inexpensive and deniable means. In 2011, the police sought to make the Naxalites unpopular by claiming that they were supported by China and Pakistan.[19] Fighting continues to the present, although it is widely underreported, both in India and more widely.

Maintaining order is never easy, a point that critics of imperial rule, British and other, are apt to neglect. India suffers from a lack of cohesion in such tasks, with a range of competing agencies generally failing to get to grips with the problem and being far too dependent on the army.[20] Thus, in 2015, in Gujarat, the army, as well as five thousand paramilitaries, were deployed to support the police in resisting demonstrating crowds of upper-caste Patels who, demanding reserved jobs and college places, attacked the police. The episode was described as an "uprising" as well as a riot. In the state of Haryana in 2017, troops were deployed after thousands of rioters overcame thousands of police and paramilitaries trying to keep order following the conviction of Gurmeet Ram Rahim Singh, a powerful guru, for rape. In Kashmir, the army and paramilitaries are to the fore in suppressing Muslim separatist pressure, and with considerable bloodshed and the apparent murder of some militants.

This point about the difficulty of maintaining order is not only relevant for India. It is instructive to consider criticisms of British responses to the Mau Mau in light of recent Kenyan moves against Somali separatists and Islamic terrorism within Kenya, as well as of electioneering and ethnic violence in Kenya. A similar contextualization can be offered for the United States and Israel.

Turning anew to World War II, the Cellular Jail returns to attention as Subhas Chandra Bose (1897–1945) visited it while the Andamans were under wartime Japanese occupation between 1942 and 1945,[21] and at a time when the Japanese were treating those islanders they suspected of supporting the British with murderous harshness. Public executions were to the fore. As a prominent nationalist, Bose received German backing and supported the Japanese. Attempts to extenuate his conduct are unconvincing,[22] and even more so given Japanese conduct in other parts of what became India that they occupied: Nagaland and Manipur. This point has reference to the more general one that British politicians of the period, such as Churchill, understandably viewed more favorably those who provided Britain (and not its enemies) with support, in his case Jinnah, the leader of India's Muslims, rather than Bose, or Gandhi's pacifists in World War II, or the Palestinian Muslims in World War I and, indeed, in the shape of the Mufti of Jerusalem, in World War II.[23]

The situation was paralleled in the case of Burma (Myanmar), with the People's Revolutionary Party and the Ba Maw puppet government both cooperating with Japan. Given that several of the anti-imperialist movements during World War II (including the IRA) were pro-Axis, frequently with Fascist inclinations, it is not surprising that a racist essentialism played a role in their postwar identity. Looked at differently, such racism was linked to their pre-war proto-nationalism, and this factor, as much as opposition to the colonial powers, led them to turn to Hitler, Mussolini, and imperial Japan.

If the agency emphasized in Indian independence is (understandably) not that of cooperation with Japan, as with Bose, but of the Congress Party, which came to power in 1947, then the focus is on the latter's "Quit

India" campaign of 1942. This was a large-scale campaign of all-out civil disobedience. In part, this campaign arose from anger at the Viceroy's commitment of India to war against the Axis in 1939 without consulting nationalist leaders. In practice, "Quit India" failed, although it did have a highly disruptive effect. Railway tracks were uprooted and communications with the frontline on the Burmese border against Japanese forces disintegrated. Most of the Indian police and civil administration remained passive and the government had to deploy fifty-five battalions of the Indian Army, as well as to use aircraft to overawe crowds threatening strategic railways.[24] Over 100,000 people were arrested. The British realized that, in case of a further dispute, they could not rely wholesale on the police or the administrators.

The army in 1942 was loyal, indeed the largest volunteer army in history. Moreover, against Japan, the army became increasingly professional and highly effective between 1943 and 1945. Wartime Indianization, notably in command positions, was an aspect of the impressive potential of British India and arose from competition between empires. Britain would have found it difficult to resist the 1944 Japanese attack on the Burmese frontier without the support and effectiveness of the Indian Army. At the same time, Japanese forces lacked the capability to exploit victory there. Japanese logistics in Myanmar were very poor, while much more of an effort was devoted by Japan to launching a major offensive in China and to opposing the American advance in the western Pacific. Indian forces went on to play a key role in the re-conquest of Burma in 1945, and would have done so in Operation Zipper, the projected re-conquest of Malaya and Singapore, had the American atomic bombs not brought a close to the war.

There were murmurings within the army about a desire for independence once the war ended. Moreover, after the war, the British government, struggling with challenges and commitments across much of the world, failed adequately to appreciate the pressures under which the soldiers served.[25] Post-1947, Indian historiography underplays the genesis of Indian nationalism in the army and overplays the nonviolent culture of Congress. In addition, many Indian politicians and others who cooperated with the British against Japan are generally ignored.[26]

British rule is discredited in the standard nationalist account by reference to the terrible Bengal famine of 1943 and 1944, an epic disaster of global proportions in which an estimated 2.1–3 million people died, and to the unsuccessful and unsympathetic nature of the British response to this calamity.[27] This, however, is an account that, searching for racist motivation in British policy and its implementation, greatly underplays, if not ignores, the wartime difficulties of the British position, not least grave shortages of food and shipping, as well as the major disruption to the rice trade arising from Japan's conquest of Myanmar in 1942, the problems created by a harvest shortfall, the local (Muslim League) administration of Bengal, local hoarders, and a soaring inflation rate, and the efforts made by the British to try to address the problem. Moreover, it is important to consider comparisons. In particular, Japan's determination to direct the movement of rice helped to cause large-scale famine in Java and serious difficulties in Korea and the Philippines. In short, a perspective of racialist attitudes on the part of Britain in India is emphasized, attitudes that certainly existed, rather than the context of the difficulties and practicalities of the period.[28] The debate is frequently highly politicized.

The idea of successive wars of independence emphasizes the Indian role in obtaining independence, as opposed to stressing the British willingness to cede control and, earlier, to seek to conciliate Indian concerns by granting a considerable degree of autonomy. In practice, there was no second war of independence. It is necessary, instead, as in 1949 with the Dutch in Indonesia, where there was such a war, and a bitter one, to focus on metropolitan factors in leading to independence: first, to emphasize British exhaustion as a result of World War II, and secondly, to stress the sympathy of the Labour government elected in 1945 for Indian independence. American support for decolonization was also significant, and notably so for Indonesia.

Separately, it is also appropriate to note the extent to which the very logic of British imperialism was to move colonies toward independence and cooperation with Britain, a course already followed by those colonies that had gained Dominion status. In part, British policymakers failed to understand that, once independent, India, which they had sought to keep united,[29] would take an independent geopolitical course, and more so than Australia and New Zealand, let alone Canada and South Africa.

The preferred historical narrative in India is not only one of independence won by Indian efforts. In addition, the Congress Party ruled India, on its own or in coalition, for most of the period from 1947 to 2014. It has consistently drawn in part on support from the country's large Muslim minority (while at the same time allowing them to remain very much second-class citizens and ignoring this condition), and has sought to keep confessionalism at bay. Partly as a result, there is an emphasis not on focusing on sectarian violence today, but on commemorating the victims of British imperial rule. This is an agenda that is "ahistoricist," in that it deals with a situation that is long past but presented as if somehow still relevant. Thus, there is a convenient approach, but it's one that provides little guidance for the contemporary situation, other than in terms of outrage, about Britain.

Of course, the situation was, and is, more complex. In 2005, speaking publicly at Oxford, where he had been a student, Manmohan Singh, the prime minister from 2004 to 2014, and a Congress figure, acknowledged a mixed legacy, saying, "Our notion of the rule of law, of a constitutional government, of a free press, of a professional civil service, of modern universities and research laboratories have all been fashioned in the crucible where an age-old civilisation met the dominant Empire of the day." He argued that the struggle for independence was more an assertion of a "natural right to self-governance" than an outright rejection of the "British claim to good governance."[30] So also with the infrastructural inheritance India received from the efforts of British engineers, albeit efforts heavily dependent on local labor and expertise.[31]

BJP opponents, who, with a characteristic bellicosity, preferred to stress links to armed resistance to British rule, criticized Singh's approach.[32] In practice, there is no one national myth, and no one treatment of Britain's imperial presence in India, or of its consequences. Criticism of Britain is in part a matter of the bitter partisan politics within independent India and rival groups can be castigated for allegedly being pro-British. This point tends to be overlooked or downplayed in the British response.

Moreover, attacking Britain for its imperial role and, specifically, for being allegedly unsympathetic to Hindus (for which there is no evidence) provides the BJP with a way to locate the Mughals, and Muslims in general, as also non-Indian. Much is now invested, politically and culturally, in anti-Muslim sentiment,[33] and that stance leads to pressure to remove the Mughals from textbooks. In this approach, British imperial rule is apparently part of a hostile sequence.[34] At the same time, to delegitimize Muslims, the role of Islam, in opposition to British rule in nineteenth-century India, was/is downplayed.

In the Indian election of 2014, Hindu nationalist groups, notably the *Rashtriya Swayamsevak Singh* (RSS), argued that, in the rise of the BJP, which won the election, the nation was being restored, correcting losses over the previous millennium. Collective grievance thus becomes empowering. The RSS has benefited from the social dislocation linked to economic change and modernization.[35]

In academic terms, the situation in India, as in other former colonies, can be very differently contextualized by noting not only the complexities and ambiguities of imperial rule, but also of the concept of modernity and the extent to which imperialism itself was always being shaped and reshaped in the processes of imposition and continuation.[36] For example, in Indian port cities there was collaboration between Indian merchants and European merchants, with wealthy Indians seeing Europe rule, as Macaulay did, as an agent to impart useful knowledge. Almost every major college in the port cities was co-sponsored by rich Indians and the state.

Such complexities are scarcely addressed by some of the populist writing on the economic consequences of empire. They tend to make a sharp distinction between state and subject, which, in practice, underplays the diversity of both. Aside from arguing that Indian resources were used to help Britain expand its empire, it is presented there as a vehicle for plunder and economic exploitation, therefore making it look like an economic burden that delayed the development of the country and affected subsequent views of it. Alongside the undoubted damage and problems caused, the value and creativity of British rule with Indian cooperation were, and are, not part of the equation for many commentators. Nor are the problems within the Indian economy prior to British rule, such as the restricted degree of market integration in India,[37] or the extent to which Britain had only limited control over its developing economic relationships with India and the United States.[38] Imperial powers neither deserve all the credit nor all the blame, a point that is more generally true.

IRELAND

If India was the most populous part of the British Empire, indeed, according to Gandhi, what makes it an empire, then Ireland was the part of empire closest to home and the oldest part outside of Britain. Moreover, it was the sole part of empire represented (from the start of the nineteenth century) in the Westminster Parliament. Ireland's position was a major source of political contention in British politics from the late nineteenth century, and Ireland became independent at the time when the empire was at its apogee. The legacy of empire remains highly contentious in Ireland and among the numerous Irish diaspora, not least due to the difficult Northern Ireland issue and related sectarianism, factors that can be reversed to give a different impression.

The imperial amnesia in question is that of the major role played by the Irish in the development of the English, and then the British, empire. The positive aspects of English/British control from the twelfth century (more completely the seventeenth) to the Anglo-Irish Treaty of December 1921 were underrated once Ireland became independent, and this remains the case to this day. Museum displays on Irish history concentrate on the glories of Celtic civilization in the "Dark Ages" of the second half of the first millennium CE, emphasizing Ireland's contribution to European (including English) culture at a time when Europe was assailed by "barbarians." There is a related Celtic mythology, most evident in Thomas Cahill's *How the Irish Saved Civilisation* (1995). This bestseller credited the Irish with preserving civilization from the collapse of Rome to the Middle Ages.

In contrast, in the Irish museums there is then relatively little on the period of British rule, until the story resumes with the struggle for independence and the subsequent period of history. The established Irish image is of lost centuries, a standard motif in former colonies. In the case of Ireland, their gloom is punctuated by cruel episodes, notably the harsh fate of the besieged towns of Wexford and Waterford at the hands of Oliver Cromwell and his invading English troops in 1649, and the Great Famine of 1845 all the way to 1852, the deadly consequences of which are blamed on the British government. These episodes are presented in an overwhelmingly bleak fashion, indeed as if they were genocidal. There is scant mention, for example, of the brutalities inflicted by the native population on recent Protestant settlers in the Irish Rising of 1641, brutalities that inflamed politics in England then and that played a part in the treatment subsequently meted out to Catholics in 1649.[39]

Mid-century conflict and that in the early 1690s led to the expropriation of more land from Catholics, with religion (misleadingly) taken as the definition of loyalty.[40] The amount of land owned by Catholics fell to 14 percent by 1703. The seizure of land in Ireland, and the settlement of English people in so-called "plantations," very much drew on imperialism as profit, as well as security. This was scarcely novel as far as Ireland was concerned, and had been seen with the Anglo-Norman nobles who went to Ireland in the 1160s and subsequently. Then, as in the sixteenth century, there was an ideology of improvement, with religious and cultural factors blended in. From the late 1560s, English rule in Ireland became increasingly military in character and intention, leading to fresh attempts to extend and enforce control. These were at the expense of Gaelic Irish opposition, but English rule also had little support from the Anglo-Irish, most of whom were Catholics.

This was not a conducive environment for the expansion of Protestantism, and, as Catholic energies were revived from the mid-sixteenth century by the Counter-Reformation, so religious differences became a more important feature of the situation, symbolizing, reflecting, and strengthening, a political rift and hatred felt between those who were increasingly seen as conquerors and, on the other hand, a subject population. In every term, short, middle, and long, this rift was to undermine imperial rule and identity in Ireland. Moreover, in each of these terms, religious tension helped give imperial rule much of its character, not least a frequently embattled sense of identity: for the Catholic majority and for the Protestant minorities, both Anglican and Presbyterian. At the same time, earlier handpicked Catholic peers had done well and had been able and willing to adopt and adapt to English legal, administrative, political, and economic structures.[41] Subsequently, the Irish played a key part (as part of a "fiscal-military state" that was aligned with Britain, as well as run on its behalf[42]) in supplying food for the navy in the eighteenth century and, even more, troops for the army in the nineteenth century. As a result, the demobilization of much of the army in 1815 caused acute problems in Ireland. Being part of an imperial system, nevertheless, brought many benefits, benefits that were widely, albeit unequally, shared.

While some Irish colonial civil servants were affected by Irish nationalism, and sufficiently so to criticize aspects of British rule, notably in India, the commitment of most to the empire, albeit an improved empire, was clear.[43] Thus, in the late-nineteenth-century Punjab, Irish civil servants played a central role in carrying through an economic development that included the provision of security of tenure, while Irish doctors also took a crucial role in the Indian Medical Service.[44] The networks created by the Irish within the empire bridged with those created outside the empire, notably in the United States, and served the individual and family strategies of large numbers, leading to an experience that was simultaneously individual and varied.

This crucial contribution is underplayed in the Irish account of national history. More generally, the survival of the Irish Union in the nineteenth century has been described as "the great elephant in the room of modern Irish historiography."[45] So also with the riches of Anglo-Irish culture, famously represented by the writers Jonathan Swift and Oscar Wilde. These are undervalued or treated essentially as Irish, as also with James Joyce, who did his best to leave Ireland, a point not generally pointed out, and certainly not in Dublin.

In 1997, the newly elected Tony Blair marked the 150th anniversary of the Great Famine by declaring that those "who governed in London at the time failed their people by standing by while a crop failure turned into a massive human tragedy." In response, the *Daily Telegraph* claimed that Blair had given support to "the self-pitying nature of Irish nationalism." The empire certainly plays a major role in the nationalist account of Irish history, both in Ireland and in the Irish diaspora, most significantly the United States. The Famine allegedly demonstrated that Ireland had been extremely harshly, if not murderously, treated when linked to Britain, and, therefore, apparently showed that Irish commentators who defended the link were wrong. On Cambridge Common near Boston, Massachusetts, "The Great Hunger. Ireland 1845–1850," a statue dedicated in 1997 by Ireland's president, Mary Robinson, bears the inscription NEVER AGAIN SHOULD A PEOPLE STARVE IN A WORLD OF PLENTY.[46]

Moreover, the Great Famine and the Easter Rising of 1916 against British rule were, and are, despite being very different, linked, thus each supporting a particular interpretation of the other. This can be seen in what is deliberately presented as double remembrance, as in *Twinsome Minds: An Act of Double Remembrance* (2017) by Richard Kearney and Sheila Gallagher. Published by Ireland's Great Hunger Museum at Quinnipiac University and Cork University Press, this book aims to retrieve "micro narratives of Irish historical trauma to illustrate how memory occurs at the cross section of story and history."[47]

The emphasis on Irish nationalism led to a marked neglect of the large numbers of Irish volunteers (Catholics and Protestants) who fought for George V in World War I. If built, war memorials in the Republic were obscure.[48] In contrast, the far smaller number (about 1,200) involved in the Easter Rising were actively commemorated, even though their rebellion directly helped Germany with which Britain was then at war, just as in 1798, the nationalist rebellion had directly helped France with which Britain was then a war and was linked to a French invasion.

The first person killed by the rebels in 1916 was an Irish policeman. Indeed, there was much Irish-on-Irish violence in the Rising, and more generally in Irish nationalist violence. However, that is not an echo seen in public memorialization. The emphasis, instead, is on the execution of fifteen resistance figures by the British after the suppression of the Easter Rising. In 2015, Thomas Kent received a state funeral in Ireland, with the president present, even though he had been executed in 1916 for murdering a policeman whose life was not thus commemorated. In practice, the Rising was handled in an extremely less rigorous and bloody fashion than that of the rebellion against Russian rule that year in Central Asia.

Endowed with great symbolism, the Rising at the time had little general effect on Irish cooperation in the war effort, but was subsequently presented as a crucial element in winning independence,[49] although there is room for some doubt on this head. That a survivor of the Rising, Eamon de Valera, leader of the Sinn Féin and very much a product of the Irish diaspora, was in power in Ireland for much of the period from 1932 to 1973, contributed greatly to this situation. Fighting resumed after World War I, with the Irish Republican Army (IRA) relying on raids, ambushes, assassinations and sabotage. The British use of auxiliary police, especially the black and trans people recruited from ex-soldiers, became associated with contentious reprisals against IRA terrorism, and the use of civilian clothes by the IRA helped encourage a lack of care in the targeting of reprisals.[50]

Although the army and police benefited from improvements in their methods,[51] while the outnumbered IRA was short of arms and explosives; the IRA was still able to take the initiative and to benefit from the limited options available to those trying to restore control. Moreover, political and public opinion in Britain lacked enthusiasm for a long, tough struggle. The Liberal prime minister, David Lloyd George, who, with his Welsh radical background, had long had sympathy for nationalist causes, initially used bellicose rhetoric against the IRA, but later changed his attitude. His belief that the government stance was not working led, in July 1921, to a change of policy toward granting effective independence. That month, Lieutenant-General Sir Philip Chetwode, the Deputy Chief of the Imperial General Staff, claimed that victory was possible, but only if the army was given more power and support:

> The full incidence of Martial Law will demand very severe measures and to begin with many executions. In the present state of ignorance of the population in England, I doubt very much that it would not result in a protest which would not only ruin our efforts, but would be most dangerous to the army. The latter have behaved magnificently throughout, but they feel from top to bottom that they are not supported by their countrymen, and should there be a strong protest against severe action it would be extremely difficult to hold them.[52]

Whatever the truth of this, public opinion in both Britain and Ireland would probably not have stood for a tough policy (although that was not tested), while the government, confronting the need to increase the number of troops sent to Ireland,[53] was also faced, as it was to be in the later 1940s, by a range of difficult imperial and international commitments. The IRA benefited from such issues as the Russian Civil War and from new British commitments in the Middle East, including war in Iraq in 1919 and difficulties in Egypt, India, and Iran. British imperialism helped ensure that the legacy in Ireland was that of disengagement.

In contrast to the subsequent celebration of the Easter Rising, there was an ambivalence about the commemoration of the Irish Civil War from 1922 to 1923 that followed the British departure. This was in part because de Valera had been a member of the defeated rebels, rebels who had rejected the peace with Britain which had been based on the compromise of partition. This conflict led to more brutal government conduct than that of the British, notably the execution of 77 insurgents and the internment or sentencing of 8,338.[54] This has received far less attention than the Rising, and particularly so among the Irish diaspora. So also with the extent to which subsequently, under de Valera, the Protestant

Irish living in the newly independent Irish Free State were denied equality: many had already been driven out by intimidation and violence.[55]

Ireland was in the Commonwealth as a Dominion from 1922 to 1949, with the governor-general appointed by the Crown and MPs obliged to take an oath of allegiance to the Crown. The first Irish prime minister, William Cosgrave, believed that his government worked well within the Commonwealth. For example, Ireland played a significant part in the making of the Statute of Westminster whereby no law enacted after 1931 by the Westminster Parliament should extend to a Dominion unless that Dominion had requested and consented that it should be so. Cosgrave, like the other Dominion prime ministers, and, indeed, the British government, saw this as "freedom within a developing system." After his Fianna Fail party won the key election victory of 1933, de Valera worked to weaken the Commonwealth links, and, by 1938, claimed that Ireland (now called Eire) was indeed a republic in all but name. The previous year, under a new constitution, the oath of allegiance was abolished. In the event, Cosgrave's Fine Gael party broke the link with the Commonwealth with the Republic of Ireland Act of 1948, probably to check Fianna Fail accusations that Fine Gael, which arose from those who supported the Treaty of 1921, was pro-British.

While being normally reasonably pro-British, Cosgrave's government also set out in 1922 on a program of "Irishing Ireland" by insisting that restoring the Irish language was its priority. In fact, he could not speak Irish and had to make his declaration about the cultural revolution using a phonetic prompt card.[56]

Irishmen who fought for Britain in World War II, including some five thousand who deserted from the Irish army, were branded as traitors and barred from jobs in the civil service. They were pardoned only in 2013. Ireland was the sole member of the Commonwealth to be neutral, a powerful affirmation of independence from Britain. Its refusal to permit Britain the use of ports in southwest Ireland, the "treaty ports" handed back in 1938, increased the grave damage to British trade from German submarine attack[57] and led to irritation on the part of Churchill and to British consideration of an invasion of Ireland. None was mounted, which was just as well in terms of the subsequent nature of the relationship, as well as relations at the time with the United States. As an ironic instance of the complex and contentious application of language, the return of the ports can be seen as a necessary and welcome step toward decolonization and/or as an act of "appeasement" or, even part of "Appeasement," as Britain struggled to reduce its potential opponents in the run-up to World War II.

Irish neutrality in the war, or what was termed there the "Emergency," was in large part sympathetic, if not supportive, to the German cause, not least given both the fate of neutral powers attacked by Germany from 1939 to 1941 and Britain's serious plight in 1940 and 1941. However, Allied aircraft were allowed to fly over Irish air space and there was cooperation on weather forecasts, wireless direction-finding aids, information about German submarine activities, and other matters.[58]

This neutrality also reflected a moral bankruptcy, notably in treating the combatants as equally valid, which extended to de Valera calling at the German Legation to offer condolences on the death of Hitler as another head of state. Indeed, although far outnumbered by those who fought for Britain, a few prominent Irish nationalists and IRA figures, such as Frank Ryan, saw British defeat as a means to pursue Irish unity and, as with their predecessors in 1916, were willing to consider assisting German imperialism. The 1939 IRA bombing campaign in Britain was linked to German support.[59] De Valera replied to Churchill's criticism of his conduct in 1945 by criticizing Churchill for not having the generosity to acknowledge that there was "a small nation that stood alone, not one year or two," as he acknowledged Britain had done in 1940, "but for several hundred years against aggression." This nationalist interpretation of Irish history was clearly partisan, as well as misleading, and was also not relevant to the more general threat from Hitler, including to the many neutrals attacked, including Denmark, Norway, the Netherlands, Belgium, Yugoslavia, and Greece.[60]

Subsequently, the IRA's border campaign in the 1950s failed, but from the late 1960s, the Catholic nationalist struggle in Northern Ireland played a major role in influencing debate in the Republic of Ireland and among the Irish diaspora. There was a tendency to see this struggle in terms of the long-standing nationalist cause, but the Provisional IRA ultimately failed to command the support of all the minority Catholic community, while the (difficult and often problematic) support of the Protestant majority for government policy, combined with the ability of the army and police to contain the situation, led to a compromise peace settlement, the Good Friday Agreement, in 1998. This was a sign of post-imperial maturity. Despite difficulties, this agreement still holds. However-er, the growing intertwining of the British question with that over Brexit has complicated debates about the future situation of parts of the United Kingdom, notably over the Irish question. As Dennis Staunton, London editor of the *Irish Times*, pointed out, the 1998 Good Friday Agreement

> has been sustained by a kind of constructive ambiguity that has al-lowed each community in Northern Ireland to interpret it in their own way. Northern Irish citizens can be British or Irish or both, a concept that made little difference as long as the UK and Ireland were in the EU. Brexit has cast a harsh light on that ambiguity, forcing the people of Northern Ireland into being British or European.[61]

In practice, such ambiguity was central (as in other countries) to the issue of multiple identities and, therefore, was not inherently a problem other than when changes led to a need to confront (or avoid confronta-tion) with this issue. Change has been pushed to the fore in the 2010s, first with the Scottish independence referendum and then with Brexit.

The expression of Irish nationalism continues to involve a process of self-definition away from Britain. Launched in 2009, and a product of Ireland's earlier economic boom, *The Dictionary of Irish Biography* was presented to Brian Cowen, the prime minister, as a "powerful statement of our Irish nationality," one that freed the country from dependence on its British counterpart, *The Oxford Dictionary of National Biography*. Pub-lished, in the event, by a British press, the *Dictionary* faced the problem of reconciling Ireland as a geographical space with the more potent idea of the Irish as a people of ancestral descent, a nation.[62]

Competing senses of Irish identity, competition which extends to the Irish abroad, including in Britain,[63] still offer room for very different nar-ratives of the past, with present developments providing opportunities for restating contradictory accounts of the past.[64] This was seen in Ireland in 2015 and 2016 with contrasting views on how to best to mark the Easter Rising.[65] The imperial legacy is crucial to these contradictory accounts. At the same time, in Ireland as elsewhere, nationalist anti-imperial (anti-British) history is a useful way of avoiding discussions of class conflict and class exploitation within one's own nation. The British are the villains, and all the Irish are the victims. The potato famine can be presented as a genocide engineered by evil British politicians, ignoring the point that the main beneficiaries were substantial Irish Catholic tenant farmers who grew more substantial still by taking over the leases of poorer tenant farmers who had died, emigrated, or were evicted. Similar points can be made about other imperial episodes and the responses, for example in India, as with the Bengal famine spanning from 1943 to 1944. These points do not extenuate imperialism or its policies and consequences, but they put them in context.

5

CHINA AND THE
UNITED STATES

eing pressed to remove the poppies they were wearing in memory
of all those who had died fighting for Britain put David Cameron,
the newly elected prime minister, and the British delegation he
was leading to China in November 2010 in a major effort to win investment and trade, in an impossible position. To the Chinese, the poppies
clearly referred to the Anglo-Chinese Opium Wars (1840–42, 1856–60).
In fact, as a reminder of the slippery case of drawing parallels, the totemic
British poppies, which symbolize French poppies from World War I bat-
tlefields on the Western Front, are very different to those from which opium is derived. In the event, the British refused to put aside the poppies.

Compared to India and Ireland, the impact of British imperialism
was less potent and intense for both China and the United States. Each,
however, have an historical account in which British imperialism serves
as the hostile basis from which national identity and political polemics are
formed. However misleading, this is not imperial amnesia. For example,
Sarah Palin, the Republican vice presidential candidate in 2008, was in no
doubt when, in her characteristically blunt fashion, she deployed history
before a sympathetic Boston audience in 2010:

> You're sounding the warning bell just like what happened in that
> midnight run and just like with that original Tea Party back in 1773.
> I want to tell him [President Obama] "Nah, you know, we'll keep

clinging to our constitution and our guns and religion and you can keep the change."

Boston brought together the Boston Tea Party, remembered as a key moment in the struggle for independence, and the extent to which Boston had a population with few affinities with Britain and many of whom are of Irish descent.

CHINA

The narrative of modern China attaches great significance to the British Empire, for, it is in reaction to that foreign and capitalist empire, that the need for Chinese modernization is located and expressed, and has been for a long while. Moreover, this approach suited a range of reformers, both nationalist and, later, Communist. The Opium Wars (1840–42, 1856–60)[1] provide the key charges for the prosecution, and much use is made of them. The first war arose from the attempt by China to enforce a prohibition on the import of opium, the profit from the rapidly rising export of which from India was important to the financing of British imports from China and of British exports to India. Moreover, the seizure of opium held by British merchants, and their expulsion from Guangzhou (Canton), the major trading port for China, led to pressure within Britain for a response. The pressure for compensation was backed up by force. Conflict developed from the Chinese demand for the handing over of a British seaman accused of murdering a Chinaman.

Maritime strength and the projection of power ensured in the subsequent war that the British could enjoy and use the initiative. Able to decide where to apply their strength, they blockaded the major Chinese positions and focused in 1842 on the Yangzi, proceeding up the river to Nanjing. British successes led China to cede Hong Kong Island by the Treaty of Nanjing of 1842. Lower tariffs on British goods were enforced at the expense of China's right and long-standing ability to regulate its economy and society, while compensation was granted for the opium destroyed by the Chinese in 1839, and five ports were opened to British trade.[2] This was the first time a Western European state had waged war on China, the first European victory over the

Chinese, and one achieved in China itself, and, indeed, in the center of Chinese political awareness.

The second war arose because, in the context of mounting competition between the Western powers, not least America's "opening up of Japan," Britain sought to expand its privileges, opening all of China to British trade. The incident that led to hostilities was the arrest in Guangzhou of the *Arrow*, a Hong Kong cargo ship with a Chinese crew that was said to be flying the British flag. Henry Parkes, the acting Consul in Canton, and Henry, 3rd Viscount Palmerston, the habitually bellicose prime minister, both of whom sought conflict, exploited this crisis. In 1856, the British bombarded Guangzhou, but the need to focus on the Indian Mutiny then led to delay: there was a sequential character to imperial effort and Britain benefited from this in the shape of being able to separate the Crimean War, the Indian Mutiny, and the major stage of the Second Opium War. The situation for Britain was very different when conflict with Germany, Italy, and Japan coincided from December 1941.

France, under Napoleon III, allied with Britain, with the incident in question for France being the Chinese execution of a French missionary. Anglo-French forces occupied Guangzhou on January 1, 1858, and attention then shifted to north China, focusing on the forts at Dagu near Tianjin. After failing in 1859, an arresting demonstration of the limitations of Western power, an Anglo-French expedition captured the forts and Tianjin in 1860. Attempts at negotiation, however, failed. British diplomats were seized and some were tortured to death, after which the Anglo-French forces defeated a Chinese army outside Beijing and entered the city, a major blow to Chinese prestige. The Summer Palaces were destroyed, an action that still rankles, but this destruction was a reprisal for the Chinese atrocities, a point not made to visitors to the site or, indeed, in Britain and France today.

This is similar to the British burning of the White House in Washington in 1814, which was a reprisal for the pyromanial destructiveness of invading American forces in Canada. This is a point that is rarely made in the United States, and certainly not in 2018 at the state banquet for the visiting French president Emmanuel Macron, when the latter raised the issue.

In 1860, peace with China was then made. Under the Convention of

Beijing, Kowloon was added to Hong Kong, Britain and France received an indemnity, freedom of religion (in other words, Christianity) was established in China, and China was further opened to foreign trade, including of opium.

By then, China focused many of the aspirations of the British Empire, including trade and missionary activity, but not territorial control. Like other European imperial powers and the United States, the British sought to impose their definitions and their rules, as well as their interests. In the case of China, and indeed elsewhere, there was a move by the British from a presentation of themselves as merchants and suppliants for favor, instead, to an emphasis on state representation from a superior background. This shift was central to a more assertive British position in China from the outbreak of the First Opium War onward. Nevertheless, although maritime and commercial strength had a political edge,[3] the British position in China was not essentially that of a territorial power. There was no attempt, then or subsequently, to gain control of large tracts of territory, and no parallel between British policy and subsequent Japanese policy.

In turn, however, rather like France and the Seven Years' War (1756–63), the defeat and humiliation of China greatly hit the prestige of the Qing (Manchu) system, as well as of a Chinese political culture based on superiority to outsiders. This humiliation led to attempts at reform, beginning with the "Self-Strengthening Movement," a term that deliberately distinguished aspirations and policy from that of borrowing Western archetypes.

In a very different context, the Opium Wars remain important to the ethos of Chinese modernization, including to the historical account of Chinese Communism. National coherence, both political and territorial, is very much the goal of presentist history in China, and nationalism (as well as history) is intensively employed to that end. The suppression by the government of the pro-democracy demonstrations in 1989, a suppression in which thousands of peaceful protestors were slaughtered (and amnesia then imposed by the state), was followed by a major effort to use nationalism to support the Communist system. Flag-raising ceremonies became mandatory in schools, museums were presented as "patriotic education bases," and, in 1991, Jiang Zemin, the General Secretary of the Communist Party, praised patriotic education as a means to stop the young from worshipping the West. They were supposed to worship the Party.

A portrayal of past humiliation for China, notably in the nineteenth century, justified from then on an assertion of Chinese values in the present, with the Communist Party, from 1949, as their exponent and protector.[4] Xi Jinping, the general-secretary from 2012 and president from 2013 onward, has pressed for the fulfillment of a "Chinese Dream," in which national self-assertion is linked to the end of what is presented as historical humiliation. The first mention of his dream of "the great revival of the Chinese nation" was made at the National Museum in Beijing, where the "Road to Revival" exhibit counterpoints humiliation at the hands of colonial powers with revival under the Communists. This is a central theme of Chinese Communist ideology, one to which history contributes. In 2013, Xi Jinping returned to the theme when accepting the presidency, and its inclusion in school textbooks was ordered by Liu Yunshan, in effect the Party's propaganda head. The theme has also been taken up by figures linked to the military. Abolishing in 2018 the limit on his period as leader, Xi adopted a strongly nationalist stance.

The Opium Wars, the very title of which reflected a reductionist and pejorative account of British motivation that is definitely less than complete, were, and are, seen in China as a national humiliation, and are presented to the public accordingly, as with Xie Jin's film *The Opium War* (1997). Ironically, but not surprisingly, in both Britain and China, the past misrepresentation of the situation satisfied partisan political arguments. In Britain, there were divisions over policy toward China before, during, and after the Opium Wars. When it came to deploying rhetoric, William Gladstone used the opium trade and the conflicts to attack the government. In 1840, he claimed to be in dread of the judgment of God over the issue, and he later criticized "Palmerston's Opium War." The issue played a role in the 1857 election, with Palmerston, however, attacking the patriotism of his critics and, partly as a result, winning a greater parliamentary majority. This prefigured Salisbury's success in the "Khaki election" of 1900 during the Boer War in overcoming opposition among the Liberals who were divided by the war. On at least these occasions, the public thoroughly backed imperial conflicts.

In turn, Chinese reformers of the time denigrated existing arrangements with Britain on the grounds that they had failed to protect the country. Moreover, the *Guomindang* (National) government of the 1920s under Jiang Jieshi, which, not least when it was initially backed by the Soviet Union, took nationalistic steps against British interests and supporters, argued that these interests were a product of past Chinese weaknesses from the time of the Opium Wars. This analysis was adopted and adapted by the Communists who, as it were, renationalized it.

The depiction of British imperialism in China in terms of opium is the case not only in governmental and pedagogic discussion, but also in fiction, both in China and, more generally, as part of the critique of the British Empire. Thus, the Indian novelist Amitav Ghosh, in *Sea of Poppies* (2008) and *River of Smoke* (2011), presented empire as resting on the commercial logic of opium. In an interview published in the *Times* on June 11, 2011, Ghosh claimed: "It was their financial basis for Empire. In India it was the single largest sector of the economy. Everyone was connected to it." Moreover, with an ahistoricism that is all too common in the discussion of empire, Ghosh compared the Opium Wars to the 2003 Iraq War, "when national identity, a colonising power and a battle for control for profitable natural resources collide. People may not know it, but the Opium Wars were as important as the French Revolution." The extent to which the nineteenth-century empire readily served to inscribe critical accounts of power was apparent from this article. In addition, the theme taken by the paper was clear, as the interview was headlined OPIUM WAS THE SINGLE LARGEST SECTOR OF THE EMPIRE'S ECONOMY.

This claim would have surprised the shipbuilders and financiers of Britain, just as the emphasis on slave-produced sugar drives out a more appropriate focus on coal as the key product underpinning British economic growth and providing British exceptionalism.[5] France also had large quantities of slave-produced sugar, but not large-scale coal production. Placing the emphasis on coal encourages one on the metropole, rather than one on the colonies that come from a stress on the empire, sugar and slavery.

In addition, the involvement of many Indian merchant princes in the opium trade tends to be underplayed, as do contemporary views and practices toward opium taking in Britain and elsewhere: its consumption was widely accepted. The principal cause of Chinese weakness in the 1850s and 1860s in practice was the large-scale and traumatic Taiping Rebellion that spanned from 1851 to 1866, and not the Second Opium War. The

Taiping Rebellion was deadlier and far more destructive. Moreover, as far as Chinese relative decline in the nineteenth century is concerned, there was already, prior to the European, principally British, pressure from the 1830s, major signs of difficulties in Chinese government, including widespread corruption, losses of tax revenue, the deleterious role of the tax farmers, and the insufficient control of the central authorities over the provincial viceroys. The costly and large-scale White Lotus Rebellion that spanned from 1796 to 1805, which arose mostly due to the treatment of non-Han minorities, had exposed many faults in administration, while China faced difficult regional problems on the northwest and southwest frontiers after the Taiping Rebellion.[6] So also with India and the problems it faced in the early eighteenth century before British (and French) imperial pressure rose to a height, problems that continued significant during the remainder of the century.

However, it understandably proved more attractive, in China as in India and elsewhere, to focus on Western imperialism, and this approach has linked the Maoist Period to those that came before and after. In 1939, Mao Zedong discerned Marxist-derived continuity in some very diverse struggles, a process that placed British imperialism in the position as the first cause of trouble for China:

> The history of China's transformation into a semi-colony and colony by imperialism in collusion with Chinese feudalism is at the same time a history of struggle by the Chinese people against imperialism and its lackeys. The Opium War . . . all testify to the Chinese people's indomitable spirit in fighting imperialism and its lackeys.[7]

Works produced in China followed this line, such as the volumes published by the Foreign Languages Press, translated from the *History of Modern China*, compiled by members of the history departments of Fudan University and Shanghai Teachers' University, and published by the Shanghai People's Publishing House. Chapter headings for *The Opium War* (1976) included "The Covetous British Invaders," "British Aggression Brings War to China," "Popular Anti-British Struggles in Fukien, Chekiang and the Lower Yangtze Valley," "The U.S. and French Invaders Follow Suit," and "Birth of a Semi-Colonial and Semi-Feudal Society." The text matched the titles. The topic and approach were clear-cut:

With foreign capitalism undermining China's social economy, the contradiction between the forces of aggression and the Chinese people deepened. The five trading ports became the bases for capitalist aggression against China.... Foreign gangsters and adventurers gathered in these places where robbery, murder and other crimes were common occurrences.[8]

The Taiping Rebellion was presented in this volume as a sequel to the contradictions between foreign aggression and the interests of the Chinese, and the Taiping citizens were praised for a struggle against foreign capitalism as well as feudalism. This approach permitted a castigation of the Qing (Manchu) dynasty as imperialist "lackeys."[9] Indeed, foreign troops were used against the Taipings people. Present and past were deployed together. The role of the Communist Party in defending China against supposed American and Japanese threats was given historical resonance by stressing the earlier damage done by Western imperialism, notably that of Britain. The resulting contrast in effectiveness served to make the Communist Party appear more successful and necessary.[10] The focus on the Opium Wars, rather than the Taiping Rebellion, overlaps with, but is not identical to, that on the war with Japan from 1931 to 1945, rather than civil war within China in the 1920s and 1930s, let alone the appalling human cost of such Communist movements as the "Great Leap Forward" and the "Cultural Revolution." These were multimillion fatality events, but somehow fail to arouse the revulsion directed at killings due to British and American action.

British imperialism therefore has fulfilled a range of official goals in China. It can operate as a surrogate for the United States, and also provided ammunition for a critical focus on particular aspects of British policy. This approach is not solely historical. Thus, Britain's alignment with Japan in recent years serves China as a critique of both. To China, this alignment acts as a rejection of the Chinese, an argument, expressed by Liu Xiaoming, the ambassador in China, in *The Daily Telegraph* on January 1, 2014, that as the two powers (Britain and China) were "wartime allies" in World War II, they should "join together both to uphold the UN Charter and to safeguard regional stability and world peace."

Given the growing importance of China in the world at present and its determined effort to disseminate state-supported views, the significance of the hostile Chinese account of British imperialism will grow. It will provide a ready narrative as China pursues alliances and agreements with former British colonies, notably in Africa, but also elsewhere, such as in the West Indies, the Indian Ocean, and the South Pacific.

THE UNITED STATES

Visiting Liberty Hall in Philadelphia, repeatedly a moving sight even for a Brit, I was much struck to hear George III (r. 1760–1820) referred to by a guide as a tyrant. However, that description very much reflects the standard American response to the Declaration of Independence (1776) and its role in American public history.[11] In criticizing George, the Americans drew not only on the sense that monarchy, in contrast to an elected president, is an anachronism, but also on British opposition to, and criticism of, George, notably the contemporary (and misleading) Whig myth about his subverting the British constitution.[12] Moreover, the history of countries under republican governments, such as Classical Athens, republican Rome, and the Netherlands in the early modern period, was scrutinized in order to provide constitutional guidance and political ammunition for use against Britain and the monarchy. The hostile portrayal of George endures to this day and is reiterated in popular academic works. Thus, in 1982, Robert Middlekauff found virtue essentially an American prerogative in his *The Glorious Cause: The American Revolution 1763-1789*.

The situation was made more complex in the Gilded Era and then in the twentieth century by a marked degree of anglophilia among part of the American elite. This anglophilia was political, social and cultural. The Anglo-American alliance created in 1941 became the key plank of foreign policy for both powers.[13] Moreover, in what can be seen as a reaction within the United States in the 1920s, and notably the Republican governments of the period, against "Bolshevism," progressivism, and immigration, there was an emphasis on an early America that was under the British Crown. This situation was given visual form in the 1920s in John D. Rockefeller's sponsorship of Colonial Williamsburg. In the 1950s, this combination recurred in the Eisenhower Cold War years.

"Culture wars," however, then changed the situation in the United States. The rise of a new historical consciousness reflected a more radical stance from the 1960s. In part, this radical stance involved a foreshortening and misunderstanding of American history, with a stress on the period from the Civil War providing a backdrop to an engagement with Civil Rights and other contemporary issues. As a result, earlier American history, and certainly the Colonial Period, and that of the Early Republic, dropped from attention. There is an old American parenting joke in which the family is driving in Idaho or another state in the West. The children in the back of the car want to know what a monument they are passing by is for, and the parents reply, "It is for the War of 1812." The joke refers to parental ignorance, as there were no battles then in Idaho or nearby, but the parents can rely on that war being so unknown that their reply will not be questioned.

Indeed, a lack of knowledge as well as reflection was reflected in the addition of a British example to the more general American citing of Pearl Harbor in 1941 when seeking to locate historically the terrorist attacks on New York and Washington on September 11, 2011. John Lewis Gaddis, a prominent Yale historian with links to the George W. Bush administration, saw a precedent in the British burning of Washington in 1814, during the War of 1812 (in other words 1812–15). Describing "this now barely remembered violation of homeland security,"[14] Gaddis provided a ridiculous comparison. Whereas there was no reciprocity in devastation in 2001 and the atrocities there were aimed at civilians and staged without warning, the situation was very different in 1814. Invading Americans had burned freely in Canada in 1813, notably destroying what is now Toronto, then the capital of Upper Canada, while, unlike in 2001, the only people killed in Washington were those who fired on British forces. In a passive-aggressive fashion, Donald Trump followed French president Macron in bringing the issue up in 2018, albeit (wrongly) at the expense of Canada. Most so-called British imperial atrocities lack the sources and discussion devoted to that in Washington in 1814. Scrutiny of the fallacious nature of the general public discussion of the latter invites consideration as to whether other atrocities deserves reconsideration.

In so far as the Colonial and Early Republic periods now receive public (and even educational) attention, it is in large part in terms that would have made sense from the 1960s. Thus, signs of social radicalism have attracted more attention. From this perspective, the British and the

Loyalists can appear anachronistic and reactionary, opponents not only of the new America fought for from 1775, but also, more relevantly, of its fruition being contested from the 1960s. The War of Independence becomes the American Revolution, and, therefore, offers a different "lesson" for today. This presentist approach underrates the complexities of the conflict. Reconsidering the War of Independence in terms of later values certainly leads to a major misunderstanding of empire. This was especially so from the 1960s, when the war was compared with the Vietnam War, a comparison, notably of British forces from 1775 to 1783 with American forces in the later war, that was seriously misleading as well as conveniently arresting for its progenitors. In particular, this approach underrated the extent to which the War of Independence was very much a civil war, especially, but not only, in the southern colonies.

Very different contexts continue to be offered when considering the War of Independence. The Tea Party movement of the 2000s and 2010s drew on a key moment that was part of the foundation account for America, the illegal seizure and destruction of 340 chests of tea in Boston on December 16, 1773, an episode that had a distinctive resonance in terms of modern American society. The process of reaching and redefining a consensus that underlay and often constituted government in the Colonial Period had broken down.[15] The drama of the Boston Tea Party, however, is a very poor model for politics within a modern civil society, let alone the rule of law and order. Moreover, the events of 1773 scarcely describe modern America, not least given the role of colonial Boston as a slaving port.[16] The treatment of Loyalists in Boston was to be extremely harsh, but so earlier with those of different religious views. Indeed, in 1732, Thomas Sherlock, an influential bishop, argued that it was ironic that those Puritans who had claimed religious freedom in England left for North America where they had turned persecutors of those who wanted freedom there.[17]

Relations with Native Americans and blacks put the War of Independence (1775–83) in an instructive context. Ironically possibly (although looking ahead to tensions in Australia) the British were more mindful of the interests of the former than were the exponents of the new state, and this helped alienate colonial opinion, notably in Virginia. Moreover, numbers of black slaves escaped their masters and fled to the British during both the War of Independence and the War of 1812. This flight

offered and offers a complication that was/is not really wanted by commentators, and it was/is generally ignored. Take Fort Apalachicola in West
Florida (significantly known as Fort Negro by the Americans), which was
established by Lieutenant Colonel Edward Nicolls of the British army,
who sought to use the support of runaway slaves and Native Americans
in the last stages of the War of 1812.[18] Once the war was over, Nicolls faced
pressure from the Americans to return runaway slaves. He responded
defiantly that they had been sent "to the British colonies where they are
received as free settlers and land given them."[19] Rear Admiral George
Cockburn, who had established a base on Cumberland Island, Georgia,
in the closing stages of the war, rejected similar pressure.[20] After the war,
in July 1816, an American expedition attacked Fort Apalachicola, which
was destroyed when a shot ignited the powder magazine. The surviving
blacks were enslaved.[21] From a variety of motives, the American government and some prominent interest groups were to support the idea of a
free black state or federation of states in Africa, but freedom for blacks
was only acceptable at a distance from America, eventually in Liberia.[22]

The muddy reaches of the Apalachicola River conjure up a different
world, one in which Native Americans and blacks could maintain or seek
their independence, autonomy, or freedom. Alongside the aspirations
of Nicolls and Cochrane[23] for Britain to take a role in a new order, this
serves as a reminder of the ways in which Britain's empire could develop,
and the limitations of seeing it as either good or bad. Subsequently, the
Americans pressed the British hard and repeatedly for compensation for
the runaway slaves, and eventually gained it. The pressure for compensation was also seen in France's treatment of Haiti.

Cochrane himself was to play a key role in helping secure the independence of Chile, Brazil, and Peru during their independence wars of the
1820s, and also became a major influence in later fiction about the British
navy, as in G. A. Henty's adventure book for young men, *With Cochrane
the Dauntless* (1897). Politically, Cochrane was a radical and a supporter
of parliamentary reform. He very much serves as a reminder of variations
in the possible image, or rather images, of empire, British and otherwise.

Differently, this point about Britain and the United States can be
approached by a comparison of the United States up to 1865 with the Caribbean islands that were under British rule. Slavery had been abolished
in the latter. This comparison can then be brought forward by presenting

these islands and those under the United States, notably, from 1898, Puerto Rico, but also by considering the situation in the Bay Islands in the Gulf of Mexico, especially Roatán, which is now part of Honduras, but was for a while under British control. It is by no means clear that British imperial rule was notably worse than that of others, a situation that lasts to the present, and in some respects it was better. Some of the critique of the British Empire has come from American commentators whose own country not only acted with enormous brutality against indigenous people, but maintained slavery longer than most Western states (all bar Brazil and Spain), and did not abandon imperialism while urging this approach on others. That does not invalidate the criticism, but it contextualizes this criticism and does not mean that American commentators cannot point out the imperial excesses of other nations.

The focus on the Civil War in America's potent "history wars," rather than the brutal and even more lengthy civil war that the War of Independence entailed,[24] has ensured that Britain and the earlier colonial link has dropped from American public attention and is far less controversial for American history than would probably have been the case had there been no Civil War. Nevertheless, with the exception of Churchill, as in *Darkest Hour* (2017), the British and British actors frequently recur in American historical films as the villains. This is an instructive indication of national attitudes. Moreover, some stars that succeed in the American media adopt American accents, as with Angela Lansbury. The global significance of Hollywood then ensures that the image of British villainy, as well as that of the British as class-obsessed, is widely disseminated. In the seriously misleading *The Patriot* (2000), which deals with the War of Independence, a German atrocity from World War II (people being confined to a church which was then set alight at Oradour in France in 1944) is misleadingly extrapolated onto the British.[25] This egregious rubbish is part of a pattern, as with the highly inaccurate, as well as extremely hostile, treatment of medieval England in the film *Braveheart* (1995), a film that proved very convenient for Scottish nationalism. Moreover, in lighter adventure stories intended for the young, such as the *Pirates of the Caribbean* series (2006–), villains are often British officials. As with China, although very differently, the global importance of American views and images is such that they play a significant role in forming images of the British Empire. These images are largely negative, and often very negative.

In the United States, Britain plays a continuing but nevertheless secondary role in the "culture wars" through which political values, indeed a degree of tribalism, expresses itself. This situation was made abundantly clear in Virginia in 2007. A debate then over whether Virginia should apologize for slavery was contentious. It was decided to express "profound regret," but not an apology. Frank Hargrove, a Republican member of the House of Delegates, whose ancestors were French Huguenots who had come to America in search of religious freedom, was strongly criticized for remarking:

> The present Commonwealth [Virginia] has nothing to do with slavery.... Nobody living today had anything to do with it. It would be far more appropriate in my view to apologise to the Upper Mattaponi and the Pamunkey [Native Americans who had lost their lands]. I personally think that our black citizens should get over it. By golly, we're living in 2007.

This controversy overlapped with the celebrations of the four-hundredth anniversary of the foundation of the Jamestown settlement by English settlers, the first settlement that has lasted to the present and the basis of Virginia. Donald E. McEachin, a descendant of slaves, who had sponsored the proposal for state contrition, also called on Queen Elizabeth II to "express regret." She did not do so, but later that year at a Special Joint Session of the Virginia General Assembly, the queen noted the difference between her visit in 2007 and that in 1957, for the 350th anniversary, when there had been no pressure for an apology. She sagely concluded: "It is right that we continue to reassess the meaning of historical events in the changing context of the present." That, of course, is not the same as understanding what happened.

6

AUSTRALIA, CANADA, AND NEW ZEALAND

On Australia Day, January 26, 2018, Aboriginal (indigenous) activists defaced monuments dedicated to Captain James Cook and other British explorers of Australia. A statue of Cook in Melbourne was covered in pink paint with the words NO PRIDE painted beneath his feet alongside the Aboriginal flag. Paint was thrown on a monument to an expedition across inland Australia in the nineteenth century, and the word STOLEN was added. Statues of Lachlan Macquarie, the most prominent colonial governor of New South Wales, have also been defaced. Alan Trudge, the Citizenship Minister, declared on radio, "These people are trashing our national heritage." The date of Australia Day is that when, in 1788, the "First Fleet" of British convict ships arrived and Captain Arthur Phillip claimed the land for George III, which was a form of compensation for the loss of the Thirteen Colonies. To some, it is what they termed "invasion day" and a celebration that whitewashes earlier history.

The attack on statues, a form of public re-inscription, is not new, and George III suffered in statue form during the War of American Independence, losing his perch in New York. In August 2017, a statue of Cook in Hyde Park in Sydney was given the additions CHANGE AND DATE and NO PRIDE IN GENOCIDE. Politics as usual are involved. Malcolm Turnbull, the prime minister in early 2018, criticized activists, while his

Labour opponent, Bill Shorten, backed a change to the inscription which claims that Cook discovered "this territory," which, in 1879 when it was erected, meant the colony of New South Wales. Cook was indeed the first person to see the entire coast of New South Wales. Turnbull has argued for debate, not censorship: "A free country debates its history – it does not deny it. It builds new monuments as it preserves old ones, writes new books, not burns old ones." In 2018, the Australian government decided to build a monument in Botany Bay, where Cook had arrived in 1770 on his voyage of exploration.

In 2011, new tensions had arisen when the Left-dominated Sydney City Council insisted that the words "European arrival" be replaced in official documents with the term "invasion or illegal colonisation." This decision was reached after pressure from the council's Aboriginal and Torres Strait Islander Advisory Panel, and the council voted 7–2 in favor of the change. Academic opinion was divided, the historian Alan Frost pointing out that the intentions of William Pitt the Younger, the British prime minister from 1783 to 1801 and from 1804 to 1806, could not be accurately described as an invasion:

> My notion of invasion is armed forces arriving to dispossess someone else. What happened to the Aborigines subsequently was dispossession but that was not the intention of the Pitt Administration. For the first 15 to 20 years, Sydney was just a tiny thing on the edge of a vast continent. It seems to me that to use the word "invasion" to describe it is an abuse of language.[1]

Such an abuse is very common, and Frost correctly focused on the misuse and impact of language. In April 2018, Aboriginal protestors unsuccessfully sought to disrupt the opening of the Commonwealth Games on the Gold Coast in Australia, referring to it as the "Stolenwealth Games."

LAND AND INDIGENOUS PEOPLES

In Australia, Canada, and New Zealand, the focus of the debate and controversy about empire is not on the policies of the imperial government, although they attract a fair amount of discussion and some opprobrium,[2] but rather on those of settlers. Whereas the former can be detached from the present for many former colonies, the latter interact far more clearly with present politics and tensions, and that interaction makes these past policies contentious or rather in an instructive distinction, a focus of contention. It is necessary to reconcile a colonial past with a continuing indigenous presence.[3] In place of beginning Australian history in 1788, has come an interest in the long human occupancy of the country. Moreover, there is now a presentation of this occupancy as more sophisticated and adaptable than in terms of a simple and static description of the early inhabitants as "hunter gatherers," who, therefore, were unable to develop unless confronted by the example of Western rule. That approach gives all agency to the settlers.

A major cause of contention is that of control over land. Bound up in those disputes were issues over the moves and treaties by which this control had been obtained by settlers or by their descendants. In New Zealand, this contention has made the Treaty of Waitangi (1840) an issue. Although presented as a means by which Maori and Pakeha (Europeans) jointly founded modern New Zealand and by means of an agreement, this treaty has since been rejected as a misleading account that sought to sanitize settler colonization. As a result, sparked by the Māori Affairs Amendment Act (1967), which aided the compulsory acquisition of land, there were protests on Waitangi Day from 1971.[4]

Charges of racism and a lack of recognition were issues in the questioning of the purpose and implementation of historical treaties. This was a topic in both Canada and New Zealand. In contrast, in Australia, where there were no such treaties, the focus was on the challenging of colonial doctrines, the dispossession to which they had led, and the erasure, both real and alleged, of the Aborigines from national memory.[5] The latter responded with complaints, as in 1938, when a "Day of Mourning" for Aborigines was held in Sydney by the Australian Aborigines' Progressive Association at the same time that the sesquicentennial celebrations for the original British landing were being held. Formed in 1925, the association pressed for full citizenship rights and for land as a compensation for dispossession.

In the 1990s, tensions rose, with the *Bringing Them Home* report of 1997 on the "Stolen Generations" of Aborigines (an issue also in Canada), and, in 2008, Kevin Rudd, the Labour prime minister, apologized for relations with the Aborigines since 1788. There was a pronounced trend from the 1960s, through legislation and judicial rulings, to abandon discriminatory practices, recognize original occupancy, and concede land rights (notably a High Court ruling of 1992 and the Native Title Act of 1993),[6] although some of the arguments made were questionable.[7] In 1985, the government transferred Ayers Rock National Park to the traditional Aboriginal owners. Scholarship was also affected, as with the marked difference in content and tone between Charles Manning Clark's *A History of Australia* (1962–87) and the more clearly political *The Cambridge History of Australia* (2013) edited by Alison Bashford and Stuart McIntyre.

In New Zealand, there has been an attempt to give greater voice to Maori accounts of the past, as part of a national reconciliation that has been sought on the basis of equality. These attempts have been challenged from both "sides." In 1996, the term "holocaust" was used by the Waitingi Tribunal, which investigated Maori grievances. This was in *Taranaki Report: Kaupapa Tuatahi*, its report on Taranaki, a district in the North Island, which saw conflict, land confiscation, protest, and dispossession in the nineteenth century:

> As to quantum, the gravamen of our report has been to say that the Taranaki claims are likely to be the largest in the country. The graphic *muru* [plunder] of most of Taranaki and the *raupatu* [confiscation] without ending describe the holocaust of Taranaki history and the denigration of the founding peoples in a continuum from 1840 to the present.

In 2000, Taria Turia, a prominent Maori and the associate minister of Maori Affairs, gave a "Maori holocaust" speech and, in the resulting furor, referred to the report. This clashed with the decision, made just days earlier, by Helen Clark, the prime minister, that the word "holocaust" must never again be used in a New Zealand context. In turn, the Indigenous Peoples Conference held a few days later in Wellington endorsed both the *Waitangi Tribunal* statement and Taria Turia.

In the general election of 2005, the unsuccessful center-right opposing National Party attacked what its leader termed the "grievance industry" centered on Maori land claims. He promised an end to the numerous claims and the reversal of any legislation granting special privileges to Maoris. The Maori themselves had markedly expansionist tendencies in the early nineteenth century, as, at the expense of non-Maori, in the Chatham Islands, but, more particularly, at the expense of other Maori. To blame these tendencies on guns obtained by means of trade with Europeans is to make the means the cause, which is inappropriate but parallels the habit of blaming the Atlantic slave trade simply on Europeans rather than allocating due agency to enslavement and sale of Africans by Africans.

The legacy of empire came to play a much more polarizing role in Australian public identity and even politics from the 1990s, as the long-standing issue of Aboriginal claims became more central. A conservative position was strongly advanced by John Howard, the prime minister from 1996 to 2007. He argued that a positive interpretation should be advanced in contrast to what he presented as the "Black Armband view" which he claimed, under the goal of offering a multicultural account that accepted Aboriginal perspectives, was negative about Australian achievements. In his Australia Day Speech in 2006, Howard called for a "root and branch renewal" in the teaching of Australian history at school level, an argument that was also to be taken up by politicians in Britain, both Labour and Conservative.

The impact of changing views can be seen by comparing the centenary of the beginning of British settlement in Tasmania in 1803 (the city of Hobart itself was founded in 1804) with the bicentenary. For the centenary, in front of several thousand spectators, the governor unveiled a monument to the founder of the colony and praised the settlers. No Aboriginal people are known to have been present, and no mention was made of the subsequent "massacre" of Aborigines on May 3, 1804, which, in practice, was most likely three Aborigines who were shot by troops when found molesting a settler and his wife at their hut. In 2003, in contrast, no formal ceremony was held to mark the landing at Risdon Cove, the site of both the landing in 1803 and the "massacre" (or killings) in 1804. Indeed, on May 3, 2004, the "massacre" was commemorated from an Aboriginal perspective. The monument erected in 1904 was covered with a white sheet splattered with blood, as a supposed mark of respect to the victims of the "massacre," and the Secretary of the Tasmanian Aboriginal Centre, the representative group of the northern Tasmanian people, declared, "They killed us off in this place 200 years ago, stole our land, took away our people and imposed their religion on us. But our presence here today shows they have not destroyed us." After Aboriginal pressure, including the disruption of a re-enactment of the 1803 landing held in 1988 to celebrate the bicentenary of the establishment of the first British colony in Australia (in New South Wales), Risdon Cove was declared an Aboriginal Historic Site and transferred to the Tasmanian Aboriginal Land Council.[8]

The southern Tasmanian people, the Lia Pootah community, adopted a more conciliatory approach. Both groups have more British ancestry than the Aboriginal, but only the southerners chose to celebrate it in 2004. This is an instance of the need to appreciate that the "middle-ground" is very much a matter of the present as it is of the past. Jacinta Price, a Warlpiri-Celtic politician, in an interview in early 2018, commented, "Most of the self-identifying indigenous members of our community who claim to feel hurt by Australia Day being held on January 26 would also have white ancestors in their family trees and may not even have been born if the First Fleet hadn't come."[9] The point is also the case for many Maori. Indeed, the call, in Australasia as elsewhere, to "decolonize" the past is, in its own way, quite racist (unwittingly so) as it underplays, ignores, or slights the wide range of activities, drives, and practices that undermined what can be presented as colonial barriers of race and religion.

The British decision to establish a settlement in Tasmania should be placed in the context of bitter competition with France. In 1802, the French explorer Baudin had appeared in Tasmanian waters which excited British concern. Moreover, there was a quest for new sources of timber for British warships. So also with British expansion into West and South Australia and in New Zealand. William Pitt the Younger and his mentor on the Board of Trade, Henry Dundas, also saw a much bigger picture than competition with France, with which war resumed in 1803, and the quest for timber. They grasped the potential of a genuinely global empire linked by trade across the oceans as well as the means for holding strategic harbor locations that could contain the ambitions of all of Britain's imperial rivals. The vision also provided a trade outlet for the new British manufactured products from the emerging industrial revolution, and would potentially be based on free trade. Having read Adam Smith, Dundas saw free trade as benefiting Britain and creating a global realm of cooperation. This was a very early version of the *Pax Britannica* that emerged after 1815. Amidst all this, gaining the benefits of civilization, it was believed, could please the natives of the colonies.[10]

In addition, museums were, and are, controversial in their accounts of the past. Public policy played a major role in the controversy over the National Museum of Australia, which opened in Canberra in 2001, the centenary of federation. The Howard government, which had commissioned the museum, regarded its contents as overly devoted to the Aborigines, not least in the First Australians Gallery, the largest of the museum's permanent exhibitions. In 2004, the director was replaced. That the museum incorporated the zigzag employed in Daniel Libeskind's Jewish Museum in Berlin, providing a possible parallel with the fate of the Aborigines, a totally inappropriate one, was a cause of further controversy.[11] In 2018, the National Gallery of Victoria accompanied its impressive exhibition *Colony: Australia 1770–1861*, with *Colony: Frontier Wars*, which included modern paintings of anger, many by Aboriginal artists. The content and tone of such works vary, one of the more striking being *Tunnerminnerwait and Maulboyheener* (2015) by Marlene Gibson, which depicts an execution in 1842 in Melbourne "in accordance with European law," an approach that is inherently critical. The second exhibition was presented as celebrating "Aboriginal resistance and the resilience of culture and community through art, and memorializes the trauma of the past by making space for First Peoples' voices in the now."

The critique of the historical treatment of the Aborigines was seen at many levels. In 2018, the national airline Qantas issued instructions to its staff that they were to refer not to the settlement of Australia but to its invasion.

MOVING AWAY FROM BRITAIN

Historical issues focused on the indigenous population were not the only ones. There was also a more general disengagement from the imperial link during the twentieth century by the Dominions. In the case of Australia, Peter Weir's iconic film *Gallipoli* (1981) offered a political dimension to disenchantment, one directed against the imperial link with Britain. In this deeply distorted account, the British contribution to the campaign was downgraded and misrepresented. The impression offered was of British inefficiency, cowardice and dilatoriness leading to the sacrifice of the Anzac troops. World War I remains far more important in Australian national identity than World War II, with the Gallipoli expedition presented as the key episode that demonstrated Australian mettle and advanced its nationhood.[12]

In practice, imperial identity was changing in the late nineteenth and early twentieth centuries, and notably so in Australia, where empire appears to have had somewhat shallow roots. This can help explain why imperial sentiment evaporated so quickly in the decades after World War I. In this approach, there was an instrumentalism in the Australian response to imperial themes—the empire was of importance only at particular moments and in certain contexts. Defense was the key to imperial enthusiasm, whereas Antipodeans appear to have been considerably less impressed by vague notions of imperial unity that were presented in the form of imperial federation. Once the Boer threat had receded and it became clear that the empire was not endangered, it became difficult during the Boer War (1899–1902) to retain popular enthusiasm. Returning troops were not greeted by the large crowds seen when they had set out. Subsequently, the memorialization of World War I was divided, with imperial identity less central a theme than could have been expected.

At the same time, a more positive account of imperial identity in the late nineteenth and early twentieth centuries can be advanced. Splendid memorials to service in the Boer War were erected, such as the ones erected in Adelaide, as also in Canada, for instance in Halifax. In 1901, the English painter William Strutt (1825–1915) produced his impressive *Sentinels of the British Empire (the British Lion and his Sturdy Cubs)*. This painting, which hangs in the Tasmanian Museum and Art Gallery in Hobart, was produced to coincide with the federation of the Australian colonies and offered an idealized notion of the relationship, with the still vigorous lion surrounded by a large number of well-grown young lions. Strutt had lived in Australia and New Zealand from 1850 to 1862, producing popular history paintings.

Clearly, it was possible to hold more than one sense of identity at the same time, a point that remains relevant, and for the United States, as well as Britain. In the late nineteenth century, Australian identity was defined through heroic rural activity, as in Tom Roberts's painting *Shearing the Rams* (1890) and Frederick McCubbin's painting *The Pioneer* (1904). There were tensions between the strong sense of Australia as egalitarian and that of Britain as class-based, but that tension was not incompatible with a strong sense of Britishness.

In addition, there was a sense of change through empire and in its shadow. This can be presented through two very different paintings hung by the Gallery of South Australia in Adelaide. *Zenobia's Last Look on Palmyra*, painted in London in 1888 by Herbert Schmalz (1856–1935) and acquired by the gallery in 1890 thanks to the South Australian Government Grant, shows the Romans taking over the stormed and burning city, while the striking Zenobia, its queen, is in chains. Britain is the successor of Rome, and Australia shares in its heritage. Separately, H. J. Johnstone's *Evening Shadows, backwater of the Murray* (1880) shows an Aborigine family camping in the twilight, and reflects the widespread idea that the Aborigines were trapped in the past and would not survive the present day. This was a version of Enlightenment stadial thought taken on through the medium of Social Darwinism.

The extent to which new Australian, Canadian, New Zealand, and South African identities emerged during, and because of, World War I is a matter of current debate. Most historians argue that this was much less than modern popular opinion, especially in Australia, thinks. For example, the First Battalion of the Australian army thought of themselves as English. More generally, Australians shared British views and opinions.[13] At the same time, there was a sense of separate and superior military identity among the Canadians.[14]

The war left a powerful legacy of memorialization, with an emphasis on Australia, Britain, and empire as shared identities. However, as the imposing memorials were being built across the country, notably in Canberra, Hobart, Melbourne, and Perth, the impact of American culture was a crosscurrent. Imperial films had less of an impact than American counterparts. While youth became international in a different context to their parents, urban culture was, as a consequence, reshaped.[15]

American political influence came to the fore even more as a result of the changing geopolitics created by World War II, notably by the Japanese successes between 1941 and 1942, and the subsequent determination by the United States and Australia to contain Communism in Southeast Asia and more generally. The British link, like the broader British presence in the Pacific, increasingly came to appear irrelevant politically, a point captured in Ian Fleming's James Bond novel *You Only Live Twice* (1964).

Growing cultural affinity between the United States and Australia was an important part of the changing situation. In so far as imperial legacies were concerned, Australia had increasingly to adapt to the informal American empire, rather than the formal British one.

Australian-born John Curtin, prime minister from 1941 to 1945, declared: "This nation will remain forever the home of sons of Britishness who came here in peace to establish an outpost of the British race. Our laws have proclaimed the standard of a White Australia.... We intend to keep it, because we know it to be desirable." Also Australian-born, Harold Holt, the immigration minister from 1949 to 1956 (and prime minister in 1966–67), declared in 1950: "This is a British community, and we want to keep it a British community living under British standards and by the methods and ideals of British parliamentary democracy." Also Australian-born, Robert Menzies, prime minister from 1939 to 1941, and from 1949 to 1966, claimed, "A migrant from Britain to Australia is not lost to Britain; he merely serves the true interest of Britain in another part of the British empire." Close to 1.5 million Britons immigrated to Australia from 1947 to 1981. However, in contrast to the earlier dominance of immigration by Britons, notably as late as the 1970s, the principal groups of immigrants are now Asian. The same change has occurred with Canada with resulting shifts in notions of nationality and identity accordingly.

By the 2010s, the question in Australia was rather that of competition between two informal empires, those of the United States and China. The British legacy remained, notably in institutions and in the family connections of many individuals, but was largely individual; there was pressure for an end to the link represented by a shared monarch, and a widespread belief that it would end after the death of Elizabeth II. So also, albeit not to the same extent, with New Zealand. Empire had passed and the imperial legacy has become much weaker.

7

RESPONDING TO
THE WORLD
THAT EMPIRE MADE

About two hundred men invaded Sabah in Malaysia on February 9, 2013. They did so to reject a territorial legacy of the British Empire. Sabah, an area in the Malaysian-ruled northern part of the island of Borneo the size of Ireland, had been ceded to the Sultan of Sulu (an island in the southern Philippines) by the Sultan of Brunei (in northern Borneo) in 1658. However, in 1878, at a time when Britain was strong and Sulu weak, the Sultan of Brunei leased it to the British North Borneo Company. As a result of this action, Sabah became part of Malaysia in 1963, while descendants of the Sulu sultans received a nominal rent. The invasion was on behalf of Sultan Jamalul Kiram III, who claimed the (now honorary) throne of Sulu from 1986 until his death in October 2013, and was led by the Sultan's brother. It led to a clash with the Malaysian police and army in which the invaders were killed, captured or escaped.

The variety and complexity of the imperial legacy are fully exemplified by states that were creations of the British Empire, for example, in a far-from-complete list, Kenya, Malaysia, Nigeria, Pakistan, South Africa, Sri Lanka, Tanzania, Zambia, and Zimbabwe. At present, their public history shows a reaction against the empire, although the nature of this reaction is very varied. For example, in South Africa, the focus of opprobrium is on the apartheid that drew on the Dutch settler group that arrived under Dutch imperial rule from 1652 but that, in the nineteenth century, fought hard against becoming part of the British Empire. So, differently, in the United States where concern about the Civil War has partly or largely pushed out earlier issues.

These, however, are exceptional cases. In general, divisions within postcolonial independent states make criticism of Britain more attractive. This criticism is made easier by arguing not that Britain created the postcolonial state, but instead that British conquest and rule ruptured an historical continuity.

MALAYSIA

This argument can be readily seen in the case of Malaysia, a state with a Muslim Malay majority, but also including other groups, principally Chinese. In the National Museum of Malaysia, an impressive building that was opened in 1963 in the capital, Kuala Lumpur, the focus is on the medieval Malay sultanate of Melaka, which is presented as a peaceful multiracial society. This approach implies that Malaysia's current communal tensions are a consequence of British imperialism. However, it is the Malaysian government, in its consistent affirmative action policies (in effect, positive discrimination) toward the Muslim Malays, that has very much disadvantaged the native Chinese and Indian populations, both of whom did well under British rule.

Resistance to Western imperialism is discussed and approved of in the Museum, for example the murder of the British Resident in Perak in 1875. In addition, the language used can look toward more recent times. For example:

> British intervention in the administration of the Malay States, the rule of James Brooke in Sarawak, and the North Borneo Company's management of Sabah all sparked reactions from the local populations. Freedom fighters emerged who defended the dignity and sovereignty of their individual lands.

The Museum's treatment of the twentieth century scarcely emphasizes Malaysia's role in the British Empire. World War I, in which Malaysia was an important support for the imperial economy, is ignored, while, for World War II, accommodation from 1941 to 1945 between Japanese invaders and Malays is emphasized instead of the harshness of rule by Japan or opposition to it. The Communist insurrection against British rule after the war is ignored, which is scarcely surprising, as it was a Chinese-Malaysia movement. Within Malaysia, this insurrection is not presented as contributing to independence, a correct evaluation, and one that throws light on the memorialization of other insurrections. Somewhat differently, the independence movement against Britain in Singapore is presented in a way that underrates the role of the trade unions, a clear political choice.

AMNESIA?

So also with other museums. In Singapore, the emphasis in museums is on the Asian Civilisations Museum, the most impressive of the museums under the care of the National Heritage Board. Although part of this museum occupies the Empress Palace Building, designed in the 1860s to house British government offices and named in honor of Queen Victoria, British imperial rule has only a small impact in the museum. Instead, the museum aims to reconnect Singapore with its cultures of origin, notably in East and South Asia; more particularly China and India. At the same time, Singapore takes a more positive view than Malaysia toward British imperial rule.

To visit other national museums is similarly instructive. Indeed, this is very much a case of amnesia. The impact of empire, and certainly of the British Empire, is underplayed, and notably so if the impact was in practice positive. The major extent of accommodation to empire also tends to be ignored. The theme, instead, is one of opposition and liberation. History, thereby, becomes both one-dimensional and adversarial. At the same time, the idea of an account of the past that is not so shaped by the present as to be objective possibly is not only unhelpful, but also naive in so far as public history is concerned, and maybe often for academic history. Given that nationalism is such a part of modernity, it is mistaken, unless we wish for nations to dissolve away into the cosmopolitan ether, to expect that the construction of national identities will not inevitably come with nationalistic conceits. More particularly, many nations in the developing world will construct their identities against the British Empire.

A most dramatic form of deliberate postimperial amnesia, or, alternatively, a necessary correction to the former period of imperial enforced amnesia was offered by renaming, which has been widespread and continues. On independence in 1964, Nyasaland was renamed Malawi and Northern Rhodesia became Zambia, with Southern Rhodesia eventually becoming Zimbabwe in 1980. Not all the changes occurred at the same time as independence. Ceylon did not become Sri Lanka until 1972, while, in 1989, Burma became Myanmar, the name of the country in Burmese. Cities were also renamed. The capital of Southern Rhodesia, Salisbury, named after a British prime minister of the imperial age, the Third Marquess of Salisbury, became Harare. So also with some natural features. Lake Edward was renamed Lake Idi Amin Dada in 1973 after the Ugandan dictator Idi Amin; after his fall in 1979, it reverted to the earlier name. More generally, streets and squares have been extensively renamed. Most people (including most current Britons) would have no idea of the identity of the past Britons thus commemorated, other than the awareness that they were British.

So also with other aspects of memorialization. In 2002, the life-sized bronze statue of the explorer David Livingstone located near Victoria Falls was defaced. More commonly, statues of imperial rulers, ministers, generals, and heroes have been moved from prominent sites, as in India. Thus, the urban landscapes of empire have been transformed, and these alongside a process of urban change in which previous points of importance have lost their significance and often their centrality. Most commonly, the central parts of cities have moved and/or been rebuilt, while the cemeteries, churches, and fortresses of old appear redundant, as in Penang in Malaysia. The cemeteries are closed and overgrown, the churches generally closed or with very small and aged congregations, and the fortresses crumbling. Other buildings, both pre-colonial and colonial, have had new or renewed symbolic meanings inscribed on them.[1]

CYPRUS

The approach to empire varies by communities, reflecting their particular history with British rule. Thus, in Cyprus, hostility to empire is much more common among Greek Cypriots than from their Turkish counterparts. The former focus on their "liberation struggle" in the 1950s, but for

Turkish Cypriots, this simply moved a new and more serious adversary to a position of control. *Enosis*, or "reunion," with Greece was the goal of many Greek Cypriot nationalists, but not of the Turkish Cypriots. In 1955, EOKA, a Greek Cypriot nationalist movement, launched bomb attacks on the British imperial authorities, beginning, depending on one's perspective, an insurrection or a terrorist movement. Lacking adequate intelligence information, the British were unable to separate EOKA from the civilian population or to protect the latter from often-murderous EOKA intimidation. As a result, EOKA could be checked, but could not be destroyed and was not deprived of its means of regeneration.[2] Those murdered in insurrections and riots tend not to receive much attention unless they support the movement in question. This is true of Cyprus, as earlier, of the (far-fewer) British people killed by rioters before the unnecessary response at Amritsar.

As with Ireland in 1916, Amritsar (a very different episode) and on other occasions, the British response in Cyprus provided fresh material for the nationalist cause, both at the time and subsequently. Those killed by the British were memorialized as Greek national heroes, with their photographs prominently displayed. The Greek Cypriot account, which treated Greece as the motherland and taught a love of Greece, left no positive role for the Turkish Cypriots. The latter were regarded as interlopers under the rule of the Ottoman Empire who had then cooperated with the British. In fact, the Ottomans had conquered Cyprus from the Venetian empire between 1570 and 1571, holding it until it was ceded to Britain in 1878; Cyprus was then ruled by Britain until 1960, and, in the 1950s, was a military base compensating Britain for the loss of that of Egypt, as, also, albeit differently, was Aden. In practice, there had been no "union" with Greece, in the shape of rule by Byzantium or a Byzantine prince, for many centuries, in fact, since 1191. Moreover, Cyprus had been ruled as an Arab-Byzantine condominium in some form or other for most of the period from 649 to 965.

DECOLONIZATION AND FORCE

As Cyprus, Ireland, and other cases show, the number of civil conflicts, or of full-scale civil wars, in former imperial colonies ensured that this question of "placing" British rule is further complicated by the extent to which groups within colonies are composed of individuals who make their own responses to the legacy of the past. As a result, the tendency to agglomerate responses in the terms of a national account is in part a matter of shaping a complex situation. While such shaping is understandable, it is also misleading. This is because the responses are presented as if they were national in character whereas the unit in practice more commonly that of family, locality, or ethnicity.

In Cyprus and elsewhere, British counter-insurgency policies showed less evidence of the policy of minimum force that was subsequently to become important in British military doctrine.[3] British policy benefited from a largely supportive or apathetic, or at least not-too-critical, domestic public opinion.[4] Nevertheless, there was some criticism in Britain of the methods of control, including detention without trial and the enforced movement of people into villages, as had happened on a large scale in Malaysia. The use of coercion was in part a response to imperial overreach, and notably to the weakness of Britain after the costs of World War II and the loss, with Indian independence, of the highly important manpower of the Indian Army. As with the employment of air power, force was a response to a sense of weakness and to the realities of a shortage of troops and of a lack of local control and intelligence. Force was seen as the way to maintain authority.

At the same time, concern about the Cold War and the repeated tendency to see Communist planning behind nationalist pressure, a tendency that was generally (although not always) misplaced, encouraged this reliance on force, a reliance that extended to a manipulation of judicial systems and regulations. The political concessions that were subsequently praised, notably in the handling of Malaya, were not the first step and came only after the use of force. Indeed, the British concept of opposition as a threat to a benign bulk of the population who accepted imperial rule ensured that such a use of force was regarded as very necessary. The British reliance on force and the use of collective punishments appears anachronistic from the perspective of imminent decolonization, but the latter was less apparent in the mid-1950s than by the end of the decade. Moreover, in the aftermath of World War II, attitudes toward the use of force were very different to those that were to follow.

In the case of colonies for which there was no decolonization conflict, there was (and is) still the problem of defining postcolonial identity and, even more, the consequences that could, or can, be expected to stem from it. This again puts empire at the center of recent and current political narratives. The very notion of a political narrative captures the degree to which speculation about national identity and purpose is best captured in the form of a narrative that often has epic and mythic proportions. From that perspective, Britain emerges as a villain, the strength and villainy of which have to be inflated in order to enhance the value of overcoming it, and thus the inheritable and inherited virtue of this achievement. Political ownership makes this an important process.

This observation can be enhanced further by noting what was (and is), in practice, the salience of religion and ethnicity as factors in the divisive internal politics in many former colonies, such as Nigeria and India. British imperial rule appears as a safe target in this respect, not least because Christianity and "whiteness" are not part of the subsequent internal politics. However, this targeting is a cul-de-sac in terms of the more serious issues and divisions that currently engage political attention, however much these issues and divisions may be traced to this rule, and often in a questionable fashion. There are few former parts of the empire in which British imperial politics can very readily be inscribed in terms of current religious or ethnic divisions, and vice versa, although they can be in Northern Ireland and, less credibly, Sri Lanka.

LOOKING AHEAD

This point about exemplary political narratives invites speculation about the way ahead. The British Empire clearly will remain a matter of contention, and especially so in the British Isles, as issues of "four nations" (English, Scottish, Welsh, and Irish) history and, very differently, post-imperial multi-culturalism, are addressed. Scottish nationalism is the key issue in the former case.[5] This situation, however, is likely to be less the case in many former colonies. Despite the efforts to keep issues alive, notably those made by academics working in the field of postcolonial studies, the period of empire will recede and is already affected because we are, in the twenty-first century, a post-(British)imperial century, rather than the twentieth century, a period when empire did not seem so distant. Every day, the number of those who can remember being born under imperial rule falls, as do those who served, or fought against, empire. Each day, the apparent relevance (and interest) of the experience of British rule recedes, and such rule, if remembered, appears simply to be one among a number of historical episodes. Moreover, British imperial rule becomes one, albeit usually the latest, and definitely what is presented as the latest, in a sequence of periods of imperial control. Any "deep history" captures this sequence, whereas an only slight engagement with the past, whether or not conceived of in terms of amnesia, leads to the overwhelming focus on British imperial rule. Most people have only a slight engagement and welcome a simple account, a process encouraged by an emphasis on the relatively recent past.

In particular parts of the world, this process is pushed to the fore by geopolitics. Thus, Britain was already overshadowed by the United States as an imperial presence and issue in many areas from the 1960s, such as in the Caribbean, and, from the 1970s, in the Middle East and Far East. Britain then might still be the imperial ruler, but America was the focus of much political and economic criticism, a process encouraged by American economic penetration and Cold War issues and propaganda. Now, the spread of the Chinese presence, notably in Africa, takes that to the fore when discussing informal empire.

Separately, the most violent recent episodes in former colonies, such as Aden (South Yemen), Israel, Cyprus (with the Turkish invasion of 1974), British Somaliland, Nigeria (with the Biafran War of 1967–1970), and Zimbabwe, rarely relate to Britain other than indirectly, despite efforts to present the British as responsible, a point that will also become increasingly relevant for the United States. In Zimbabwe, the *Gukurahundi* (early rain that washes away the chaff), the brutal treatment of Matabeleland, an area of opposition to President Robert Mugabe in the early 1980s, was far more brutal than British rule in the region, and has left a lasting grievance. However, the government of Zimbabwe, when under Mugabe from 1980 to 2017, tended to present its difficulties as derived from the legacy of British imperial control and the continuing reality of British economic pressures; rather than addressing serious issues in its government composition, policies, and structures. Aspects of the British legacy that might have helped greatly in economic regeneration, such as the security of legal contract that greatly encourages investment, were neglected, as, in general, was the rule of law.

More generally, by the 1970s, newly independent African and Asian states were increasingly apt to discredit what was called Westminster-style parliamentary democracy as an expression of Western imperialist and neo-colonial designs. As a result, they were able to rebut foreign criticism of an authoritarianism that was sometimes more marked than that of colonial powers. This pattern continues to this day, with the criticism more commonly focused on the application of human rights legislation. Thus, especially from in 2013, there was African criticism about the International Criminal Court at The Hague, notably as it sought to prosecute senior Kenyan politicians, such as Uhuru Kenyatta, for murderous electoral violence at the time of the presidential election of 2007. This rejection of international jurisdiction by Kenya took place at the same time that the British courts and press were used, and more successfully, to pursue claims for redress arising from the brutal treatment of Kenyans during the Mau Mau insurrection against British imperial rule in the 1950s.

The habit of modern authoritarian governments attacking past Western colonialism is not only an issue for Britain. In March 2018, President Recep Tayyip Erdogan of Turkey, in criticizing France's attempt to act as a peacemaker between Turkey and the Kurds, who were subject to Turkish imperialism, claimed that France "has yet to give an account for its dirty and bloody past." In 2017, Erdogan had attacked France's record in Algeria.

The diminishment with time of the shadow of postcolonial rule will presumably alter the historical narrative, and most so in the former colonies. Indeed, there may open up a disjuncture. On the one hand, British public discussion, and that of the traditional national narrative in former colonies, may focus on the British Empire. On the other, the current debate over history in recent colonies may come to depart from this traditional narrative. Indeed, the critique of empire among commentators may become a political and politicized "discourse" that scarcely captures changing opinion around the world or, rather, seeks to place it in an established context. The historical focus may increasingly be on the policies of the major states of the moment, matching the focus of historical concerns.

ISRAEL

As a reminder of the range of postcolonial examples, Israel was also a state that emerged from the end of British imperial rule. The focus there was not on a long period of anti-imperial struggle, because it was the British who had driven out the Ottoman Turks between 1917 to 1918, ending an imperial rule that had begun in that case in 1516, replacing the earlier Egyptian-based Mamluk empire which had ruled from the thirteenth century, in turn replacing the Crusaders who had conquered the region from the late 1090s. The key opposition to the British in the 1930s, the Arab Rising, was led by the Palestinians, and not by the Jews. Indeed, Palestinian activism was very much hostile to Jewish settlement.

The path of decolonization from Britain remains a major issue of dispute in Israel, not least the terms employed. For example, in the 1970s and 1980s, the powerful rival political parties, Labour and Likud, offered differing views of the Jewish opposition to British rule in 1945–1948. In particular, the use of terrorist violence by the *Irgun Zvai Leumi*, a group that later was to be influential in the genesis of Likud, was controversial. So also was the use of the term "terrorist," not only because it delegitimized past and present but also with reference to Israel's position with regard to Arab terrorist attacks from which it has suffered grievously. Menachem Begin, prime minister from 1976 to 1983, had been the head of the *Irgun*, while Yizhak Shamir, his successor as prime minister (1983–1984, 1986–1992), was a member of the more radical *Ohamei Herut Yisrael*, which was called by the British the Stern Gang. Streets were named after members of the group, and Yair, the *nom de guerre* of Avraham Stern, served as a name for Kochav Yair, a West Bank settlement, as a well as for the sons of prominent Likud figures.[6] Contesting responsibility for winning Israeli independence, a prime form of contention between Labour and Likud, was a means to affirm a right to govern.

At the same time, British policy, both imperial and later, was criticized in the Arab world as pro-Jewish/Israeli; but also during the imperial period for enforcing division on the lands of Islam in a pattern allegedly going back to the Crusades. In 2014, Islamic State Report, the online voice of ISIS, presented the movement as seeking to reverse what it claimed was a long-standing Western attempt to divide the Muslim world, one in which the British allegedly took a major role. The 1916 Anglo-French Sykes–Picot agreement to partition the Ottoman Empire was presented as a key episode:

> It was 98 years ago that the Allies of WWI forged a secret agreement to carve up the territories of the Muslim lands. They would form a

symbolic precedent for subsequent partitioning of Muslim lands by crusader powers. Years after agreement, invisible borders would go on to separate a Muslim and his brother, and pave the way for ruthless, nationalistic *tawaghit* [idolatry] to entrench the *umma's* [Muslim world's] division rather than working to unite the Muslims under one imam carrying the banner of truth.[7]

In practice, the political and religious division of the Muslim world was entrenched from the eighth century and was very violent from the seventh century. Paranoia about non-Muslims is not an appropriate guide.

Differences over Israeli policy became more significant in British politics from the mid-2000s and, by the mid-2010s, were closely related to contention over the extent of anti-Semitism, notably in the Labour Party. Although there were references to the impact and legacy of British imperial rule, the differences and contention in this case were not really a matter of the empire coming home. Instead, the focus was on the consequences of Israel-Arab conflicts from 1948 on. Many treated Israel as an anti-colonial and postimperial state in the late 1940s and 1950s, but, from the late 1960s on, critics, both in Britain and elsewhere, increasingly presented it as neo-imperial. Whatever the approach, the stress was not on Britain's role. This was not a matter of "amnesia," but rather of a distinctive trajectory and debate, and one in which the United States took a far greater role. Britain was criticized as being historically pro-Arab, while Israel, instead, identified with the United States.

MALTA

Political division over empire did not always involve or focus on violence. In Malta, a British colony from conquest from France in 1800 to independence in 1964, division between the two main political groupings, Labour and the Nationalists, affected both the path to independence and its subsequent memorialization. In the 1920s and 1930s, in opposition to British rule of what was then a key naval base, prominent Nationalists played up the Italian character of Malta (and the Maltese) as an adjunct to Sicily, of which it had been part until 1530. This *italianatà* also served as a way for the social elite to monopolize jobs and to exclude working-class Maltese, who did not speak Italian and who were the basis of Labour support. The powerful Catholic Church was seen as close to the Nationalists. The latter played down the extent to which being linked with Italy would simply mean exchanging one empire (Britain) for another, albeit a Catholic one, and also moving from rule by a liberal empire to a Fascist one, that of Benito Mussolini from 1922 to 1943, a regime that had settled Italy's differences with the Papacy in 1929. Claims, then and now, by the nationalists that being pro-Italian in the interwar years meant opposition to colonial rule are flawed as well as self-serving.

After World War II, this Nationalist theme was discredited as a result of the wartime failure of Mussolini. Moreover, the Italian role in the bitter Axis air assault on, and serious attempted blockade of, Malta in the war ensured that the memorialization in Malta of the conflict had political consequences. Indeed, focusing on independence for Malta, the nationalists downplayed their earlier support for Italy, most of which was ignored and written out of the record. Modern scholarship on the point therefore resonates with its significance for the historical legitimacy of the Maltese political parties, a situation also seen with India, Ireland, and other cases. Legitimacy is a problematic concept, but one that can be employed by considering what each movement said, and says, about its goals and history.

The Maltese Nationalists' treatment of their history is as one with a more general rewriting of nationalism against the Western imperial powers in order to ignore, minimize, or extenuate support by the nationalists for Germany, Italy, or Japan during World War II. In contrast to this approach, opponents of particular nationalists who were heavily implicated in such support, for example, critics of the pro-Japanese Bose, draw attention to it. These tensions contribute to debate about what a postcolonial history should contain.[8]

SRI LANKA

In another, more divided island, Sri Lanka, criticism of Britain focuses not on the process of gaining independence, which was peaceful on both sides, but on the alleged policies of the British as imperial rulers. These policies are held responsible for subsequent issues and identities that can therefore conveniently be blamed on them. In particular, the emphasis, in the independent Sri Lanka, on a Sinhalese Buddhist national identity has led to a downplaying of the integral role of the Tamil population of Sri Lanka, many of whom are Hindu. The accurate presentation of the Tamils as more likely to serve British imperial rulers serves to imply that they were (and therefore are) somehow less patriotic and nationalist, and, instead, are more like the British than Sri Lankan. The two themes are linked in British colonial support for education, which proved of particular benefit to Tamils seeking employment in public service, while the Sinhalese then preferred to focus on agriculture. A harsher tone is offered by seeing this as an instance of British policies of "divide and rule," which is an overly easy accusation to make, for Sri Lanka and elsewhere. While criticizing Britain, this approach serves to present Tamil assertiveness, let alone separatism, as a legacy of imperial misgovernment, and one that is out of place in modern Sri Lanka.

CONCLUSION

Similar analyses and narratives can be found elsewhere. These exemplify the contentious political legacy of history. There is scant amnesia as far as ignoring empire is concerned. However, there is amnesia about its benefits, the degree of cooperation with it, and the extent to which the history and experience of particular countries that were once part of the empire need to consider not only that background, but also that the imperial experience was as part of a greater historical and geographical whole that included earlier periods of imperial rule of particular colonies, other British colonies, and the imperial history of other Western powers.

8

THE SLAVE TRADE
AND RACISM

Bishop's Palace. Henry Philpotts, Bishop of Exeter, received a share of £12,729 4s 4d, which was a portion of the £20 million paid to compensate slave owners for the loss of their human property, following the Abolition of Slavery Act of 1833. The Bishop's Palace was also the site of one of Exeter's sugar processing factories linking Exeter to the plantation economies.

Telling our Stories, Finding our Roots: Exeter's Multi-Coloured History," a project by Devon Development Education, funded by the British National Heritage Lottery Fund, offered, in 2013, a very different account of the city's history to that with which its inhabitants (and others) were familiar. The self-guided tour drew attention in the history of Exeter to long-standing ethnic minorities, and, more particularly, to uncomfortable links with the past. Alongside the references to slavery above came: "Royal Clarence Hotel. Well-known Black British singer Leslie Hutchinson (Hutch) visited that city during WWII and was not allowed to stay in the Royal Clarence Hotel," Exeter's leading hotel.

This is a somewhat different legacy to such surviving signs in Exeter as the public lamp put up in memory of General Gordon's death at Khartoum in 1885, which remains a very different presence in Exeter's suburb of Heavitree (one acknowledged by a notice), to the long-past hanging tree after which it takes its name, which is not acknowledged. Other legacies include street names recording victories (Alma in the Crimean War, 1854) and successful generals (Roberts).

There is also a prominent equestrian statue of Sir Redvers Buller, member of a local landowning family, who was a major general of empire, ultimately being replaced in 1900 due to the failure in the early stages of the Boer War. Put up by public subscription, the base declares that, "He

Saved Natal." It is frequently decorated with wreaths, not in continued memory of the attempt to rehabilitate Buller, but because students at the nearby Exeter College have climbed it for self-display, only for some to fall to their fate. Buller himself is often crowned with a traffic cone. As part of the complexity of the past, and the mistaken nature of focusing only on one element, Exeter had also had large attendances at Abolitionist (ending slavery) meetings.[1] Moreover, the minorities who were treated well in Exeter included Jews.

These are not the only contrasts. In 2008, the Racial Equality Council complained when a pub in Plymouth, a city close to Exeter, was named after Sir John Hawkins, an English naval hero of the sixteenth century who was also a prominent slaver. Two years earlier, a descendant of Hawkins and a group of twenty friends publicly locked themselves in chains in Gambia to demonstrate their sorrows, before being forgiven by the vice president.

In Bristol, the role of Edward Colston (1636–1721), slave trader and philanthropist, is even more controversial. Since 1999, there has been controversy in Bristol over the 1895 statue to Colston and over the name Colston Hall. "Countering Colston," a local campaign, has drawn attention to the annual church service in his name, as well as to the names Colston Girls School and Colston Primary School. A new plaque is to be placed on Colston's statue, which is intended to avoid recourse to graffiti. The Wills Memorial Building in the university is also controversial as Wills' bequest is seen as "slave-profited money" dating back to the eighteenth century.

Slavery and the slave trade are the most difficult and contentious aspect of the imperial legacy, one that captures the full viciousness of power, economic, political, and military, and that leaves a clear and understandable hostility to empire in the Atlantic world. Moreover, within Britain, slavery and the slave trade became and become, ready ways to stigmatize empire, and increasingly so, notably as Britain becomes a multiracial society. In 2007, Tony Blair, the Labour prime minister, expressed "deep sorrow and regret" for the "unbearable suffering" caused by Britain's role in slavery. The previous year, the Church of England apologized to the descendants of victims of the slave trade, its General Synod acknowledging the "dehumanising and shameful" consequences of slavery. Indeed, in his 1957 sermon "The Birth of a New Nation,"

Martin Luther King had noted the role of the Church of England in giving slavery moral traction.

While arguing that slaves should not be treated brutally, the Society for the Propagation of the Gospel in Foreign Parts, founded in 1701 with the Archbishop of Canterbury as its first president, presented slavery as compatible with the social order and claimed that the Christian instruction of slaves was crucial to sustaining the stability of this order. In 1727, Edmund Gibson, Bishop of London and the key Church of England adviser to the first minister, Sir Robert Walpole, issued a pastoral letter in which he supported both slave conversion to Christianity and the biblical sanctioning of slavery. Gibson's use of freedom is instructive:

> The freedom which Christianity gives is a freedom from the bondage of Sin and Satan, and from the dominion of men's lusts and passions and inordinate desires; but as to their outward condition, whatever that was before, whether bond or free, their being baptised, and becoming Christians, made no manner of change in it.[2]

The attitude of the SPG was harshly displayed on Barbados where, in 1710, it became the owner of the valuable Codrington plantation. The subsequent treatment of the slaves on this plantation was scarcely different from the norm. Public whippings were designed to maintain order, runways were branded with the word "Society," children were forced to work, and families were separated by sales.[3]

Liverpool, Britain's major slaving port when the slave trade was at its height, made a public apology in 1994 for its role in the slave trade, and the International Slavery Museum there is very candid about the city's involvement in slavery. So also with the situation in Bristol, another prominent slaving port, although, in each case, and notably the latter, there are complaints that "more should be done." While an easy claim to make, this claim reflects deep anger. For example, on January 5, 2012, in an interview with the *Sunday Times*, Chiwetel Ejiofor, the lead actor in *Twelve Years a Slave*, a much-watched film about slavery in 1840s America, demanded that British schools face up to the country's slave-trading past. The film's British director, Steve McQueen, argued that slavery should be remembered in Britain in the same way as the Holocaust. This is a stark comparison, although the Holocaust was totally different in being genocidal in intention and impact.

Both slavery and the slave trade were vile and all the details of both confirm this vileness. They also were aspects of the more general coercion of labor seen across much of the world for much of its history. To abstract slavery from other forms of coerced labor, such as convict labor, serfdom and indentured labor, is not always helpful to our understanding of it. Nor, as a related issue, is it wise to ignore the extent to which slavery could also be indigenous to areas from which slaves were taken, notably, but not only, sub-Saharan Africa, where it was very important, and for many centuries. Control over people generally proved as significant as control over territory; even more so.

Slavery played a crucial role in the British Atlantic world, from the arrival in Virginia in 1619, only twelve years after the colony was founded, of the first cargo of African slaves.[4] Between 1691 and 1779, British ships transported over two million slaves from Africa, the conditions of their transit being degrading, cruel, and harsh.[5] In the colonies, slavery was central to the production of plantation crops, notably sugar, cotton, tobacco, indigo, and rice, as well as to the world of work more generally, both directly for the economy and household tasks. The majority of the slaves in the Caribbean colonies worked in sugar cultivation,[6] which was arduous.

Slavery, and the money made from it, moreover, affected the economy and culture of England/Britain, the imperial metropole, a topic that has attracted much attention in recent years; although the extent to which it did so is also a matter for debate. Economic links were certainly important. Some are well known, as with the British role in the processing and re-export of plantation crops; others less so, for example, the export to the West Indies of copper equipment for sugar processing led to a major expansion in the copper industry in Britain.[7] The latter helped increase the impact of slavery.

More generally, the export of goods to Africa helped broaden the range of groups in British society who were interested in the slave trade and who, directly or indirectly, profited from its expansion. This increased the penetration of the slave trade in the British economy and in British society. Britain's largest industry, the woolen textile industry, benefited greatly from the development of the slave trade. The share of these textiles in the export of British-made goods to Africa rose from 6.5 percent in 1660 to 64.9 percent in 1693, a year in which European markets were greatly affected by war; and from then until 1728 never dropped below 47.1 percent. Moreover, the percentage of British exports to Africa produced in Britain rose from less than 30 percent in the 1650s and 1660s to about two-thirds between 1713 and 1715. This helped manufacturers to cope with difficulties, including protectionism in their usual European markets, and led to innovations, notably in the production of lighter cloth as the African market was pursued.[8]

Although "white slavery" existed in the British world, notably in the 1650s in Barbados, including for Irish prisoners, slavery, as a condition, was increasingly affected by racial attitudes. This approach served to preserve Englishness at the expense of Africans, who were the key labor supply for plantation agriculture; and, to a far more ambivalent extent, at the expense of Native Americans.[9]

In 1800, after nearly three centuries of the transport of African slaves across the Atlantic, there were major slave economies in the Americas, principally in Brazil, the Caribbean, and the southern part of the United States (formerly British colonies), with the Caribbean and British Guiana (now Guyana) being the British slave societies. Abolitionism, however, became a significant cause in Britain from the mid-1780s, with providentialism playing a key role.[10] Abolitionism led, first, to the ending of the slave trade, notably by Britain in 1807, and then of slavery itself, particularly in the British colonies between 1833 and 1838, in the French colonies in 1848, in the United States in 1865, and in Brazil, the leading slave state, in 1888.

Thanks to Abolitionism, former slave societies changed greatly. Nevertheless, across the world, for most former slaves, there was no sweeping alteration in their lives, and many remained dependent, in some form or other, on either their ex-masters or new masters, and could be treated harshly. In addition, racism remained an issue. Moreover, it was multifaceted, like in Brazil, Cuba, and Venezuela, where, in what have been termed "pigmentocracies," those with a darker skin found themselves discriminated against, a situation that is still very much the case. In part, this attitude is a reflection of white racism.

In the British West Indies, many ex-slaves left to seek unsettled land for their own where they followed subsistence agriculture. This hit the productivity and profitability of the sugar estates. Free labor proved more expensive and less reliable than slaves. As the exports of former plantation economies declined, so they were less able to attract investment, afford imports from Britain and elsewhere, and develop social capital. This hit local society hard. The CARICOM action plan in 2014 called for funding from the former slave-trading nations for education and health in the West Indies to eradicate illiteracy and chronic health conditions, an aspect of a generally less-focused pressure for reparations for slavery.[11] Sir Hilary Beckles, a historian from Barbados who chaired the CARICOM Reparations Commission that produced the action plan, argued:

> This is about the persistent harm and suffering experienced today by the descendants of slavery and genocide that is the primary cause of development failure in the Caribbean.... The African descended population in the Caribbean has the highest incidence in the world of the chronic diseases hypertension and type 2 diabetes, a direct result of the diet, physical and emotional brutality and overall stress associated with slavery, genocide and apartheid.... The British in particular left the black and indigenous communities in a general state of illiteracy and 70 per cent of blacks in British colonies were functionally illiterate in the 1960s when nation states began to appear.[12]

Flows of labor in the globalizing, expanding economy of the nineteenth century included not only coerced workers, but also the continued practice of indentured labor, which, earlier, had been plentifully used in the seventeenth and eighteenth centuries to send white workers to North America. In return for their passage, indentured workers accepted hard terms of employment for a number of years. In the British world, after the end of slavery, the main source was India; and the British West Indies, especially Trinidad, British Guiana, South Africa (notably Natal), East Africa, Fiji, Malaya, and other colonies, received plentiful cheap Indian indentured labor. This was largely part of an Indian Ocean world that was an important section of the British Empire, as well as one that both changed and was varied. Similar systems were also employed elsewhere. In Cuba and Peru, indentured Chinese workers were treated harshly and found that, although "free," they could not buy their way out of their contractual obligations. Chinese workers also moved to Australia and the United States. Critics claimed that indentured labor was another form of the slave trade: there were certainly similarities as well as differences.

The standard defense of the empire makes much of Britain's role in ending first the slave trade and then slavery. This is essentially true, although, seeking to keep pace with Britain, Denmark, in the end, anticipated Britain's move against the slave trade. Moreover, Abolitionism, in practice, drew on international networks of opinion and support.[13] Abolitionist legislation certainly challenged important interests in the empire, both in the colonies and in the metropole, as well as racist attitudes.[14] Slaveholding was a major investment, and there was no sense on the part of slave-owners that Abolitionist pressure would invariably succeed. Indeed, their response to metropolitan pressures was hostile, and there was an often-violent reaction to agitation for change by the black population. The destruction of the newly built mission chapel at Salter's Hill, Jamaica by white militiamen at the beginning of 1832 was a significant attack intended to shock and intimidate black Christian converts and their allies.

It was, however, not the only face of empire. Slavery was abolished while the Salter's Hill mission was reestablished in 1834. In addition, the West Indian colonies did not defy the empire to protect slavery, becoming, as it were, a pre-figurement of the outbreak of the American Civil War in 1861, in the shape of a series of secessionist South Carolinians.[15]

Critics have attacked the British stance over Abolition, emphasizing self-interest, a view that needs to note the strength of the colonial connection in Parliament.[16] Connected to that, the compensation paid to slave-owners attracts sharp criticism,[17] because it appears to endorse the legitimacy of slave ownership as well as offending moral views. Separately, although reforming ideas played the key role in metropolitan support for Abolitionism, there was also the role of black agency, ranging from revolution in Haiti, a French colony but one that appeared to offer a fiery warning to other colonial powers, to the example of the British free-slave colony of Sierra Leone,[18] in challenging racist assumptions.

Self-interest and ideology were related in the subsequent implementation of British policy. As a key instance of the fusion of materialist and idealist drives, trade and Abolitionism were linked, as slave economies (notably the Spanish colony of Cuba) were a threat to the economic viability of the British West Indies once slavery and the slave trade had officially ended in the latter.[19] In pushing Abolitionism, Britain came up against most of the powers of the world, whether other European oceanic empires, notably Spain, newly independent New World states, especially Brazil, or non-Western countries. Moreover, the casualty rates, largely to disease, suffered in British navy operations against slavers, were high, as were the financial costs.[20]

Drawing on the energies of governmental and social opposition to slavery,[21] senior British ministers were committed opponents to slavery and the slave trade. In 1862, Henry, 3rd Viscount Palmerston, then prime minister, responding to a deputation pressing for action to end the "barbarous practices" of King Gelele of Dahomey, who was not interested in ending the trade, replied that he, and the Foreign Secretary and next prime minister, John, 1st Earl Russell, were "quite as desirous of putting the slave trade down as any of them can be." Palmerston's language made clear his grasp of the cruelty involved and his emotional commitment: "Half the evil has been done by the time the slaves are captured in the American waters. The razzia [devastating raid] has been made in Africa, the village has been burnt, the old people and infants have been murdered, the young and the middle aged have been torn from their homes and sent to sea." This was an accurate account of conflict within Africa, which, to a degree that is not welcome to all today, was an origin, as well as means, of slavery and the slave trade. Russell noted three years later: "I hate slavery and the slave trade beyond measure."[22]

In public debate today, the emphasis to be placed on ideology or self-interest as motives for Abolitionism can be linked to political preferences. This is most clearly seen with the often-misleading focus on self-interest in order to argue for hypocrisy on the part of those propounding the moral character of Abolitionism. As a result of such linkages, there is scant reason to anticipate an end to such debate.

Because slavery and the slave trade were closely linked to racism, as well as to economic advantage, it is appropriate to ask what happened to racism after Abolitionism. The cultural values of empire were certainly positioned within a context of racial and religious assumptions, and related hierarchical and often pejorative assumptions, all of which affected attitudes to imperial subjects, albeit without necessarily determining them. A whole host of norms and values were involved, as in attempts to incorporate existing hierarchies, interests and rituals within a patron-client relationship. This was particularly apparent in India, Malaya, and northern Nigeria.[23]

Moreover, the extent to which the empire was a monarchy made it easier to fit other rulers into the system as subordinate. This was true of those who retained independence or a degree of autonomy, for example rulers in southern Africa, the Middle East, India, the Himalayas, Malaysia, and northern Borneo. The emphasis on an Anglicized hierarchy led to a stress on status, not race. Status proved an intermediary and expression of imperial rule and cooperation. Alongside this process, which, in a reference to the idea of orientalism, has been referred to as "ornamentalism,"[24] the British search for support was a multi-layered one. It extended to the co-option or creation of professional and administrative groups able to meet local as well as imperial needs.

Yet, there was also a strongly racist dimension. Thus, in Africa, where slavery continued, as did much British effort to end it,[25] much British investment was linked to the imposition of a white settler and company control that had a clear racial dimension. In Kenya, both the African and the Indian population suffered discrimination, while white settlers greatly extended their control over the land, especially the most readily cultivated life. The continuation in peacetime of the pass system introduced for Africans during World War I was both indicative of attitudes and a cause of hostility. In addition, the treatment of workers in tea production in South Asia was harsh, a subject that has attracted considerable attention.[26]

Racism and slavery are issues in the present day. Often tendentious accounts of past circumstances, however, can be diversions from the present situation, although that is certainly not how they are intended. To take the slave trade, a focus on the situation in the eighteenth century deals with one that is long past. The hard work of confronting large-scale trafficking today,[27] as well as continuing slavery in Africa, notably in Mauritania and Sudan, can be overlooked in favor of the easy target of Western misbehavior in the past.

Slavery, the slave trade, and racism are scarcely alone. It has been repeatedly argued, on behalf of postcolonial states and by Western historians critical of Western imperialism, that ethnic and sectarian divisions and rivalries essentially derived from colonialism, notably from politics of "divide and rule." However, as with slavery, there is much evidence that such divisions and rivalries preceded Western colonialism and were not dependent on it. Moreover, they could be bitter and long-standing, as in India and Africa.[28] Such an assessment provides a basis for a rethinking of slavery, as part of the impact of Western imperialism, but also of much else.[29]

The role of slavery, past and present, in non-Western cultures, notably, but not only, African and Islamic ones, while present in the scholarly literature,[30] is scarcely prominent in discussion outside it. This is misleading. As in between the sixteenth and nineteenth centuries, war and debt have proved prime sources of slaves in recent decades, and continue to do so. Thus, the bitter and frequent warfare in southern Sudan from the 1960s to the 2010s led to the enslavement of captured men and women. This process was encouraged by the role of ethnic hatred in conflicts there and elsewhere, for example, in western Sudan. Across Africa, rebel groups captured women for sex slaves. In 2014, Abubakar Shekau, the head of the extremely violent Nigerian Islamic militant group Boko Haram, announced in a video: "I abducted your girls. I will sell them in the market by Allah. There is a market for selling humans. Allah says I should sell. He commands me to sell. I will sell women. I sell women." The movement also kidnapped men and children for enforced service, including as soldiers. In Iraq, the Islamic State followed both processes, and on a large scale.

These processes are specific to the present and throw much attention on the past. They also underline the questionable nature of the public treatment of the discussion. Instead of "imperial amnesia," there is an obsession with one highly important episode of slavery, to the detriment of other episodes and types, which are also very important, a focus that affects the treatment of both British and American history. "Atlantic slavery," the term for European and European American enslavement practices and slave societies in the Atlantic world, was one of the more prominent instances of a type of enslavement and slavery also seen across much of the world, notably within Africa and throughout the Islamic world. At the same time, Atlantic slavery was largely capitalist in nature, in that most of the slave traders and owners were private individuals or concerns, although there were exceptions, for example slaves in Royal Navy dockyards in the West Indies.

In contrast, "public slavery," slavery under the state, was important from Antiquity on, as in state mines and galleys under Rome, and also slave soldiers, such as in the Mamluk, Ottoman, and Safavid empires. This strand can be seen to the present, with the use of millions as slave labor under Nazi Germany and the Soviet Union, and the extent to which entire societies are enslaved in totalitarian regimes, as with North Korea today.

The willingness of those concerned with slavery to discuss, still more address, public slavery today is generally limited. That is the amnesia. It is an aspect of the preference for the total victory of moral condemnation (which is easiest when directed at the past), rather than trying to produce a more livable future; or, phrased differently, theatrical emotion instead of strategic thinking.

9

THE VIEW FROM BRITAIN

Nostalgia for a world where passports were blue, faces were white and the map was coloured imperial pink" had driven some older voters to Brexit, announced Sir Vince Cable, the Liberal Democrat leader, when speaking on March 11, 2018, at the Party's Spring Conference. He ignored the range of factors involved, including dissatisfaction across the political spectrum with the Cameron government and a wish for national sovereignty, but captured the extent to which imperialism had become a theme and language of abuse that could be employed to criticize at will. The empire also provided a source of misleading reference for at least some Brexiteers. Thus, later that month, Jacob Rees-Mogg, a prominent Conservative parliamentary supporter of Brexit, compared rowing back on Brexit to the Suez Crisis of 1956: "As with the disaster of Suez it would end up being a national humiliation based on lies."[1]

Empire has long been controversial. Criticism of particular aspects or episodes of imperialism can be found from the late eighteenth century. Many from the 1960s, however, treated empire in a consistently hostile fashion, while its political purchase had fallen markedly after the Suez Crisis of 1956. Indeed, this humiliating and very public failure led to a "bolt from Empire" from 1957 as the Macmillan government (1957–63) rapidly abandoned colonies. It did so both directly and by means of creating postimperial federations, such as Malaysia, that, it hoped, could maintain stability or, at least stability on British terms.

In Britain, there was little mainstream criticism of this move to anti-colonialism, and that is the essential background to the subsequent situation including that today. Indeed, the end of empire was relatively painless in Britain, because interest in much of it was limited from the 1950s. As a result, there was no need for anti-imperialism to be a populist cause. Indeed, far from being so, it was more a product of an increasing apathy combined with an active hostility from small groups. This lack of interest was not the case with some traditional constituencies, such as the military and those linked to white settlers in the colonies, notably Africa, but it was true of much of the middle-class support of the Conservative Party. Moreover, this support became more important for the party in the late 1950s. Rising leaders such as Edward Heath, party leader from 1965 to 1975 and prime minister from 1970 to 1974; Iain Macleod, colonial secretary from 1959 to 1961; and Reginald Maudling, his successor from 1961 to 1962; and, like Macleod, a contender for the party leadership in the early 1960s felt little commitment to the empire. In October 1961, Macleod declared his belief "in the brotherhood of man." He was chairman of the party from 1961 to 1963.

When Labour gained power in 1964, it continued the process. In turn, Mrs. Thatcher, Conservative Party leader from 1975 to 1990 and prime minister from 1979 to 1990, fought a war for the sake of the Falklands in 1982, but focused her foreign policy on the Cold War (and thus the Soviet empire), and not on the vestiges of the British Empire. Since then, the dominant theme has been that of apology, and, notably with Tony Blair, Labour prime minister from 1997 to 2007, and David Cameron, Conservative prime minister from 2010 to 2016.

That, however, does not offer any guidance to previous views. These views, indeed, can be seen as located today in an imperial amnesia with the exception of the hostile stereotyping provided by critics, both British and from former colonies. This chapter seeks to provide an historical perspective for the view from Britain. In the space available, there is not the intention of providing a history of the British Empire. Instead, the emphasis is on the attitudes developed and expressed during imperialism. The intention is not to ignore drives for economic, geopolitical, and military benefit, which are more generally true of imperialism and, indeed, of governmental policy as a whole. Instead, the focus is on an ideology that sought to provide benefit to those under imperial sway, and this whether they were living in Britain or elsewhere in the empire. Much of that ideology for Britain, as for other imperial powers, was self-satisfied, misleading, and self-serving, as in the provision of security and stability, but that reflection does not exhaust the topic.

ENGLAND CONQUERED

Imperialism in the British context was initially a matter of being the recipient of imperial conquest and control from Rome (43–410). This was the first power to wield power over all of England (and also Wales), as well as some of Scotland.[2] As such, Rome, bringing a measure of unity, operated in a similar fashion, as Britain was to do later in Australia, Canada, India, and New Zealand, albeit doing so in very different contexts and with very different consequences.

England was later conquered by the Angles, Saxons, and Jutes from the fifth to ninth centuries, and, in large part, by the Vikings in the late ninth century, but, as a unit in the shape of a newly formed kingdom, it was not subsequently conquered until the eleventh century. Then it was, first by Cnut of Denmark (r. 1016–35) and then by William, Duke of Normandy, "William the Conqueror," William I (r. 1066–87). Their rule, notably that of Cnut, rested in part on maintaining existing practices of governance in Church and State.

Moreover, although the rule of Cnut's dynasty ended in 1042, the descendants of William I had significant, indeed larger, possessions in France until 1453. In part thereby, they encouraged, in response, a development of national autonomy and identity within England. Opposition to outside interests, indeed, was important to this process of national formation, from that to the Vikings in the tenth century, via such episodes as opposition first to French intervention and later to foreign favorites during the reign of Henry III (1216–72), to the lengthy Hundred Years' War with France that closed with total English failure in 1453.

The extent to which imperialist interests and consciousness had a separate identity to the views of the ruler and his advisors is open to discussion. Certainly, there was a process of imperialism, as the ruling house of Wessex established the Old English state in the tenth century. This was a matter of a strong, expanding state benefiting from the destruction of rivals, notably of the independence of Mercia (the state in the Midlands), by the Vikings. Again, this was a process similar to that, which was to be seen in the case of British imperialism. At the same time, there was, with the Old English state, an ideology, a compound of Englishness and Christianity in the shape of a Christian kingship ruling fairly over a people from a variety of backgrounds, although also exercising hegemony elsewhere in Britain.

A less attractive ideology, however, underpinned the Norman and Angevin position in England and their expansion into Wales and Ireland. In the case of attempted expansion into Scotland and France, the basis advanced for rule was jurisdictional-hereditary and focused on the sup-posed rights of the Norman, and then the Angevin/Plantagenet, dynasty. England, for these monarchs, was one among a number of inherited rulerships. Military conquest, in contrast, was, from the outset, more to the fore in expansion into Wales and Ireland.

A process of English national development took far deeper political and cultural roots in the long wars with France and Scotland from the 1290s to the 1450s. These wars helped link conflict to an emergent na-tional identity, one that had an institutional formulation in Parliament. Symbols of collective identity were advanced, such as the cult of St. George as a national saint,[3] while the interest of the kings of England in the claim to the throne of France slackened markedly from the 1520s.[4]

REFORMATION AND EXPANSION

In the sixteenth century, alongside the new opportunities and com-petition stemming from the prospect of trans-oceanic trade,[5] a further element was added in the case of the Protestant Reformation, as well as of the intellectual and cultural development of ideas of empire within the British Islands.[6] The Reformation very much saw opposition to outside interests, especially the Papacy which in part was stigmatized as foreign, linked to the development of national identity. In the preamble to the Act in Restraint of Appeals (to Rome) of 1533, an act that proclaimed jurisdic-tional self-sufficiency and rejected appeals to Rome, it was claimed that "by divers sundry old authentic histories and chronicles, it is manifestly declared and expressed that this realm of England is an empire, and so hath been accepted in the world, governed by one supreme head and king, having the dignity and royal estate of the imperial crown of the same." This assertion, on behalf of Henry VIII, looked back to the House of Wessex's claims of overlordship in Britain in the tenth and eleventh centuries, an overlordship that was rooted in control of England but not restricted to it. The English were now depicted as a chosen people with a divine mandate. Protestant England was presented as God's New Israel, a providential state forwarding the right goals, notably the expansion of a godly Christianity. There was also a strong sense of Englishness in the plays of William Shakespeare.

Imperialism was at stake for England, unsuccessfully so in Scotland in mid-century and, eventually, successfully so in Ireland by the 1600s. In each case, imperialism was poised on the cusp of ambition and fear. Anxiety about what Scotland and Ireland, if independent, might mean to England looked to English fears of France and Spain respectively, fears that were more potent due to the strength of Catholicism in each, and notably in Ireland. Again, this was a process that was later to be seen with British imperialism.

In the seventeenth century, the range of English imperialism can be readily gauged by contrasting the trading companies with the settlement colonies, for example the East India Company with Virginia, which was founded as a colony in 1607: less than a decade later. At the same time, there was no uniformity in either category. Thus, the Virginia colony had a very different ethos and governance to those in New England founded from 1620. Moreover, companies such as the East India, Royal African, and Hudson's Bay, controlled territory and forces, in a totally different fashion to the Levant and the Russia companies. Yet, this control was not intended to provide the basis for "plantation" settlement on the Irish model. Nor did the English in India or West Africa produce a settlement pattern comparable to that of the Portuguese in Angola and Mozambique, or the Dutch at Cape Town. Instead, they relied largely on bases without adding any territory.

Despite being a different kingdom, Scotland did not have much separate imperialism. That, however, was not through a lack of effort. Aside from the major plantation of Scots in Northern Ireland, there were attempts to establish colonies, notably in Canada, Central America, and West Africa. None succeeded, the most spectacular failure being that of the late 1690s on the Darien isthmus in Central America.[7] However, Nova Scotia, as a name, remains on the map.

WAR AND IMPERIALISM

Imperialism became more clearly presented as an English, later British, goal in the seventeenth and, even more, eighteenth centuries. In part, this was due to fortuitous political struggles, domestic and international, and to the nature and content of recovered memory in the shape of politicized history. A key point of departure was England's intractable war with Spain (1585–1604) under Elizabeth I (r. 1558–1603). Despite the serious multiple problems involved, and the many failures encountered, this war, particularly the attacks on Spanish colonies and ports and the success over the Spanish Armada in 1588, was subsequently held up as the correct model for English action (and notably so in the 1620s, 1650s, 1720s, and 1730s), and, as such, as a corrective for current policy, which was presented as pusillanimous and/or a failure. Francis Drake was the leading figure among a pantheon of heroes. In his poem "London," published in May 1738, the young Samuel Johnson used Elizabeth's successful stand against Spain as a tool with which to berate Sir Robert Walpole, first minister since 1720, for not fighting Spain:

> In pleasing Dreams the blissful Age renew,
> And call Britannia's Glories back to view;
> Behold her Cross triumphant on the Main,
> The Guard of Commerce, and the Dread of Spain,
> Ere Masquerades debauch'd, Excise oppress'd,
> Or English Honour grew a standing jest.[8]

Elizabeth's war with Spain involved not just conflict on the continent, but also across the oceans, notably in the West Indies. The idea of Spain as a threatening force, politically and ideologically, in Europe and across the globe, was to be transferred in the late seventeenth century onto France. The threat could also be inscribed onto domestic groups and alleged tendencies, notably Catholicism, crypto-Catholicism, and autocracy, although, in practice, many Catholics were loyal supporters of Britain.

Empire as essentially a Protestant project, to protect England/Britain against international Catholicism, and to spread Christianity and thus save souls, ironically was in accord with earlier Portuguese and Spanish interest in the late fifteenth century in exploration and empire. This was the case, for Portugal and Spain, in North Africa, West Africa, the Indian Ocean, and more broadly, as a means in an existential Christian conflict with Islam that was designed finally to lead to the "liberation" of Jerusalem. In short, building on the *Reconquista*, Iberian expansionism had a crusading component. In England, the concept of a Protestant project helped explain interest in a Caribbean "design," notably by Robert, 2nd Earl of Warwick in the 1620s and 1630s and by Oliver Cromwell in the 1650s. The last marked the first English attempt at a large-scale invasion in the New World. It failed on Hispaniola (now divided between Haiti and the Dominican Republic) in 1654, in part due to poor execution, but also as a result of the strength of the Spanish opposition, only to succeed on more lightly defended Jamaica,[9] which then remained a colony until 1962.

At the same time, imperialism drew on mercantilist currents, particularly notions of a zero-sum gain in global wealth, and of overseas commercial expansion and colonial establishment as means to pursue national advantage within this context. These were the views not only of publicists, notably from the late sixteenth century on, but also of influential politicians, such as George, 2nd Earl of Halifax, the president of the Board of Trade from 1748 to 1761,[10] after whom Halifax, Nova Scotia is named. This, again, is an aspect of imperial amnesia: it is normal to present the energy and power of imperialism as directed against non-Western peoples and thus as racist; but that is to mistake means for goals; and to a degree that modern public history seriously underplays, and notably for the period prior to the end of the Napoleonic Wars in 1815. Imperialism then, for England/Britain, was mostly about beating Spain, with which Britain fought a series of wars between 1585 and 1808, and France, with which the wars, stretching back into the Middle Ages, continued until 1815. Rivalry between Britain and France continued urgent until the Fashoda Crisis of 1898 about control in Sudan nearly led to full-scale war with France, which, however, backed down.

Moreover, there were wars with the Dutch, three between 1652 and 1674, and two more between 1780 and 1806. There were also efforts to thwart Russia that included war between 1854 and 1856 (the Crimean War) and apparently imminent war, particularly in 1720, 1723, 1727, 1791, 1801, 1878, and 1885; conflicts with Denmark in the 1800s; and confrontations with Austria and Prussia, notably in 1726–27 and 1730 with the former and 1729 and 1753 with the latter. These conflicts and confrontations were at the forefront of British strategic concern, with strategy understood as ideological and economic as well as political and military.

In the twentieth century, this situation continued with the two world wars, and with "cold" (and "hot" briefly in 1919–20) war with the Soviet Union from 1918 to 1989. Trans-oceanic power politics, conflict, and imperialism were all secondary to these twentieth-century concerns and drives; although that is a point that can be readily neglected in the debate over empire. Indeed, empire then was, in part, instrumental to power-political rivalry with other European powers, and was regarded accordingly, rather than it being central to the drive of British policy.

This is not a question of imperial amnesia, but of a misunderstanding of the purpose of empire and, therefore, of its chronology, context, and success. To argue for the primacy of great-power confrontation, and the related ideology, helps explain domestic attitudes toward empire, notably support for its expansion, and gives a particular character to imperialism. In contrast, the habit of looking for lasting cultural and social archetypes, such as racism, is important to an understanding of imperialism, but is also insufficient. It is overly a matter of the present placing its values on the past, and, as a separate, but related, point of extrapolating from the period of "high imperialism" in the late nineteenth century in order to discuss the entire history of British imperialism.

Instead, it is pertinent to consider the particular geopolitical contexts and the accompanying ideological assumptions. This approach provides a background to British imperialism; not that the approach excuses it in so far as such an interpretation is more than ahistorical. This background was of a fight for survival. This was a fight that, in the case of France, was not assured until late 1813, when Napoleon was decisively defeated (by Austrian, Prussian, Russian, and Swedish forces) at Leipzig, which was the background to the successful Allied invasion of France in 1814, to his enforced abdication that year, and to Britain's ability to take the offensive against the Americans in 1814–15 during the last stage of the War of 1812.

Full assurance followed Napoleon's defeat at Waterloo in 1815, although anxiety revived, and there were serious war panics about France between 1858 and 1862 and 1898. In the case of Germany, survival was likely from December 1941, when Hitler foolishly declared war on the USA at the same time as his forces were getting defeated outside Moscow, but success was not assured until the heavy defeats of German forces by Soviet and Anglo-American armies in the summer of 1944.

This competitive context may not appear to be the best way to approach, say, the slave trade, which, again, contributes to the current range of perception and debate. Nevertheless, this context helps explain the set of assumptions that played a role in the long period of imperial activity. Control was a response to a fear of loss of security, and profitability to one of concern about the economic and financial future. Modern views stress arrogance, domination, and vicious cultural assumptions, rather than the fear, anxiety, and insecurity that should be emphasized as well.

It would be too simple to argue that the situation changed after a measure of stability was secured with the final overthrow of Napoleon in 1815, but that is indeed part of the equation. Imperial expansion could then be pushed forward without as much fear from other powers as earlier. The situation was very different with decolonization and the aftermath of World War II, as concern about the Soviet Union replaced that with Germany. The exhaustion produced by the war was a key element.

Once Britain had defeated its rivals, early examples from English/British history became less valuable as a basis for understanding the current situation of both country and empire. Instead, there was reference back to the example of Classical Rome aplenty in the nineteenth century. The situation was of course more complex, as references to Rome could already be seen in plenty in the eighteenth century. However, the theme of empire under challenge to a degree was moved, from that between 1714 and 1759 of the true religion (Protestantism) and dynasty (Hanoverian) imperiled by Catholicism and Jacobitism, respectively (and in a joined fashion), toward the more secular opportunity offered by comparison with Rome.

Moreover, the Rome in question increasingly became not Republican Rome, but Imperial Rome, which was easier to compare with contemporary Britain. Imperial Rome was appropriate as a pattern maker. This was notably because it, eventually, spread citizenship and, subsequently,

Christianity, throughout its possessions, and defined itself accordingly. Jesus had lived and died under the empire while Imperial Rome was also the ruler of much of Britain. Furthermore, Rome's rule of much of the Hellenistic world, notably Egypt, prefigured Britain's control of its own "exotic East," especially India, but also subsequently Egypt.

Acquired in a struggle with other empires, and in order to help weaken the powers involved, the empire became a definition of Britishness, indeed of the British as being a people of the British Isles and beyond the British Isles; not that most subjects of the empire were regarded as British or saw themselves accordingly. This approach had implications for the conduct of empire, both in terms of expansion and with regard to its treatment of its subjects. Again, this was scarcely unprecedented. So also with Spain in the sixteenth century, as imperial rule in the Americas meant the need to engage there with the obligations of Christian rule.

Whereas, however, Spain had pursued empire also in Europe, notably in Italy, but also in the former Burgundian lands (principally the Low Countries), England/Britain had given up its pursuit of territories in France and did not seek another Continental land empire. There was no attempt, for example, to contest control over Norway (or Iceland) with Denmark, their imperial ruler. Indeed, to that extent, British policy was less European-minded than those of Spain, France, and Austria, and more trans-oceanic. This has been a key feature of British imperialism, albeit with the important additional concern to prevent a European rival from becoming overly powerful there, a goal that has led to interventionist pressures and episodes.[11]

EMPIRE AND PROGRESS

To the British, the progressive Whig agenda from the 1830s had to be offered to imperial subjects, although there were major contrasts: Abolitionism was definitely not the same as self-government for the Canadian and Australian colonies. Moreover, there was no self-government at this stage for the colonies in Africa. The key element was that of change. British politicians saw development as a necessary dynamic and consequence of being the leading power in the world, and development was a process in which empire was to play a role and that the empire was to experience.

There was no sense of empire as a static resource, either politically or in economic terms. Nor was there such a view of imperial subjects. Empire, in short, was not intended as a conservative force, context, goal, or means. It is excessively viewed as such today.

The engagement of Britain with its empire increased in the nineteenth century at the same time as the empire expanded greatly to become the largest in history up to then or, indeed, subsequently. This engagement was very much seen in the presentation of national history. National independence, the Reformation, and a robust international position, were all linked, as in James Froude's *History of England from the Fall of Wolsey to the Defeat of the Spanish Armada* (1856–69). Adventure stories often dealt with the expansion of Britain's imperial presence, as with G. A. Henty's many historical novels for children, for example, *Under Drake's Flag* (1883) and *With Clive in India* (1884).[12] These novels were still plentiful in my local library in the 1960s and I read them, although I am not aware that they molded my views, any more than my visits to the Commonwealth Institute in London.

The meaning of empire, in its Victorian and Edwardian heyday to the British and imperial public(s), is a matter of debate.[13] In particular, it is unclear how they saw the compound of national and imperial identities. Moreover, there is the issue of how this changed during the period. More specifically, there has been considerable debate over the imperial content of such varied, and apparently emblematic, works and events as the music of Sir Edward Elgar, notably *Pomp and Circumstance March No 1*, accompanying, for example, *Land of Hope and Glory*, and the popular celebrations for the relief of Mafeking from Boer siege in 1900. Empire was staged, but no less potent for that. Jack Hunt, a private in the Scots Guards, described the entry into Pretoria, the capital of Transvaal, in 1900, during the Boer War: "When we marched into the market square headed by Lord Roberts to raise the flag they took our photo by the cinematograph so I expect you will see it on some of the music halls in London."[14]

These and other episodes can be seen as patriotic, chauvinistic and national, rather than imperial. Alternatively, it can be argued that such a distinction is of limited value, not least because the empire was regarded as both product and part of the far-flung British nation and imperialism was inherently patriotic and chauvinistic. These points are also pertinent for the "Khaki election" held in 1900 during the Boer War, an election in which the Conservatives, who supported the war, won heavily over the divided Liberals, many of whom criticized it. At the same time, the Conservatives benefited both from military success in 1900 and from the return of prosperity.[15]

In practical terms, the situation was similar to that today. There was no uniform attitude but rather a range of engagements with empire, each of which reflected different contextual and contingent factors.[16] Moreover, the same individual could respond in a very varied fashion, for example depending on whether the local celebration of imperial effort, such as the doings of local regiments, was at stake, or a broader national engagement. Each could also differ crucially. Support for a broader national engagement in the shape of Protestant missionary activity was not necessarily the same as backing conquest or gaining economic markets.

There was also the "banal imperialism," the imperial influences on people's everyday lives of which they might not be conscious or aware, but which were still very much there framing public attitudes. These influences included not only goods but also the culture offered by advertisements, songs and newspapers, a culture that spanned the colonies. Again, however, responses varied.[17]

"Wider still and wider," the British nation was not regarded as limited to one state or country. The values that accrued to empire offered therefore an extensive fluidity that encompassed Britons abroad; although, in a racist sense, these values could also serve to exclude immigrants. Indeed, the late nineteenth and early twentieth centuries saw anti-immigrant panics directed, in particular, at Jews and Chinese. These panics affected imaginative literature, as, from 1912, in the Fu Manchu stories of Arthur Sarsfield Ward (1883–1959). Writing under the pseudonym "Sax Rohmer," Ward's adventure stories portrayed the "Yellow Peril" based in China but hitting hard in Britain. In the first, Britain's Burmese expert is murdered in London. Fu Manchu was based in London's dockyards, the entry to empire. Thus, imperialism was contested in Limehouse and the East End: contested both in terms of its meanings and with reference to the consequences. In *The Quest of the Sacred Slipper* (1919), Ward brought Islamic terror to Britain. He went on writing Fu Manchu stories until his death.[18] In Australia, the equivalent was concern about Japan,[19] alongside strong opposition to

Chinese immigration, opposition also seen in Canada and leading to an apology by the prime minister in 2007.

In Britain, there were many voluntarist bodies pledged to imperial and national assertion, while the pressure for tariff reform (protectionism) was linked to support for an "Imperial Preference" in trade that was designed to contribute to imperial federation. If such bodies and political concern were dominated by the middle class, that was more generally true of the voluntarist sector, for example sports organizations.[20] A long-established aspect of criticism of empire is to present it in class terms, and to castigate both accordingly. That approach underplays the degree of popular participation in the empire and of popular support for it, while also explaining the significance of these issues. There is a related debate about nationalism, one that is also both historical and political. Notions of false consciousness are deployed in order to discuss a degree of popularity that is unacceptable to some commentators.

Attitudes to empire, both in Britain and in its colonies, were closely related to domestic politics and related visions of the future for Britain and the wider world.[21] A key link was supplied by Ireland, a central issue that was at once British and imperial. Ireland's future status contributed strongly to crises in politics and national identity in Britain in the late nineteenth and early twentieth centuries. The Liberal Unionists, such as Joseph Chamberlain, who had abandoned the Liberals in order to join the Conservatives in opposition to Irish Home Rule, tended to press hard for measures to strengthen the empire. They and the Conservatives felt that what they saw as a Liberal threat to the empire was a matter of Liberal views on domestic politics (including the position of the established churches), Ireland, and colonial policy (including immigration). Liberals were less keen than the Conservatives on fresh acquisitions for the empire.

The backing by the Liberal Unionists and Conservatives for the social welfare particularly associated with the Liberals rested largely on a desire to strengthen the British people, in both country and empire, rather than on individual amelioration. To paternalists, there was a threat of national degeneration, which they blamed on the alleged consequences of the country's increasingly urban and industrial nature. A weaker and less virile people appeared unwilling to bear the burdens of empire. Conversely, an understanding of the call of empire would hopefully produce this virility. There were similar tensions and differences in the Dominions, notably over immigration. In Australia, the Australian Natives' Association supported trade protection and immigration restriction in the 1900s. In Canada, there was pressure to restrict immigration from Asia.

WORLD WAR I

World War I (1914–18) proved exhausting for the British economy, and eventually undermined empire in Ireland by bringing to the fore what had previously been a marginal independence movement. Elsewhere in the empire, anti-British sentiment was modest in scale during the war, and certainly so compared to the severity of the challenge. In particular, the German hope from the outset of exploiting pan-Islamism, in order to cripple the empire by supporting revolution in Egypt and India, failed. The policy was compromised by Germany's alliance with the unpopular Ottoman (Turkish) empire. At the same time, the British position in Egypt ultimately depended on repelling the Turkish attack on the Suez Canal in 1915. This was done in a campaign that included the crucial use of imperial contingents, notably Australians and Indians.

In contrast to assumptions about its collapse, the empire successfully fought together, dealing with the threats posed, severally and collectively, by Germany, its colonies, and its allies, notably the Ottoman Empire. Moreover, the collective effort led to a strengthening of empire, although the terms of service could be harsh, as with the Cypriot Mule Corps[22] and the high death rates among native bearers during campaigning against German colonies in Africa. An Imperial War Cabinet, including representatives of the Dominions, met from 1917 and provided a welcome public sign of cohesion in decision-making that countered the emphasis on distinctive interests.

The war also saw a measure of the economic union that had interested Joseph Chamberlain in the 1900s. Schemes for an Imperial Customs Union were considered, while Britain's role as a market for imperial goods was fostered by military needs and political preference. The impact of the war on European food imports to Britain ensured that the British market increased for imperial exporters such as South Africa.

THE 1920S AND 1930S

With territory transferred from other empires, the war led to a major territorial expansion of the British Empire. However, its high tide was to ebb fast postwar, due to the recent wartime weakening, the new accumulation of burdens, the strain of multiple commitments, the stress of events, and the extent to which there was more opposition in the colonies to imperial rule than there had been prior to the war, notably in India (and, in a non-colony, Ireland). As a consequence of these problems, empire required, and was felt to require, new solutions that were part of the process by which empire was always a work in being, and particularly one that responded to challenges and crises. Thus, in the 1780s, there was a reconceptualization of empire and imperial governance after the successful rebellion of the American colonies.

These solutions indeed were offered, from the establishment of the Irish Free State, a self-governing Dominion within the empire, under the Anglo-Irish Treaty of 1921, to the Montagu-Chelmsford Reforms in India in 1919 which established the principle of diarchy (responsible self-government); from the development of new patterns and practice of colonial administration, including the use of surveillance,[23] to the employment of "air policing" by the Royal Air Force, notably in the Middle East. Harsh to those who suffered air attack, which could be highly indiscriminate as well as deadly, the use of the RAF provided Britain with a more rapid and less expensive response to opposition than the use of troops, and was employed accordingly, first against Afghanistan in 1919 and in British Somaliland in 1920, and then more generally. Aircraft provided a sense of British power even if its direct impact was generally limited, especially once its putative victims had learned to take avoiding action or to fire back.[24]

"Indirect rule," long a pattern of British policy in some areas, increasingly became the goal and means in imperial policy. However, there was hostility, notably within the Conservative Party, to compromises and the erosion of imperial power. This was particularly seen with the opposition by those described by Frederick, 1st Earl of Birkenhead, the lord chancellor, as "the medievalists among us," to the Anglo-Irish Treaty of 1921 as well as to Dominion status for India.[25] There was also criticism, in the mid-1920s, of the value to maintain treaty rights in the face of nationalist opposition in China.

Meanwhile, the empire was fostered in British consciousness. The Irish transformation toward a far looser link was not matched in Scotland or Wales. This fostering had clear symbolic form. Annually, on Empire Day, May 24, schools staged pageants and displays, souvenirs were issued, and large parades were held in Hyde Park. The British Empire Exhibition between 1924 and 1925, for which Wembley Stadium was built in 1923, was a major public occasion, celebrated in the press and the newsreels, and commemorated by a set of stamps. Prince George's disappointing performance opening the exhibition was fictionally presented in the film *The King's Speech* (2010), a film that closed with a powerful affirmation of empire in 1939 with George VI, as he became, broadcasting by radio to the worldwide empire about the coming of war. In 1925, there was a congregation of 90,000 for an Empire Day thanksgiving service held at Wembley Stadium as part of the British Empire Exhibition.[26]

In the 1930s, regular sea and now air (but not, after a spectacular accident, airship) services operated by Imperial Airways helped develop the integration of British and colonial elites.[27] This integration sustained mutual interest and ensured the neo-Britishness that was characteristic of settler life and that contributed greatly to a sense of empire, and not only at the level of the comfortably off. Sports teams and touring theatrical companies, as well as officials and businessmen, used these services. There was also a network of liner services, notably to South Africa and Australia.

Family and friendship links across the empire could be readily maintained, as could associational movements, such as the Freemasons or the Boy Scout Movement, the latter very much a product of the ideal of imperial manliness. Founded in 1907 by Robert Baden-Powell, a hero of the Boer War, the movement was intended to prepare young men for the active life required if the empire was to remain a vital force. As such, empire was seen as a counter to the supposedly weakening consequences of urban life, which was associated, variously, with degeneration, effeminacy, and socialism. It also had to confront the growing appeal of American power and culture.[28]

Such views serve as a reminder of the extent to which the empire played a central part in debates about the future of the British, with accounts of the future bound up in notions of imperial identity. This was most apparent on the Right, although, in a reflection of the diffuse character of political tendencies and the varied nature of imperialism, there was no one view of empire there. In contrast, on the Left, there was a move leftward, away from the predominantly liberal or evangelical concepts of progress seen in the nineteenth century and, instead, toward more socialist views. These were often inherently opposed to imperial control or, at least, indifferent to it and notably so over India. Nevertheless, liberal and evangelical concepts of progress continued to be influential.

The economic dimension of empire remained both important and a significant aspect of the public debate. Taking forward the pre-war campaign of Joseph Chamberlain, Imperial Preference was an attempt to overcome tensions over economic benefits and to strengthen the empire. A cause championed from 1929 by Max, 1st Lord Beaverbrook, the owner of the *Daily Express*, the largest circulation newspaper, in his "Crusade" for Empire Free Trade, Imperial Preference was eventually established in agreements reached at the Imperial Economic Conference held at Ottawa in 1932. Yet, British exporters benefited less than Dominion producers because, while the Dominions raised tariffs on British imports, they were unwilling to cut tariffs on British imports, as they feared the impact on Dominion producers. Indeed, the Ottawa agreement contrasted with the bold views of the Conservative politician Leo Amery, Colonial Secretary from 1924 to 1929, who pressed for a common economic policy and currency. Amery had established the Empire Marketing Board in 1926 in order to promote the "Buy Empire" cause, and also to support scientific research that would help Imperial producers. Amery was its first chairman.[29] He was an example of the extent to which the empire was regarded not as redundant, but as offering new options and opportunities.

The Ottawa agreement was part of a new footing in Anglo-Dominion relations, one seen in compromises, for example, over assisted migration and empire settlement, in which the British government had to give way.[30] Nevertheless, in light of rising protectionism elsewhere during the Depression, the agreement was promising. Thanks to Imperial Preference, the empire took 49 percent of British exports between 1935 and 1939 compared with 42 percent a decade earlier. British policymakers, instead of thinking, as in the Victorian era, primarily in terms of the global economy theoretically made possible by free trade, were increasingly discussing the future in terms of an economic bloc (led by Britain with major contributions from the Dominions) that operated as a sterling area and that played a central role in strategic planning. The empire was presented as a leading world power that possessed coherence and had distinct political interests.[31]

As part of a conviction in the importance of empire, there was a general sense among policymakers in the 1930s, both British and Dominion, that empire had to change. This sense reflected political expedience, but also the application of new ideas in the shape of searching for viable policies. Reform of the Indian government was, alongside Imperial Trade Preference and more equal relations with the Dominions, presented as the best means to strengthen the empire. Looking back to the changes in goals, policies and governance that were apparent from the outset, empire was not to be seen as static, as critics frequently dismissed it. This approach looked forward to the ideas of British modernity being linked to the democratization of empire that played a role in the preparation for the 1951 Festival of Britain, an occasion, however, that, in the event, had little to say about the empire and the Commonwealth.[32]

As with Prayer Book reform in the 1920s, the parliamentary time devoted to the Indian government in 1935 underlines what seemed important and controversial to contemporaries. Ignoring their values can ensure a failure to understand what was at stake. British policy was in a state of flux toward empire in the 1930s: that toward India representing a stage between the traditional co-option of local support and democratization. The attitudes of the constituent parts of the empire, and between them, were also in a state of flux. There were important changes in both policy and symbolism. In the case of Ceylon (Sri Lanka), the throne and regalia of the last independent kingdom, that of Kandy, were captured by the British when it was conquered in 1815 and taken to Windsor to be presented to George III. In 1934, they were returned as part of the British attempt to ease relations with the population in the colony, a process that led to constitutional reforms, including universal suffrage in 1931. Although the context was different, British policymakers would have agreed with the observation of George Orwell that "When the white man turns tyrant, it is his own freedom that he destroys." Orwell served in the Burma Police Service from 1922 to 1927, an instance of the degree to which imperial service attracted many of the best and the brightest.[33]

Britain itself was changing. Both political culture and ideological drive, or rather cultures and drives, were altering before the inroads of World War II were to cause a crisis of imperial survival. The Americanization of culture was already significant in the 1930s. Nevertheless, these changes were not leading away from a commitment to empire.

WORLD WAR II

Empire was linked, in the *Guardian* of February 13, 2014, to a bellicosity that was allegedly bad for British society. However, it was this bellicosity, as well as the empire, that enabled Britain, having been totally defeated on the European mainland, to fight on in 1940, resisting both Germany and Italy. Canadian forces proved to be a key strategic reserve against German invasion in 1940 and were also deployed to garrison Iceland after the Germans conquered its imperial ruler, Denmark. Iceland thus became an informal part of the British Empire. Australian, New Zealand, Indian, and South African forces played key roles in conquering most of Italy's African empire between 1940 and 1941. Japan became an additional opponent in December 1941, one that overwhelmed British imperial interests in the Far East and Southeast Asia, and challenged those in Australasia and South Asia. At the same time, imperial forces played key roles in containing Japanese expansionism after its initial bout of conquest.

Churchill had a very strong historical sense of empire (and much else), and liked to position himself accordingly. In October 1940, when a vulnerable Britain faced a damaging German bombing offensive in the Blitz, he wrote the foreword to an edition of *The War Speeches of William Pitt the Younger*, prime minister from 1783 to 1801 and from 1804 to 1806. Churchill saw this struggle with Revolutionary and Napoleonic France as an example to Britain in 1940, pressing the case for "our determination to fight on, as Pitt and his successors fought on, till we in our turn achieve our Waterloo."[34] The comparison, however, was less than perfect: there was no air assault on British civilians in the earlier wars.

Participation in World War II greatly altered relations within the empire, in Britain, the Dominions, and the colonies. The likely long-term consequences were unclear, but empire served politicians, in Britain and elsewhere, as an opportunity to hope and plan for the postwar world in accordance with their basic assumptions. Thus, despite tensions with Indian nationalists, Labour politicians assumed a progressive and democratic outcome for India,[35] while Conservative counterparts were less willing to think through the implications of major change. This was especially so of Churchill, who had bitterly opposed the Government of India Act in 1935 and who, in 1942, stated, "I have not become the King's First Minister in order to preside over the liquidation of the British empire."[36]

1945–64

After the war, although the imperial state was heavily indebted and colonial governance often fragile, empire was still seen in Britain as a vital economic sphere and resource. Indeed this was particularly the case due to the major problems caused by the war. Oil from the Middle East was increasingly valuable to the British economy, the discriminatory tariffs of imperial preference were crucial to trade, and imperial financial links helped maintain sterling. Ernest Bevin, the influential foreign secretary in the Labour governments from 1945 until 1951, was determined to preserve military strength in the Middle East, and hoped to use imperial resources to make Britain a less unequal partner in the alliance with America. Independence for what became India, Pakistan, Burma, Ceylon, and Israel, was not matched with other colonies, although British interests in China were abandoned (with the exception of Hong Kong). Moreover, ideas of imperial expansion, notably in Libya, were shelved.

Hopes of renewal in, and through, empire and a series of "great projects,"[37] combined with a sense of imperial and national separateness, encouraged the belief that Britain did not need to join schemes for economic cooperation in Western Europe, schemes that eventually led to the creation of the European Economic Community (EEC), which later became the European Union (EU). The French, who also showed a firm commitment to empire, proved better than Britain at combining their imperial position with advancing their European interests, especially in the EEC. In part, this contrast reflected political circumstances and skill, notably France's determination to anchor West Germany in a cooperative system, but different political cultures were also significant.

The Labour Cabinet divided over employing force against Iran in the oil nationalization crisis of 1951. The result was heavily affected by American opposition to British intervention,[38] as well as the lack of the military support offered to Britain by the Indian Army in earlier crises in the region, notably in 1919 and 1941. Nevertheless, in government (1945–51), Labour was committed to a continued imperial presence.

Like its Labour predecessors, the Conservative governments that followed from 1951 saw independence for India in 1947 as prefiguring not the end of empire, but, rather, an international presence and identity based on its continuation, albeit more in the shape of informal control than hitherto. In the 1950s, British troops were to be used to fight for empire in Malaya, Kenya, Suez, and Cyprus. There was a major commitment, through NATO (of which Britain was a founding member in 1949), to the defense of Western Europe. This commitment led to the continued presence of substantial British forces in West Germany after the end of postwar occupation. Nevertheless, much of the British defense effort in the 1950s was dominated by concern about imperial security, and continued to focus on the Mediterranean and the wider Indian Ocean. This remained the case until the mid-1960s.

As in the nineteenth century, there was a strong ethical dimension to the furtherance of empire. Support for Indian independence played an important role in Labour Party circles. There was also a conviction, which drew on aspects of the Liberal tradition (not least the nonconformist belief that there was a duty of care to protect the less fortunate), that imperial rule could serve the interests of the colonial peoples. Most, however, were regarded as less developed and ready for independence than the Indians. There was an assumption that imperial rule was a preparation for independence, but also that the African colonies would not be ready for independence for a long time. Independence was defined in terms of Westminster parliamentary democracy and considered in gradualist terms that included a fair amount of condescension, if not racism.

The apparent logic of transition, notably to the Commonwealth, helped ease the process of imperial retreat, although the latter was criticized by some influential right-wing Conservatives, particularly Robert, 5th Marquess of Salisbury, Lord President of the Council from 1952 to 1957, who had served as secretary of state for Dominion Affairs (1940–42 and 1943–45), secretary of state for the Colonies (1942), and secretary of state for Commonwealth Relations (1952), as well as president of the English-Speaking Union. Salisbury resigned in 1957 because of his opposition to the government's policy of decolonization and he subsequently became controversial for his support for South Africa. Indeed, in 1970, students at the University of Liverpool occupied Senate House to demand his removal as chancellor over his support for apartheid.

Salisbury, was also president of the Monday Club from 1962, soon after its foundation, to his death in 1972. The club was opposed to decolonization and immigration, but neither of these opposing stances proved important as policy goals for Conservative governments, let alone decisive. Like Salisbury in the 1950s, the Monday Club played a role in Conservative politics in the 1960s, but it did not determine their direction.

There was opposition within the Conservative government to the 1954 agreement ending British occupation of the Suez Canal zone, although Anthony Eden, the foreign secretary, argued that the agreement would ease relations on Egypt (an error) and lessen the strain on Britain's military situation, a significant goal. In 1956, in response to the pan-Arab nationalism of Egypt's dictator, Colonel Nasser, and in a last major flourish of imperial power, Britain, in the Suez Crisis, unsuccessfully sought to intimidate Egypt, only to fail totally. This led to a rethinking of the pace of imperial retreat, which was markedly speeded up. There was subsequent opposition to imperial retreat, for example to concessions over Cyprus.[39] Nevertheless, despite domestic criticisms of Harold Macmillan, prime minister from 1957 to 1963, notably over the fate of the settler colonies in Africa, those with a powerful minority of British settlers, especially Kenya, he still won a landslide in the general election in October 1959.

More generally, there was a breakdown in the ability to ensure the incorporation of native elites and peoples within the empire, and a lack of support at home for continued imperial effort. Loss of political will, and the related unwillingness to pay the requisite political and military costs of empire in the context of a difficult fiscal situation in the colonies and Britain,[40] were different from the inability to maintain control; but all played a role. Keeping going no longer seemed the best choice, or even an option; and the hope that something would turn up was, by the late 1950s, increasingly focused on granting independence to colonies. Muddling through now involved a bolt from empire, prefiguring that, very differently, seen with the United States and IndoChina in the 1970s.

Decolonization in the late 1950s and early 1960s did not prove as divisive for the Conservatives as relations with Europe did from the late 1980s. In part, this was because, despite what can be regarded as the anomaly of the Falklands War in 1982, decolonization was presented (however complacently and even misleadingly) as a benevolent process[41] and the empire was seen as being transformed into the Commonwealth, rather than lost. Indeed, Empire Day was renamed Commonwealth Day in 1958. Thus, the logic of Britain's imperial mission, allegedly bringing civilization to backward areas of the globe, allowed the presentation of independence as the inevitable terminus of empire. As with previous shifts in imperial thinking, this argument was far more than simply a case of presentation, as the government, in practice, reshaped its imperial mission to respond to the condition, needs, and opportunities of the postwar world.

Opposition views were also significant. Hugh Gaitskell, the Labour leader from 1955 to 1963, who had opposed military action at Suez in 1956, declared in 1962 his opposition to Britain joining the EEC. Gaitskell added that he would not sell "the Commonwealth down the river" and, with reference to World War I, that "We, at least, do not intend to forget Vimy Ridge and Gallipoli," battles in which Dominion forces (respectively Canadian, and Australian and New Zealand) had played a major role. There were memories that had had meaning for Clement Attlee, Labour prime minister from 1945 to 1951, and Bevin, and drew on ideas of a shared kinship that also had meaning on the Right.[42] Gaitskell was the son of a member of the Indian Civil Service, while his mother's father was consul-general in Shanghai, and he spent his childhood in Burma. He was also much affected by the unanimous hostility to British entry expressed at a meeting of Commonwealth socialist leaders he called in late 1962. Yet, under Macmillan, the view developed that the Commonwealth would not in practice be able to meet or, indeed, contribute greatly to, Britain's economic, political or security needs, a view that was to be fully justified by subsequent events.

Other factors were also important. The more powerful impact of American culture from the 1950s lessened a sense of British distinctiveness, exceptionalism and pride; and this impact had serious implications.

Americanism and globalization compromised native styles, and thus imperial models, whether in food or in diction, with all that that meant for national distinctiveness and continuity. The decline in the position, popularity and relevance of the Established Churches, as well as of the strands of anti-Catholicism and Protestant exceptionalism that had been significant to national identity and imperial purpose, also affected links and identities that had been important to empire. The shifting values were also seen with the decline in the idea of a distinct religious mission and Protestant character for Britain. National days of prayer ended in the 1950s as part of a more general decline in religious observance.[43] Furthermore, just as evangelicalism had helped to encourage opposition to slavery, so Protestant ecumenicalism contributed both to support for decolonization and to interest in European integration.[44]

Notably among the young across the political spectrum, and increasingly so,[45] commitment to empire was perceived as the antithesis of what is meant to be "modern," as an obstacle to economic reform, an emblem of outdated social values, and as a view out of kilter with democratic political values. Interest in becoming a member of the EEC, which Macmillan finally applied to join in 1961 (only to be vetoed by France), accentuated these assumptions. With the end of patterns of imperial trade and careers, "abroad" became more focused on the USA and Europe, although there is an important exception in the case of migrants and their descendants. In the 1960s and 1970s, moreover, both Conservative and Labour attempts at modernization, notably through state planning, failed, which meant that Britain had fewer resources to spare to protect, let alone develop, the imperial fragments that remained. Very differently, the rise in "New" Commonwealth immigration, from the arrival of West Indians on the *Empire Windrush* in 1948, meant empire "coming home" in ways in which certain politicians (and some of their constituents) found distinctly troubling. The British Nationality Act of 1948 gave citizenship of the UK and Colonies to all people living in either, and the right of entry and settlement in the UK. This situation led to major divisions over immigration, divisions in which war-charged memories of empire played a role, but a decreasing one.[46] Subsequently, the grant of British citizenship was restricted for those from colonies (e.g., Hong Kong) and former colonies.

England People Very Nice, a thoughtful play by Richard Bean, began a run at the National Theatre in 2009, albeit drawing protestors claiming that its account of immigration was critical of Bangladeshis. Set in Bethnal Green, the play deals with the waves of immigration to this cockpit of the East End of London. At one level, the play is about assimilation, with immigrants becoming Cockneys (working-class Londoners), so that the barmaid ends up as a woman of Irish-French extraction married to a Jew and with grandchildren who are half Bangladeshi. Yet, there are darker currents. There is the backdrop of a xenophobic mob angry at the Huguenots (French Protestants) for taking jobs, the Irish for being Catholics, and the Jews for producing Jack the Ripper (for which there is no evidence), and also accusing the Bangladeshis of being "curried monkeys." The British National Party is an ugly element in the story. Even darker are the young Bangladeshis who hate everyone else as infidels and admire Osama bin Laden. The prospect of the Thames running "with blood" is frequently mentioned in the play. The ability of England to cope with its diversity is left unclear, but room for optimism is limited.

THE 1960S TO THE PRESENT

Intellectual and cultural changes were also significant. *The Whig Interpretation of History*, a long-standing progressive account strongly linked to a Protestant character and mission for Britain and the empire, lost support. This was an aspect of the withdrawal of the intellectual elite from the needs and concerns of much of the population,[47] a withdrawal that led to overt hostility to empire and to imperial history. Cultural change was rapidly apparent. The heroic historical imagination at play in such notable films as *The Charge of the Light Brigade* (1936) and, in a more qualified fashion, *Zulu* (1964) was replaced by darker and more critical accounts.

Under Harold Wilson, the Labour leader from 1963 to 1976 and prime minister from 1964 to 1970 and 1974 to 1976, there was initially an attempt to maintain Britain's former imperial links, notably in the Indian Ocean regime. However, economic failure and financial crisis led to the devaluation of sterling in November 1967 (the month in which the British abandoned their unsuccessful presence in Aden),[48] and to the announcement in January 1968, that Britain's remaining military presence "East of Suez" was being discarded. Already, the building of new through-deck aircraft carriers had been abandoned. This plan, eventually for three air-craft carriers, had ended up (at least initially) as the projected CVA-01, announced in Parliament in 1963, and the Type 82 escort destroyers, but it was abandoned in the 1966 Defence White Paper.

The Conservative opposition under Edward Heath criticized the de-cision to withdraw from East of Suez, but, in office under Heath from 1970 to 1974, found it impossible to reverse the policy of withdrawal and, instead, implemented it. The Americans took over the British military presence, with an aircraft carrier entering the Gulf in 1974. Able to cut expenditure on empire, more attention and money was available for social policy in Britain.[49]

Under Margaret Thatcher, Conservative prime minister from 1979 to 1990, there was a self-conscious return to earlier values and interests. However, there was no revival of imperial concerns and scant interest in the Commonwealth. This was notably so over tighter sanctions against apartheid South Africa, especially, but not only, in 1987.[50] The Cold War dominated her view of the world,[51] and the Falklands War of 1982 did not lead to a change of policy. This conflict had marked historical roots, both in that it related to a long-standing British territorial position in the South Atlantic, and because the government's decision to fight in order to expel the Argentinean invaders was criticized by some as anachronistic. A correspondent in the *Times* enquired whether an editorial supporting military action had been misdated by a century. Thatcher mentioned in-ternational law, but said that the British action was to free British citizens and to rescue British territory. In 2004, Nestor Kirchner, the populist president of Argentina, termed the British effort "a blatant exercise in nineteenth-century imperialism."

Until 1947, Britishness was, for many, quintessentially imperial and, as a result, empire meant an international Britishness, and not an island one. Conversely, the "loss" of empire in South Asia in 1947–48 saw, despite hopes, plans and policies to the contrary, the beginning of a different state, a "Great Britain" that came into being to run a global colonial and trading system that rapidly disintegrated, or, at least, to direct a Com-monwealth of Nations that largely failed.

In the event, the Commonwealth did not meet British hopes that it would serve as a continuation of imperial cohesion. The creation of an equal partnership proved a goal that was incompatible with British leadership. There was skepticism about British intentions and moral authority, notably over apartheid in South Africa and Southern Rhodesia.[52] Moreover, the British were unable or unwilling to provide large amounts of economic aid and financial support for Commonwealth countries. In some respects, there is a comparison with criticism, fair and unfair, of the German use of the "European" concept, in the shape of what critics present as the German dominance of the European "project."

Separately, the dimming of empire encouraged an emphasis on Europe or, as with Churchill, on "the English-Speaking Peoples" of which he published a four-volume history in 1956–58. This was a basis for later ideas of the Anglosphere—the Dominions plus the United States, ideas that became increasingly influential from the 1980s and, even more, 2000s.[53]

In turn, the "Great Britain" morphed into a fretful "Little British-ness" that was associated, in particular by her critics, with Thatcher, and that her successors found it difficult to maintain. The decline in global power affected the Union with Scotland and the extent there (and elsewhere) of working-class Conservatism. Having ceased to be possible to be Canadian and British or New Zealander and British, it became harder for many to be Scottish and British, although, in 2014, a referendum in Scotland rejected independence, and, despite continuing commitment by the Scottish National Party, subsequent support for it has not reached a majority.

A different ethos, in Britain and elsewhere in the world, and declining relative power, were the key elements in the retreat from empire, while the practice of multilateralism in an America-directed international order was a crucial means. The past was rejected. In 1988, the tercentenary of the Glorious Revolution proved a damp squib, rather like other national and imperial anniversaries, for example the 250th anniversary of the capture of Quebec from France in 1759. Indeed, the past appeared forgotten, or, as with the bicentenary of Trafalgar in 2005, embarrassing; and this at both the British and the English levels, although not at those of Ireland and Scotland.

In 1997, Peter Mandelson, the ideologue for New Labour, declared "We are defining ourselves by the future." Novelists, others, and much of the public, were not so sure. In Ian McEwan's novel *Solar* (2010), the protagonist is stuck on an aircraft circling while waiting to land at Heathrow, an image of dystopia:

> Whichever direction his gaze fell, this was home, his native corner of the planet. The fields and hedgerows, once tended by medieval peasants or eighteenth-century labourers, still visibly patterned the land...teeming like a charnel house with ghosts. One day this brash and ancient kingdom might yield to the force of multiple cravings.[54]

Bathos intervened for the protagonist en route from Heathrow by train into London. He finds a Union Jack presented on a packet of salt and vinegar crisps: "an artful laboratory simulation of the corner fish and chip shop, an enactment of fond memories and desire and nationhood. That flag was a considered choice."[55]

The closing of the Commonwealth Institute in London was more widely symptomatic. Originally the Imperial Institute, established by royal charter in 1888, its name was changed to the Commonwealth Institute in 1958, but following its sale in 2007, it became, in 2016, the home of the Design Museum. After a very brief and unsuccessful history, the British Empire and Commonwealth Museum in Bristol closed in 2009. Some of the literature of empire remained popular, for example that of the novelist John Buchan,[56] but its political resonance had gone.

Amid the muddle, there was talk of European identity, internationalism, and a special relationship with the United States. The reality was a loss of independence and a lack of autonomy. Empire, as a series of possessions, as a community and continuity, and as a potent and multi-faceted expression of power, identity and independence, was no more.

IO

CONCLUSIONS

Gestures serve so often as politics and lead to controversy. In early 2018, Justin Trudeau, the somewhat-gushing Canadian prime minister, got it wrong when he made a governmental visit to India. In particular, Jaspal Atwal was invited to an event hosted by the Canadian government in Mumbai. Atwal, a Sikh separatist with Canadian citizenship, had been convicted in 1986 of being part of a gang that opened fire in Vancouver on Makiat Singh Sidhu, a visiting Indian cabinet minister who, in the event, was assassinated in the end in India in 1991. The attack in Vancouver was part of a campaign to draw attention to the long-standing campaign for Khalistan, an independent Sikh state. The Mumbai function caused outrage in India, with Trudeau being denounced for being soft on terrorism. He also refused on his visit to make a statement backing Indian unity.

As a consequence, there were claims that he was playing to the influential Sikh community in India. The Indian prime minister, Narendra Modi, also mindful of his domestic audience, some of whom had long condemned Canadian support for Khalistan, snubbed Trudeau. Few outside India cared to recall the troubled history of the Sikhs in India in the 1980s.

Judging Britain or, indeed, the United States, as an imperial power harshly frequently involves a lack of comparative rigor, or rather a marked

preference for judging across time, rather than in the context of the mores and powers of the period, for example the Cold War. Such judgment
is linked to blame for past (British) behavior. This blame is frequently
advanced in a context of excuse for postcolonial conduct on the part of
former colonies and a denial, accordingly, of moral agency by them.

In practice, as a ruler of Caribbean colonies, Britain was less harsh
than Spain in Cuba. As a ruler of settlement colonies, Britain, in Canada
and New Zealand, was less harsh than the USA; although the situation
in Australia was less favorable for the indigenous population than that
in Canada. In terms of territorial expansion, the British Empire behaved
in the late nineteenth century not only like other Western empires, but
also like non-Western states such as Thailand, Ethiopia, Afghanistan,
and China.

Yet, there were also important differences in the goals and means of
its imperialism. On April 29, 1904, Churchill, breaking with the Conservatives and declaring his candidacy as a "Free Trade" supporter backed
by the Liberals, asked the voters of Manchester North-west:

> Whether we are to model ourselves upon the clanking military em-
> pires of the Continent of Europe, with their gorgeous Imperial
> hierarchy fed by enormous tariffs, defended by mighty armies, and
> propped by every influence of caste privilege and commercial monop-
> oly, or whether our development is to proceed by well-tried English
> methods towards the ancient and lofty ideals of English citizenship.

The following April, Churchill referred in a speech to the "regular,
settled lines of English democratic development" underpinning the "free
British Empire,"[1] again without contradiction. As an imperial system,
indeed, Britain was far less totalitarian than the Soviet Union or Nazi
Germany. Ironically, when the Soviet Union collapsed, left-wing commentators safely at a distance, such as Jeremy Corbyn, then a markedly
left-wing backbench Labour MP, and from 2015 the leader of Britain's
Labour party, regretted the damage done to the "anti-imperialist" cause,
which is a richly and typically vague term, ready for the use of guilt by
association.

The criticisms visited on British imperialism are frequently ahistorical.
At times, they also appear to reflect an anger that Britain was more suc-

cessful than other powers, an anger that then sustains a mistaken belief that there was something inherently wicked about British intentions and policies.

Some of the criticism sometimes suffers from a lack of relevant contextualization, as is apparent with the environmental critique, instructive as that can be. Imperial attempts to reframe "eco-cultural networks,"[2] and influence, if not control, the environment dislocated traditional economic relationships and brought opportunity and profit very differently to particular groups. However, that was also true of change as a whole, while the ideology of "improvement" was more generally the case with reform policies.

Thus, in Sudan, the Gezira plain was used to grow grain for the nearby capital of Khartoum, but the attempt, under British rule, to develop cotton cultivation there was pressed with the construction of an expensive irrigation scheme that was officially opened in 1926. An aspect of a British "cotton imperialism" already seen prior to World War I, this scheme served to produce a cash crop designed to further the imperial economy, and was an instance of the process by which distant regions were more intensely integrated into the imperial economy. Production of cotton in Sudan lessened British dependence on India and was also part of a strategy focused on imperial self-sufficiency and, therefore, not needing to rely on cotton imports from the United States.

Similarly, imperial economic links that did not focus on Britain were developed. Burma became the largest rice exporter in the world, in large part in order to help feed India, especially highly populous Bengal. This helps explain the problems caused in World War II, when Japan conquered Burma in 1942. The terrible Bengal famine of 1943 (see chapter 4) now used as a major basis for criticism of imperial rule by Britain is best approached in its context, although there is insufficient sign of a willingness to do so.

Moreover, returning to the Gezira plain, dams and irrigation, and the environmental change and damage they could cause, were not solely the works of empire. Indeed, dams and strategies were central to the development strategy of independent states, for example, Egypt and Turkey, as well as left-wing states, notably the Soviet Union and Communist China. These policies continue, as with the Ethiopian attempt to build a large dam on the Blue Nile, much to the anger of Egypt, which has repeatedly threatened to bomb it. There was a broad-ranging determination to control the environment and to benefit from this control, which was seen as a central aspect of modernity.

Formal or informal, Britain was the dominant imperial power across much of the globe from the 1750s to the 1960s, prefiguring the situation of the United States. This was the period of the onset of modernity, as defined by such criteria as large-scale industrialization, urbanization, and the spread of literacy. Empire, in the nineteenth century, and for part of the twentieth century, was a major part of a narrative of British success and an exceptionalism that were closely related to economic strength. In turn, this strength was part of a narrative of success and an account of exceptionalism closely related to empire. The notions of progress inherent to the Whig approach were, as with "the first industrial nation," readily applied to define modernity. In this account, Britain and its empire were intrinsically linked to a big bang of modernity, in which the Industrial Revolution played a crucial role, indeed was a definition of modernity. In the colonies, the pressures and problems stemming from this process of modernization could be accentuated by British rule, and frequently were, but this rule was not the root causes of change.

It is also difficult to separate the later changes in the former colonies resulting from, or related to, decolonization, from broader patterns of development, such as the disruptive as well as beneficial consequences of increasing urbanization and literacy. Moreover, much that was associated with imperialism and is criticized, such as environmental change, in practice, remains important and more insistent under independent government. This assessment is not a welcome reflection for many, not only because it challenges the habit of blaming outsiders for unwelcome developments, but also because it questions the ability of postimperial regimes to cope with the continued effects of globalization. Looked at differently, the blame is shared.

Global demographics will greatly affect official and popular history around the world. Ninety-five percent of the world's population increase is taking place in the "developing world," with the highest growth rates in Africa. It is in the "developing world" that the pressures to provide a readily comprehensible popular history, both of individual countries and of the world as a whole, will seem most acute. Governments in developing countries need to sustain unifying national myths, especially as the liberation accounts employed in the immediate postcolonial period become less potent. So also for the world's most populous country, a status in which India is supplanting China. Indeed, the historical salience of Britain is partly explained by its significance for the national accounts of the world's three leading countries by population: India, China, and the United States.

There is also major change in Britain as a consequence of demographic transformation. Polls in the early 2010s indicated not only that the percentage of the population from ethnic minorities was due to rise significantly, but also that their sense of national identity and pattern of political allegiance was very different from those of the indigenous white majority.[3] In particular, minorities are less likely to vote Conservative, and, separately, are more prone to see themselves as British rather than English. Britishness today in part comes from the experience of the empire, and, separately, from an identification (largely unfair) of Englishness with the Far Right.[4] This Britishness is focused not on an approach to the history and politics of the British Isles, but on a wider ex-imperial legacy.

To arrive at a more perceptive and accurate account of empire, British, Western, or non-Western, it is helpful to try to avoid being ahistorical in so far as that is possible. Imperial conquest does not conform to current mores, and there is profound ambivalence, not to say hostility, within Britain toward its imperial past. At the time, however, few deplored victories, conquests, and imperial rule. Britain was ruled not by pacifist Quakers, but by a political elite prepared to pursue national interests and destiny across the oceans; and this quest resonated with the aspirations of the wider political nation and their sense of the future. It is truly a world that is lost, but one that cannot be disentangled from the history of the country and people, nor separated from that of the rest of the world.

This issue is confused by reference to "decolonizing" studies, as was urged, for example, by Lady Amos, the director of SOAS and a former Labour politician, in March 2018, and by other commentators in Britain, the United States, and South Africa. She argued for including studies of more works by thinkers from ethnic minority backgrounds, but, in practice, "decolonization" is frequently a call for a hostile engagement with the supposed legacy of the past, whether imperial or not. Ironically, that can lead to an exaggeration of the significance of British imperial rule at the expense of other influences and periods. Thus, in India, and elsewhere, there is a focus on this imperial rule, and not on earlier and other historical influences including those of the period since British control.

There is a tendency in India to blame Britain rather than, for example, to probe the significance of the economic policies of successive Congress governments, the impacts of environment, religion and social structures, and the contrast with China from 1949. To look for historical wrongs, it is easier to beat the drum of Amritsar, 1919 (see chapter 4), than to consider Mughal expansion in the Deccan in the seventeenth century, or the political economy of Maratha raiding and military power in the eighteenth century, or the extent to which Britain was but one of a number of post-Mughal political/imperial players in the eighteenth and nineteenth centuries, or the events in Amritsar in 1984. The largest battle of the eighteenth century was not Plassey, the British victory over the Nawab of Bengal in 1757, but the Afghan defeat of the Marathas at Third Panipat near Delhi in 1761. Britain was not the sole player in the imperial stakes.

Repeatedly, such contextualization is necessary and missing. It is noteworthy that most Indian commentators, like most British commentators, have only a limited grasp of their own country's history. Moreover, blaming the British can also lead to an underplaying of the agency of those who were ruled, namely their capacity for taking independent initiatives and molding the situation, even in the face of the power of the imperial state.[5]

A variety of factors make the misunderstanding of empire more dynamic, pressing, and significant. This variety includes the volatility of societies in the developing world, with the relatively large percentage of their populations under the age of twenty-five; the disruptive impact of urbanization and industrialization; the breakdown of patterns of deference and social control and the lack of a stable replacement; and pressures on established political, social, religious, and cultural networks, identities, and systems of explanation. There is also the challenge posed by particular constructions of ethnicity and religion within many states, and how they interact with historicized notions of national identity and development. The cutting edge of historiography is not, as most academics assume, university work, but instead it is how dynamic societies, especially those with rapidly growing populations, come to grips with their recent, and more distant, past. This is notably so if these societies are under authoritarian regimes and, therefore, have a more shaped or controlled (the choice of word is instructive) approach to identity.[6]

This is a process in which British imperialism is nearly invariably found wanting: Britain is the rejected "other." That approach is scarcely surprising. A British political pamphlet of 1757, commenting on a recent passage of popular agitation within the country, claimed:

> History shows ages are necessary to obliterate national prejudices, when the populace of a nation have once been raised to acts of resentment...by this means the people are made a party in the cause, and each individual thus imposed on thinks himself interested, that it should not be proved he was or could be imposed on.[7]

So also with empire. The "amnesia" is not concerning empire, but about how and why it worked, and for so long, both in the British Isles and more widely.

NOTES

PREFACE

1 *The Times* (London), January 30, 2018. For a more helpful view, see Warren Dockter, *Churchill and the Islamic World: Orientalism, Empire and Diplomacy in the Middle East* (London: I.B. Tauris, 2015), and for a vigorous rejoinder to criticism, see Zareer Masani, "Churchill a War Criminal? Get Your History Right," open essay, June 29 2018, http://www.openthemagazine. com/article/essay/churchill-a-war-criminal-get-your-history-right.

2 See, for example, the controversy in *Times Higher Education*, April 26, May 3, 2018.

CHAPTER 1 — INTRODUCTION

1 John Coffey, "'Tremble Britannia!' Fear, Providence and the Abolition of the Slave Trade, 1758–1807," *English Historical Review* 127, no. 527 (August 2012): 844–81.

2 Elizabeth George, *A Place of Hiding* (New York: Bantam, 2003; reprint, New York: Bantam, 2009), 504.

3 Peter S. Onuf, *Jefferson's Empire: The Language of American Nationhood* (Charlottesville, VA: University of Virginia Press, 2000), 18–52; quotation on p. 51.

4 For example, see Toyin Falola, *Colonialism and Violence in Nigeria* (Bloomington, IN: Indiana University Press, 2009).

5 Employed in the preface to his highly influential *The Making of the English Working Class* (London: Victor Gollancz, Ltd., 1963).

6 See, for example, Ashley Jackson, *The British Empire: A Very Short Introduction* (Oxford: Oxford University Press 2013).

7 Christine Noelle-Karimi, "Afghan Politics and the Indo-Persian Literary Realm: The Durrani Rulers and Their Portrayal in Eighteenth-Century Historiography," in *Afghan History Through Afghan Eyes*, ed. Nile Green (London: Hurst Publishers, 2015), 77.

8 Francis O'Gorman, *Forgetfulness: Making the Modern Culture of Amnesia* (London: Bloomsbury Academic, 2017).

9 Niall Ferguson, *Empire: How Britain Made the Modern World* (London: Penguin Books, 2003) and critical accounts, including Frederick Cooper, "Empire Multiplied: A Review Essay," *Comparative Studies in Society and History* 46, no. 2 (2004): 247–72; and Andrew Sartori, "The British Empire and Its Liberal Mission," *Journal of Modern History* 78, no. 3 (2006): 641–42.

Britain is the key player in A. G. Hopkins, *American Empire: A Global History* (Princeton, NJ: Princeton University Press, 2018). See also, for very different treatments, Kori Schake, *Safe Passage: The Transition from British to American Hegemony* (Cambridge, MA: Harvard University Press, 2017) and Kathleen Burk, *The Lion and the Eagle: The Interaction of the British and American Empires, 1783–1972* (London: Bloomsbury Publishing, 2018).

CHAPTER 2 — COMPETING HISTORIES

1   *The Times*, January 29, 2018.
2   Ian Campbell, *The Addis Ababa Massacre: Italy's National Shame* (London: Oxford University Press, 2018).
3   Edward B. Westermann, *Hitler's Ostkrieg and the Indian Wars: Comparing Genocide and Conquest* (Norman, OK: University of Oklahoma Press, 2016).
4   On "our disregard of the Boer War," Matthew Parris, "Forgotten Wars," *Times*, April 4, 2018.
5   David Edgerton, *The Rise and Fall of the British Nation: A Twentieth-Century History* (London: Allen Lane, 2018).
6   Bruce D. Graham, *Hindu Nationalism and Indian Politics: The Origins and Development of the Bharatiya Jana Sangh* (Cambridge: Cambridge University Press, 1990).
7   For this concept, see Francis Fukuyama, "The End of History?" *The National Interest* (spring 1989): 2–18.
8   Henry Chauncy, *Historical Antiquities of Hertfordshire* (London, 1700), p. 1.
9   Judith M. Brown, "Epilogue," in *The Oxford History of the British Empire: IV: The Twentieth Century*, ed. Brown and Wm R. Louis, (Oxford: Oxford University Press, 1999), 710.
10 Karim Bejjit, *English Colonial Texts on Tangier, 1661–1684: Imperialism and the Politics of Resistance* (Farnham: Ashgate, 2015).
11 P. Talloen, *Cult in Pisidia: Religious Practice in Southwestern Asia Minor from Alexander the Great to the Rise of Christianity* (Turnhout: Brepols Publishers, 2015); Pieter M. Judson, *The Habsburg Empire: A New History* (Cambridge, MA: Belknap Press, 2016).
12 Antoinette Burton, *The Trouble with Empire: Challenges to Modern British Imperialism* (Oxford: Oxford University Press, 2015).
13 For a selection of valuable works from a massive literature, see Richard White, *The Middle Ground: Indians, Empires and Republics in the Great Lakes Region, 1650–1815* (Cambridge: Cambridge University Press, 1981); Gabriel Paquette, *Imperial Portugal in the Age of Atlantic Revolutions: The Luso-Brazilian World, c. 1770–1850* (Cambridge: Cambridge University Press, 2003); Jace Weaver, *The Red Atlantic: American Indigenes and the Making of the Modern World, 1000–1927* (Chapel Hill, NC: University of North Carolina Press, 2014); *Exploring the Dutch Empire: Agents, Networks and Institutions, 1600–2000*, eds. Catia Antunes and Jos Gommans (London: Bloomsbury Academic, 2015).
14 Carina E. Ray, *Crossing the Color Line: Race, Sex, and the Contested Politics of Colonialism in Ghana* (Athens, OH: Ohio University Press, 2015).
15 Daniel Branch, *Defeating Mau Mau, Creating Kenya: Counterinsurgency, Civil War, and Decolonization* (Cambridge: Cambridge University Press,

2009) corrects Carloine Elkins, *Imperial Reckoning: The Untold Story of Britain's Gulag in Kenya* (New York: Henry Holt and Company, 2005) and David Anderson, *Histories of the Hanged: The Dirty War in Kenya and the End of Empire* (London: W. W. Norton, 2005). –

16 *Report of the Committee Appointed by the Government of India to Investigate the Disturbances in the Punjab, etc.* (London, 1920), 112; D. George Boyce, "From Assaye to the *Assaye*: Reflections on British Government, Force and Moral Authority in India," *Journal of Military History* 63, no. 3 (1999): 643–68; M. Doyle, "Massacre by the Book: Amritsar and the Rules of Public-Order Policing in Britain and India," *Britain and the World* 4, no. 2 (2011): 247–68.

17 Nick Lloyd, *The Amritsar Massacre: The Untold Story of One Fateful Day* (London: I.B. Tauris, 2011).

18 Anonymous reader's report enclosed in Lynn Luecken to Black, February 25, 2014.

19 Benjamin Grob-Fitzgibbon, *Imperial Endgame. Britain's Dirty Wars and the End of Empire* (Basingstoke, UK: Palgrave Macmillan, 2011); David French, *The British Way in Counter-Insurgency 1945–1967* (Oxford: Oxford University Press, 2012).

20 Myles Osborne, "'The Rooting Out of Mau Mau from the Minds of the Kikuyu Is a Formidable Task': Propaganda and the Mau Mau War," *Journal of African History*, 56, no. 1 (2015): 77–97; Huw Bennett, *Fighting the Mau Mau: The British Army and Counter-Insurgency in the Kenya Emergency* (Cambridge: Cambridge University Press, 2013).

21 Karl Hack, "The Malayan Emergency as Counter-insurgency Paradigm," and Huw Bennett, "'A Very Salutary Effect': The Counter-terror Strategy in the Early Malayan Emergency, June 1948 to December 1949," *Journal of Strategic Studies* 32, no. 3 (June 2009): 383–444.

22 Martin Thomas, *Fight or Flight: Britain, France, and Their Roads from Empire* (Oxford: Oxford University Press, 2014). For an excellent analysis of the dynamics of bureaucracy, colonial violence, and the media, see Nicholas Owen, "'Facts are Sacred': *The Manchester Guardian* and Colonial Violence, 1930–32," *Journal of Modern History*, 84 (2012): 643–78.

23 Martin Thomas, *Empires of Intelligence: Security Services and Colonial Disorder after 1914* (Berkeley: University of California Press, 2008).

24 Wavell to Lieutenant-General Sir Thomas Blamey, 25 June 1940, Australian National War Memorial, Canberra, Department of Manuscripts, 3 DRL/6643 1/27.

25 Michael Kenny and Nick Pearce, *Shadows of Empire: the Anglosphere in British Politics* (Cambridge: Cambridge University Press, 2018).

26 Catherine Hall, *Macaulay and Son. Architects of Imperial Britain* (New Haven, CT: Yale University Press, 2012).

27 Ibid., xiv.

28 Ibid., xxvii.

29 Ibid., 258.

30 Ben Maclennan, *A Proper Degree of Terror: John Graham and the Cape's Eastern Frontier* (Johannesburg: Ravan Press, 1986); and Peter Delius, *The Land Belongs to Us: The Pedi Polity, the Boers, and the British in the Nineteenth-Century Transvaal* (London: Heinemann, 1984).

31 First published in India in 2016 as *An Era of Darkness: the British Empire in India*. See the perceptive review by Nick Lloyd, *Quadrant* LXI, no. 539 (September 2017): 81–85. For Tharoor, see his contributions to "Ghosts of Empire," the Jaipur Literary Festival in London, British Library, June 10, 2018.

32 Tirthankar Roy, *The Economic History of India: 1857–1947* (Oxford: Oxford University Press, 2000); and a review of Tharoor in *Cambridge Review of International Affairs* (2018), http://doi.org/10.1080/09557571.2018.1439321; C. Allen, lecture, "*Quis custodiet ipsos custodies*: Who owns India's history?"

33 For example, Christian Wolmar, *Railways and the Raj: How the Age of Steam transformed India* (London: Atlantic Books, 2017).

34 Mark R. Frost, "Pandora's Post Box: Empire and Information in India, 1854–1914," *English Historical Review* 131, no. 552 (October 2016): 1043–73.

35 Lizz Collingham, *The Hungry Empire: How Britain's Quest for Food Shaped the Modern World* (London: The Bodley Head, 2017).

36 For the earlier situation, see Paul Maylam, *The Cult of Rhodes: Remembering an Imperialist in Africa* (Claremont, South Africa: New Africa Books, 2005).

37 *The Times*, February 21, 2018.

38 *Times*, December 22, 2015.

39 Nigel Biggar, "Rhodes, Race, and the Abuse of History," *Standpoint* (March 2016), and "The Rhodes affair," *New Criterion* (January 2017).

40 http://www.web.pdx.edu/~gilleyb/2_The%20case%20for%20colonialism_at2Oct2017.pdf. See also his "Chinua Achebe on the Positive Legacies of Colonialism," *African Affairs* 115, no. 461 (2016): 646–63.

41 "Pro-colonialism paper: how did it get published?" *Times Higher Education*, September 27, 2017.

42 Afua Hirsch, *Brit(ish): On Race, Identity and Belonging* (London: Random House 2018).

43 Elazar Barkan, *The Guilt of Nations: Restitution and Negotiating Historical Injustices* (Baltimore: John Hopkins University Press, 2000).

44 Janna Thompson, *Taking Responsibility for the Past: Reparation and Historical Justice* (Cambridge: Polity, 2002).

CHAPTER 3 — WHY EMPIRE?

1 Ernst Badian, "Alexander the Great and the Unity of Mankind," *Historia* 7 (1958): 425–44; Frank L. Holt, *The Treasures of Alexander the Great: How One Man's Wealth Shaped the World* (New York: Oxford University Press, 2016).

2 P. Mitchell, review in *TLS*, 2 (February 2018): 28.

3 Ronald Hyam, *Empire and Sexuality* (Manchester, UK: Manchester University Press, 1991). With reference to the Dutch in Sumatra, Ann Laura Stoler, *Carnal Knowledge and Imperial Power* (Berkeley: University of California Press, 2010).

4 Philippa Levine and John Marriott, eds., *The Ashgate Research Companion to Modern Imperial Histories* (Farnham: Ashgate, 2012).

5 Patrick Colm Hogan, "*Midnight*'s Children: Kashmir and the Politics of Identity," *Twentieth-Century Literature* 47, no. 4 (2001): 510–44.

6 David Armitage, *The Declaration of Independence: A Global History* (Cambridge, MA: Harvard University Press 2008).

7 Eric Richards, "British Emigrants and the Making of the Anglosphere," *History* 103 , no. 335 (2018): 286–306.

8 Jeremy Black, *Fighting for America: The Struggle for Mastery in North America, 1519–1871* (Bloomington, IN: Indiana University Press, 2012).

9 Michael B. Cosmopoulus, ed., *Experiencing War: Trauma and Society in Ancient Greece and Today* (Chicago: Ares Publishers, 2007); Edward N. Luttwak, *The Virtual American Empire: War, Faith, and Power* (New Brunswick, NJ: Transaction Publishers, 2009); A. G. Hopkins, *American Empire: A Global History* (Princeton, NJ: Princeton University Press, 2018).

10 Herman Lebovics, *Imperialism and the Corruption of Democracies* (Durham, NC: Duke University Press, 2006).

11 Mary Lefkowitz, Not Out of Africa: How Afrocentrism Became an Excuse to Teach Myth as History (New York: Basic Books, 1996); Ronald H. Fritze, *Invented Knowledge: False History, Fake Science and Pseudo-Religions* (London: Reaktion Books, 2009): 251–56.

12 Richard Hingley and Christina Unwin, *Boudica: Iron Age Warrior Queen* (London: Bloomsbury Academic, 2005).

13 Christopher Hagerman, *British Imperial Muse: the Classics, Imperialism and the Indian Empire, 1784–1914* (Basingstoke, UK: Palgrave Macmillan, 2013); Joanna de Groot, *Empire and History Writing in Britain. c. 1750–2012* (Manchester: Manchester University Press, 2013).

14 Joanne Parker, *England's Darling: The Victorian Cult of Alfred the Great* (Manchester: Manchester University Press, 2007); Roy Strong, *And When Did You Last See Your Father? The Victorian Painter and British History* (London: Thames and Hudson, 1978); Stephen Bann, *The Clothing of Clio: A Study of the Representation of History in Nineteenth-Century Britain and France* (Cambridge: Cambridge University Press, 1984).

15 Bruce Abramson, "Nation States could save the Middle East," *Standpoint*, 100 (April 2018): 30–37.

16 For an emphasis as well on commercial interests, see Anthony Webster, "Business and Empire: A Reassessment of the British Conquest of Burma in 1885," *Historical Journal*, 43, no. 4 (2000): 1003–25.

17 Jutta Bolt and Ellen Hillbom, "Long-term trends in economic inequality: lessons from colonial Botswana, 1921–74," *Economic History Review* 69, no. 4 (2016): 1255–84.

18 Barnaby Crowcroft, "Egypt's Other Nationalists and the Suez Crisis of 1956," *Historical Journal* 59, no. 1 (2016): 253–85.

19 Eve Troutt Powell, *A Different Shade of Colonialism: Egypt, Great Britain, and the Mastery of the Sudan* (Berkeley: University of California Press, 2003), 219.

20 Chris Vaughan, *Darfur: Colonial Violence, Sultanic Legacies and Local Politics, 1916–1956* (Woodbridge: Boydell & Brewer, 2015).

21 Biray Kolluoğlu and Meltem Toksöz, eds., *Cities of the Mediterranean: From the Ottomans to the Present Day* (London: I.B. Tauris); Peter Clark, ed., *The Oxford Handbook of Cities in World History* (Oxford: Oxford University Press, 2013).

22 Brain Hughes, *Defying the IRA? Intimidation, Coercion, and Communities during the Irish Revolution* (Liverpool: Liverpool University Press, 2016).

23 *The Daily Telegraph*, April, 5, 2011.

24 *The Guardian*, 3, March 18, 2017. For similar claims of collusion about this period, G. Jevon, "The Arab Legion and the 1948 War: The Conduct of 'Collusion'?," *English Historical Review* 130, no. 545 (2015): 907–33.

25 Nancy Green, "The Trials of Transnationalism: It's Not as Easy as It Looks," *Journal of Modern History* 89, no. 4 (2017): 851–74.

26 G. John Ikenberry, "The end of liberal international order?," *International Affairs* 94, no. 1 (2018): 7–23.

27 I have benefited from a conversation with Oliver Letwin for the latter point.

28 Susan Pedersen, *The Guardians: The League of Nations and the Crisis of Empire* (Oxford: Oxford University Press, 2015).

29 Tonio Andrade and William Reger, eds., *The Limits of Empire; European Imperial Formations in Early Modern World History* (Farnham: Ashgate, 2012).

30 Gregory A. Barton, *Informal Empire and the Rise of One World Culture* (Basingstoke, UK: Palgrave Macmillan, 2014).

31 Ann Laura Stoler, Carole McGranahan, and Peter C. Perdue, *Imperial Formations* (Santa Fe, NM: School for Advanced Research Press, 2007).

32 David Cannadine, "'Big Tent' historiography: Transatlantic obstacles and opportunities in writing the history of empire," *Common Knowledge* 11, no. 3 (2005): 375–92.

CHAPTER 4 — BRITISH RULE AND FOUNDATION ACCOUNTS: INDIA AND IRELAND

1 Shradda Kumbhojkar, "Politics, caste and the remembrance of the Raj: the Obelisk at Koregaon," in *Sites of Imperial Memory: Commemorating Colonial Rule in the Nineteenth and Twentieth Centuries*, eds. Dominik Geppert and Frank Lorenz Müller (Oxford: Oxford University Press, 2015): 39–52.

2 Sujatha Gidla, *Ants Among Elephants: An Untouchable Family and the Making of Modern India* (New York: Farrar, Straus & Giroux, 2017).

3 Michael Silvestri, *Ireland and India: Nationalism, Empire and Memory* (Basingstoke, UK: Palgrave Macmillan, 2009).

4 Jennifer Regan-Lefebvre, *Cosmopolitan Nationalism in the Victorian Empire. Ireland, India and the Politics of Alfred Webb* (Basingstoke, UK: Palgrave Macmillan, 2009).

5 Joya Chatterji, "Nationalisms in India, 1857–1947," in *The Oxford Handbook of the History of Nationalism*, ed. John Breuilly (Oxford: Oxford University Press, 2013), 259.

6 Faisal Devji, *The Impossible Indian. Gandhi and the Temptation of Violence* (London: Harvard University Press, 2012).

7 Kama Maclean, *A Revolutionary History of Interwar India: Violence, Image, Voice and Text* (New York: Oxford University Press, 2015).

8 Pankaj Mishra, *From the Ruins of Empire: The Intellectuals Who Remade Asia* (New York: Picador, 2012).

9 Pratik Chakrabarti, *Bacteriology in British India: Laboratory Medicine and the Tropics* (Rochester, NY: Boydell & Brewer, 2012).

10 Partha Chatterjee, *The Black Hole of Empire: History of a Global Practice of Power* (Princeton, NJ: Princeton University Press, 2012).

11 Barbara English, "The Kanpur Massacres in India in the Revolt of 1857," *Past and Present* 142, no. 1 (1994): 169–78.

12 London, British Library, India Office papers, Mss. Eur. C. 231, p. 56; K. Wagner, *The Skull of Alum Bheg: The Life and Death of a Rebel of 1857* (London, 2017).

13 Nick Lloyd, *The Amritsar Massacre: The Untold Story of One Fateful Day* (London: I.B. Tauris, 2001). For a context, see Gyanesh Kudaisya, "'In Aid of Civil Power.' The Colonial Army in Northern India, *c.* 1919–421," *Journal of Imperial and Commonwealth History* 32, no. 1 (2004): 41–68.

14 Mark Tully and Satish Jacob, *Amritsar: Mrs Gandhi's Battle* (London: Rupa, 1985); Gunisha Kaur, "Remembering the Massacre of Sikhs in June 1984," *Huffington Post*, June 3, 2013.

15 Abdul Gafoor Noorani, *The Babri Masjid Question: 1528–2003* (New Delhi: Tulika Books, 2003).

16 Christophe Jaffrelot, "Nation-building and Nationalism: South Asia, 1947–90," in *The Oxford Handbook of the History of Nationalism*, ed. John Breuilly (Oxford: Oxford University Press, 2013), 503.

17 Pav Singh, *1984: India's Guilty Secret* (New Delhi: Kashi House, 2018).

18 Jamie Doward, "British government 'covered up' its role in Amritsar massacre in India," *theguardian.com*, retrieved October 29 2017.

19 Prem Mahadevan, "The Maoist Insurgency in India: Between Crime and Revolution," *Small Wars and Insurgencies* 23, no. 2 (2012): 203–20; Alpa Shah, *Nightmarch: Among the Guerrillas of India's Revolutionary Movement* (London: Hurst Publishers, 2018).

20 Anit Mukherjee, "Facing Future Challenges: Defence Reform in India," *RUSI Journal* 156, no. 5 (Oct.–Nov. 2011): 35. For a more positive view, Steven Wilkinson, *Army and Nation: The Military and Indian Democracy since Independence* (Cambridge, MA: Harvard University Press, 2015).

21 Sugata Bose, *His Majesty's Opponent. Subhas Chandra Bose and India's Struggle Against Empire* (New Delhi: Penguin Books India, 2011), 264–5.

22 Romain Hayes, *Subhas Chandra Bose in Nazi Germany: Politics, Intelligence and Propaganda, 1941–43* (London: Hurst Publishers, 2011).

23 Warren Dockter, *Churchill and the Islamic World: Orientalism, Empire and Diplomacy in the Middle East* (London: I.B. Tauris, 2015).

24 Robert Johnson, "The Army in India and Responses to Low-Intensity Conflict, 1936–1946," *Journal of the Society for Army Historical Research* 89, no. 358 (2011): 174.

25 Daniel Marston, *The Indian Army and the End of the Raj* (Cambridge: Cambridge University Press, 2014).

26 Christopher Bayly and Timothy Harper, *Forgotten Armies* (Cambridge: MA, Belknap Press, 2006); Yasmin Khan, *The Raj at War* (London: Vintage, 2016); Srinath Raghavan, *India's War: World War II and the Making of Modern South Asia, 1939–1945* (New York: Basic Books, 2016).

27 Madhusree Mukerjee, *Churchill's Secret War: The British Empire and the Ravaging of India During World War II* (New York: Basic Books, 2010); and Janam Mukherjee, *Hungry Bengal: War, Famine and the End of Empire* (New York: Oxford University Press, 2015). For a more complex and sophisticated approach, see Cormac Ó Gráda, "'Sufficiency and Sufficiency and Sufficiency': Revisiting the Great Bengal Famine of 1943–44," in *Eating People Is Wrong and Other Essays* (Princeton, NJ: Princeton University Press, 2015), 38–91.

28 Paul R. Greenough, *Prosperity and Misery in Modern Bengal: The Famine of 1943–1944* (Oxford: Oxford University Press, 1982).

29 Barney White-Spunner, *Partition: The Story of Indian independence and the Creation of Pakistan in 1947* (London: Simon & Schuster UK, 2018).

30 *The Hindu*, July 10, 2005, gives the impressive speech in full.

31 K. Lalvani, *The Making of India: the Untold Story of British Enterprise* (London: Bloomsbury Publishing, 2010); John Broich, "Was it really the 'white man's burden'? The Non-British Engineers who Engineered the British Empire," *Britain and the World* 9, no. 2 (2016): 197–212.

32 *The Tribune*, July 10, 2005.

33 K. S. Komireddi, *The Malevolent Republic: India Under Modi* (London: Hurst Publishers, 2018).

34 Sylvie Guichard, "The Indian Nation and Selective Amnesia: Representing Conflicts and Violence in Indian History Textbooks," *Nations and Nationalism* 19, no. 1 (2013): 68–86; Allison Busch, "The Poetry of History in Early Modern India," in *How The Past Was Used: Historical Cultures, c. 750–2000*, eds. Peter Lambert and Bjorn Weiler (Oxford: Oxford University Press, 2017), 198.

35 Walter Andersen and Shridhar Damle, *Messengers of Hindu Nationalism: How the RSS Reshaped India* (London: New Hurst Publishers, 2018).

36 David Scott, *Conscripts of Modernity: The Tragedy of Colonial Enlightenment* (Durham, NC: Duke University Press, 2004); Frederick Cooper, *Colonialism in Question: Theory, Knowledge, History* (Berkeley: University of California Press, 2005).

37 Roman Studer, *The Great Divergence Reconsidered: Europe, India, and the Rise of Global Economic Power* (Cambridge: Cambridge University Press, 2015).

38 Jonathan Eacott, *Selling Empire: India in the Making of Britain and America, 1600–1830* (Chapel Hill, NC: University of North Carolina Press, 2016).

39 John Gibney, *The Shadow of a Year: The 1641 Rebellion in Irish History and Memory* (Madison, WI: Universiy of Wisconsin Press, 2013).

40 Danielle McCormack, *The Stuart Restoration and the English in Ireland* (Rochester, NY: Boydell & Brewer, 2016).

41 Jane Ohlmeyer, *Making Ireland English: The Irish Aristocracy in the Seventeenth Century* (New Haven, CN: Yale University Press, 2012).

42 Charles Ivar McGrath, *Ireland and Empire, 1692–1770* (London: Routledge, 2012).

43 Paul A. Townend, "Between Two Worlds: Irish Nationalists and Imperial Crisis 1878–1880," *Past and Present* 194, no. 1 (2007): 139–74; S.B. Cook, "The Irish Raj: Social Origins and Careers of Irishmen in the Indian Civil Service, 1855–1914," *Journal of Social History* 20, no. 3 (1987): 507–29.

44 Keith Jeffery, *An Irish Empire? Aspects of Ireland and the British Empire* (Manchester: Manchester University Press, 1996); Kevin Kenny, *Ireland in the British Empire* (Oxford: Oxford University Press, 2006); Tadhg Foley and Maureen O'Connor, eds., *Ireland and India: Colonies, Culture and Empire* (Dublin: Irish Academic Press, 2006); Michael Silvestri, *Ireland and India: Nationalism, Empire and Memory* (Basingstoke, UK: Palgrave macmillan 2009); Barry Crosbie, *Irish Imperial Networks: Migration, Social Communication and Exchange in Nineteenth-Century India* (Cambridge:

Cambridge University Press, 2012); Patrick O'Leary, *Servants of the Empire: The Irish in Punjab 1881–1921* (Manchester: Manchester University Press, 2011).

45 A. Jackson, "Ireland's Long Nineteenth Century of Union," *Journal of Modern History* 86 (2014): 125; James H. Murphy, *Ireland's Czar: Gladstonian Government and the Lord Lieutenancies of the Red Earl Spencer, 1868–86* (Dublin: University College Dublin Press, 2014).

46 For continuing scholarly enquiry, Christine Kinealy et al., eds., *Children and the Great Hunger in Ireland* (Cork: Cork University Press, 2018).

47 See also, from the same publisher in 2017, Niamh Ann Kelly, *Ultimate Witnesses: The Visual Culture of Death, Burial, and Mourning in Famine Ireland*; and Breandan Mac Suibhne, *Subjects Lacking Words? The Gray Zone of the Great Famine*.

48 Adrian Gregory and Senia Paseta, eds., *Ireland and the Great War; 'A War to Unite Us All?,* (Manchester: Manchester University Press, 2002).

49 Fearghal McGarry, *The Rising: Ireland, Easter 1916* (Oxford: Oxford University Press, 2010).

50 D. M. Leeson, *The Black and Tans: British Police and Auxiliaries in the Irish War of Independence, 1920–1921* (Oxford: Oxford University Press, 2011).

51 William H. Kautt, *Ambushes and Armour: The Irish Rebellion 1919–1921* (Dublin: Irish Academic Press, 2010); William Sheehan, *A Hard Local War: The British Army and the Guerrilla War in Cork, 1919–1921* (Barnsley: The History Press Ireland, 2011).

52 Chetwode to General Archibald Montgomery-Massingberd, July 1, 1921, London, King's College, Liddell Hart Library, Montgomery-Massingberd papers, 8/22.

53 General Staff, "British Military Liabilities," 9 June 1920, Kew, National Archives, Cabinet Office papers 24/107 fol. 256.

54 Sean McConville, *Irish Political Prisoners, 1920–1962: Pilgrimages of Desolation* (London: Routledge, 2014).

55 Gemma Clark, *Everyday Violence in the Irish Civil War* (Cambridge: Cambridge University Press, 2014).

56 K. Theodore Hoppen, *Ireland Since 1800* (London: Pearson Education Limited, 1989), 177.

57 Dermot Keogh, *Ireland in World War Two* (Dublin: Mercier Press, 2004).

58 Hoppen, *Ireland*, 185.

59 Brian Girvin and Geoffrey Roberts (eds.), *Ireland and the Second World War: Politics, Society and Remembrance* (Dublin: Four Courts Press, 2000).

60 Hoppen, *Ireland*, 186.

61 D. Staunton, "Irony of Brexit, that it pushes us closer to a united Ireland," *The Evening Standard*, December 5, 2017, p. 17.

62 Matthew Kelly, "The Kelly and the O'Kelly's," *English Historical Review*, 125, no. 157 (2010): 1481–92.

63 Mo Moulton, *Ireland and the Irish in Interwar England* (Cambridge: Cambridge University Press, 2014).

64 Evi Gkotzaridis, *Trials of Irish History: Genesis and Evolution of a Reappraisal, 1938–2000* (New York: Routledge, 2006); John M. Regan, "Southern Irish Nationalism as a Historical Problem," *Historical Journal* 50, no. 1 (2007):

197–223; and *Myth and the Irish State* (Sallins, 2013); Brain Girvin, "Beyond Revisionism? Some Recent Contributions to the Study of Modern Ireland," *English Historical Review* 124, no. 506 (2009): 94–107.

65 *The Irish Times*, February, 28, 2015.

CHAPTER 5 — CHINA AND THE UNITED STATES

1 Also given as 1839–42, 1856–60.

2 Stephen Platt, *Imperial Twilight: The Opium War and the End of China's Last Golden Age* (New York: Alfred A. Knopf, 2018).

3 Donna Brunero, *Britain's Imperial Cornerstone in China: The Chinese Maritime Customs Service, 1854–1949* (London: Routledge, 2006).

4 Peter Hays Gries, *China's New Nationalism: Pride, Politics and Diplomacy* (Berkeley: Universtiy of California Press, 2005); William A. Callahan, *China: The Pessoptimist Nation* (New York: Oxford University Press, 2010).

5 Kenneth Pomeranz, *The Great Divergence: China, Europe, and the Making of the Modern World Economy* (Princeton, NJ: Princeton University Press, 2000).

6 Kenneth Pomeranz, "Re-thinking the Late Imperial Chinese Economy: Development, Disaggregation and Decline, circa 1730–1930," *Itinerario* 24, no. 3 (2000): 49–66.

7 Mao Zedong, "The Communist Revolution and the Chinese Communist Party," in his *Select Works* (Beijing, 1967), II, p. 314.

8 *The Opium War* (Beijing, 1976), p. 115.

9 *The Taiping Revolution* (Beijing, 1976).

10 Albert Feuerwerker, ed., *History in Communist China* (Cambridge, MA: MIT Press, 1968); Jonathan Unger, ed., *Using the Past to Serve the Present: Historiography and Politics in Contemporary China* (London: Routledge, 1993).

11 Jerrilyn Greene Marston, *King and Congress: The Transfer of Political Legitimacy, 1774–1776* (Princeton, NJ: Princeton University Press, 1987); Neil Longley York, *Turning the World Upside Down: The War of American Independence and the Problem of Empire* (Westport, CN: Praeger, 2003).

12 Jeremy Black, *George III, America's Last King* (New Haven, CN: Yale University Press, 2006).

13 Kathleen Burk, *Old World, New World: The Story of Britain and America* (London: Atlantic Monthly Press, 2007).

14 John Lewis Gaddis, *Surprise, Security and the American Experience* (Cambridge, MA: Harvard University Press, 2004).

15 Peter D. G. Thomas, *The Townshend Duties Crisis: The Second Phase of the American Revolution, 1767–1773* (Oxford: Oxford University Press, 1987).

16 Jill Lepore, *The Whites of Their Eyes: The Tea Party's Revolution and the Battle over American History* (Princeton, NJ: Princeton University Press, 2010).

17 John Seed, *Dissenting Histories. Religious Division and the Politics of Memory in Eighteenth-Century England* (Edinburgh: Edinburgh University Press, 2008), pp. 62–3.

18 Benjamin Hawkins, American agent to the Creeks [largely pro-British Native American tribal confederation], to Peter Early, Governor of Georgia,

20 Feb. 1815, Auburn, Alabama, University Library, Special Collections, Frank Owsley donation, Accession No 82-08 XX.

19 Hawkins to Nicolls, March 19, and reply, April 28, 1815, Auburn.

20 Cockburn to Sebastian Kindelan, Governor of St Augustine, February 13, 22, to General Forbes, February 26, and to Admiral Cochrane, February 28, NA. (London, National Archives) WO. (War Office) 1/144.

21 Mark F. Boyd, "Events at Prospect Bluff on the Apalachicola River," *Florida Historical Quarterly* 16, no. 1 (1937): 55–93; James W. Covington, "The Negro Fort," *Gulf Coast Historical Review*, 5, no. 2 (1990): 79–91; Spencer C. Tucker, *The Jeffersonian Gunboat Navy* (Columbia, SC: University of South Carolina Press, 1993), 175.

22 E.S. Vansickle, "A Transnational Vision for African Colonisation: John H.B. Latrobe and the Future of Maryland in Liberia," *Journal of Transatlantic Studies*, 1 (2003), pp. 214–32.

23 Cochrane to Rear-Admiral Pultney Malcolm, 17 Feb. 1815, NA. WO. 1/143.

24 Holger Hoock, *Scars of Independence: America's Violent Birth* (New York: Crown Publishing Group, 2017); Virginia DeJohn Anderson, *The Martyr and the Traitor: Nathan Hale, Moses Dunbar, and the American Revolution* (New York: Oxford University Press, 2017).

25 Mark Glancy, "The War of Independence in Feature Film: *The Patriot* (2000) and the 'Special Relationship' between Hollywood and Britain," *Historical Journal of Film, Radio and Television* 25, no. 4 (2005): 523–45.

CHAPTER 6 — AUSTRALIA, CANADA, AND NEW ZEALAND

1 *The Times*, June 29, 2011, p. 27.

2 Alan Lester and Fae Dussart, *Colonization and the Origins of Humanitarian Governance: Protecting Aborigines across the Nineteenth-Century British Empire* (Cambridge: Cambridge University Press, 2014).

3 Annie E. Coombes, ed., *Rethinking Settler Colonialism: History and Memory in Australia, Canada, New Zealand and South Africa* (Manchester: Manchester University Press, 2006).

4 Patrick A. McAllister, *National Days and the Politics of Indigenous and Local Identities in Australia and New Zealand* (Durham, NC: Carolina Academic Press, 2012).

5 Miranda Johnson, *The Land Is Our History: Indigeneity, Law, and the Settler State* (New York: Oxford University Press, 2016).

6 Bain Atwood, *Telling the Truth about Aboriginal History* (Sydney: Allen and Unwin, 2005) has since been strongly challenged; Keith Windschuttle, "The Return of Postmodernism, in Aboriginal History," *Quadrant* (April 2006): 9–23; G. Davison, *The Use and Abuse of Australian History* (Sydney: Allen and Unwin, 2000); J. Hirst, *Sense and Nonsense in Australian History* (Melbourne: Black Inc. Agenda, 2009).

7 For an instructive discussion, M. Connor, *The Invention of Terra Nullius: Historical and Legal Fictions on the Foundation of Australia* (Sydney: Macleay Press, 2005).

8 Lyndall Ryan, *The Aboriginal Tasmanians* (1981, 2nd ed., Sydney: Allen and Unwin, 1997) has since been corrected; Keith Windschuttle, *The Fabrication*

of Aboriginal History. I. Van Diemen's Lands, 1803–1847 (Sydney: Macleay
Press, 2004), 11–28. See also "Risdon Cove and the Massacre of 3 May 1804:
Their Place in Tasmanian History," *Tasmanian Historical Studies* 9, no. 2004
(2004): 107–23; and Tom Lawson, *The Last Man: a British Genocide in
Tasmania* (London: I.B. Tauris, 2014).

9   M. Garrick, "Desert Wind," *Weekend Australian Magazine*, 10–11, March
2018, p. 16.

10 Alan Frost, *The Global Reach of Empire. Britain's Maritime Expansion on the
Indian and Pacific Oceans, 1704–1815* (Melbourne: Melbourne University
Publishing, 2003), 177.

11 Neil Levi, "'No Sensible Comparison'? The Place of the Holocaust in
Australia's History Wars," *History and Memory* 19, no. 1 (2007), p. 132.

12 Mark Connelly, "*Gallipoli* (1981): a poignant search for national identity,"
in *The New Film History: Sources, Methods, Approaches*, eds. James Chapman,
Mark Glancy and Sue Harper (Basingstoke, UK: Palgrave Macmillan, 2007),
41–53.

13 Dale Blair, *Dinkum Diggers: An Australian Battalion at War* (Carlton,
Victoria: Melbourne University Publishing, 2001); Jeffrey Grey, *The War
with the Ottoman Empire* (Melbourne: Oxford University Press, 2015).

14 Tim Cook, *At the Sharp End: Canadians Fighting the Great War, 1914–1916*
(Toronto, ON: Penguin Canada, 2009) and *Shock Troops: Canadians Fighting
the Great War, 1917–1918* (Toronto, ON: Penguin Canada, 2009).

15 John Griffiths, *Imperial Culture in Antipodean Cities, 1880–1939* (Basingstoke,
UK: Palgrave Macmillan 2014).

CHAPTER 7 — RESPONDING TO THE WORLD THAT EMPIRE MADE

1   Mrinalini Rajagopalan, *Building Histories: The Archival and Affective Lives
of Five Monuments in Modern Delhi* (Chicago: University of Chicago Press,
2016).

2   David French, *Fighting EOKA: The British Counter-Insurgency Campaign on
Cyprus, 1955–1959* (Oxford: Oxford University Press, 2015), 303.

3   Alex Marshall, "Imperial Nostalgia, the Liberal Lie, and the Perils of
Postmodern Counter-insurgency," *Small Wars and Insurgencies* 21, no. 2
(2010): 233–58; Benjamin Grob-Fitzgibbon, *Imperial Endgame: Britain's
Dirty Wars and the End of Empire* (Basingstoke, UK: Palgrave Macmillan,
2011); David French, *The British Way in Counter-Insurgency, 1945–1967*
(Oxford: Oxford University Press, 2012); Christopher Hale, *Massacre in
Malaya: Exposing Britain's My Lai* (Stroud: The History Press, 2013); Huw
Bennett, *Fighting the Mau Mau: The British Army and Counter-Insurgency
in the Kenya Emergency* (Cambridge: Cambridge University Press, 2013);
Douglas Porch, *Counterinsurgency: Exposing the Myths of the New Way of War*
(Cambridge: Cambridge University Press, 2013).

4   Susan L. Carruthers, *Winning Hearts and Minds: British Governments, the
Media and Colonial Counter-Insurgency, 1944–1960* (Leicester: Mansell, 1995).

5   Jeremy Black, *English Nationalism: A Short History* (London: Hurst
Publishers, 2018).

6   Patrick Bishop, *The Reckoning: Death and Intrigue in the Promised Land*
(London: HarperCollins, 2014).

7 *The Times*, June 25, 2014.
8 Henry Frendo, *Europe and Empire: Culture, Politics and Identity in Malta and the Mediterranean, 1912–1946* (Venera: Midsea Books, 2012), 1–16.

CHAPTER 8 — THE SLAVE TRADE AND RACISM

1 *The Western Times*, 6, 13, April 1833.
2 E. Gibson, *Two Letters* (London, 1727), 10–11.
3 Travis Glasson, *Mastering Christianity: Missionary Anglicanism and Slavery in the Atlantic World, 1680–1783* (New York: Oxford University Press, 2012).
4 Jeremy Black, *The Atlantic Slave Trade in World History* (London: Routledge, 2015), *The Slave Trade* (London: Social Affairs Unit, 2007).
5 Sowande M. Mustakeem, *Slavery at Sea: Terror, Sex, and Sickness in the Middle Passage* (Urbana, IL: University of Illinois Press, 2016).
6 Jack P. Greene, *Settler Jamaica in the 1750s: A Social Portrait* (Charlottesville, VA: University of Virginia Press, 2016).
7 Nuala Zahedieh, "Colonies, copper and the market for inventive activity in England and Wales, 1680–1730," *Economic History Review* 66, no. 3 (2013): 805–25.
8 Joseph E. Inikori, *Africans and the Industrial Revolution in England: A Study in International Trade and Economic Development* (Cambridge: Cambridge University Press, 2002), 407–8, 416, 513, 518–9; David Mitchell, "Three English Cloth Towns and the Royal African Company," *Journal of the Historical Society* 13, no. 4 (2013): 447.
9 Simon P. Newman, *A New World of Labor: The Development of Plantation Slavery in the British Atlantic* (Philadelphia: University of Pennsylvania Press 2013); Michael Guasco, *Slaves and Englishmen: Human Bondage in the Early Modern Atlantic World* (Philadelphia: University of Pennsylvania Press, 2014).
10 John Coffey, "'Tremble Britannia!' Fear, Providence and the Abolition of the Slave Trade, 1758–1807," *English Historical Review* 127, no. 527 (2012): 844–81.
11 Janna Thompson, *Should Current Generations Make Reparation for Slavery?* (Cambridge: Polity, 2018).
12 *The Times*, March 10, 2014.
13 J. R. Oldfield, *Transatlantic Abolitionism in the Age of Revolution: An International History of Anti-slavery, c. 1787–1820* (Cambridge: Cambridge University Press, 2013); Julie L. Holcomb, *Moral Commerce: Quakers and the Transatlantic Boycott of the Slave Labor Economy* (Ithaca, NY: Cornell University Press, 2016).
14 Paula E. Dumas, *Proslavery Britain: Fighting for Slavery in an Era of Abolition* (Basingstoke, UK: Palgrave Macmillan, 2016).
15 Christer Petley, *Slaveholders in Jamaica: Colonial Society and Culture during the Era of Abolition* (London: Routledge, 2009); and *White Fury. A Jamaican Slaveholder and the Age of Revolution* (Oxford: Oxford University Press, 2018).
16 Miles Taylor, "Empire and Parliamentary Reform: The 1832 Reform Act Revisited," in *Rethinking the Age of Reform*, eds. Arthur Burns and Joanna Innes (Cambridge: Cambridge University Press, 2003), 295–311.
17 Catherine Hall et al., *Legacies of British Slave-Ownership: Colonial Slavery and the Formation of Victorian Britain* (Cambridge: Cambridge University Press, 2014).

18   David Brion Davis, *The Problem of Slavery in the Age of Emancipation* (New York: Alfred A. Knopf, 2014).

19   D. Eltis, "The British contribution to the Nineteenth-Century Transatlantic Slave Trade," *Economic History Review* 32, no. 2 (1979): 211–27.

20   Peter Grindal, *Opposing the Slavers: The Royal Navy's Campaign against the Atlantic Slave Trade* (London: I.B. Tauris, 2016).

21   Richard Huzzey, *Freedom Burning: Anti-Slavery and Empire in Victorian Britain* (Ithaca, NY: Cornell University Press, 2012).

22   Palmerston to Russell, July 21, August 13, 1862, NA. PRO. 30/22/14C fol. 25, 30/22/22 fol. 93; Russell to Earl Crowley, envoy in Paris, 15 Ap. 1865, NA. PRO. 30/22/106 fol. 119.

23   Caroline Keen, *Princely India and the British: Political Development and the Operation of Empire* (London: I.B. Tauris, 2012).

24   David Cannadine, *Ornamentalism: How the British Saw Their Empire* (London: Oxford University Press, 1997).

25   Kevin Grant, *A Civilised Savagery: Britain and the New Slaveries in Africa, 1884–1926* (New York: Routledge, 2005); Stuart Laing, *Tippu Tip: Ivory, Slavery and Discovery in the Scramble for Africa* (London: Medina Publishing, 2018).

26   Dan Jones, *Tea and Justice: British Tea Companies and the Tea Workers of Bangladesh* (London: Bangladesh International Action Group, 1986); Sarthak Sengupta, *The Tea Labourers of North East India: An Anthropo-Historical Perspective* (New Delhi: Mittal Publications, 2009); Rana Behal, "Tea and Money versus Human Life: the Rise and Fall of the Indenture System in the Assam Tea Plantations 1840–1908," *Journal of Peasants Studies* 19, no. 3 (1992): 142–172. See also Sugata Bose, *Peasant Labour and Colonial Capital: Rural Bengal since 1770* (Cambridge: Cambridge University Press, 2007) and J. Sharma, *Empire's Garden: Assam and the Making of India* (Durham, NC: Duke University Press, 2011).

27   Kevin Bales, *Disposable People: New Slavery in the Global Economy* (Berkeley: University of California Press, 1999).

28   Gijs Kruijtzer, *Xenophobia in Seventeenth-Century India* (Leiden: Leiden University Press, 2009); Richard J. Reid, *Frontiers of Violence in North-East Africa: Genealogies of Conflict since 1800* (Oxford: Oxford University Press, 2011).

29   Martin J. Wiener, "The Idea of 'Colonial Legacy' and the Historiography of Empire," *Journal of the Historical Society*,13, no. 1 (2013): 1–32, esp. 22–32.

30   Kishori Saran Lal, *The Muslim Slave System in Medieval India* (New Delhi: South Asia Books, 1994); Ehud F. Toledano, *As If Silent and Absent: Bonds of Enslavement in the Islamic Middle East* (New Haven, CN: Yale University Press, 2007).

CHAPTER 9 — THE VIEW FROM BRITAIN

1   BBC News, March 25, 2018.

2   David Mattingly, *An Imperial Possession: Britain in the Roman Empire* (London: Allen Lane, 2006).

3   David Matthews, *Writing to the King: Nation, Kingship, and Literature in England, 1250–1350* (Cambridge: Cambridge University Press, 2010); Ardis

Butterfield, *The Familiar Enemy: Chaucer, Language, and Nation in the Hundred Years War* (Oxford: Oxford University Press, 2010); Jonathan Good, *The Cult of St George in Medieval England* (Woodbridge: Boydell Press, 2009).

4 Neil Murphy, "Henry VIII's First Invasion of France: The Gascon Expedition of 1512," *English Historical Review* 130, no. 542 (2015): 55.

5 Stephen Alford, *London's Triumph: Merchant Adventurers and the Tudor City* (London: Allen Lane, 2017).

6 Jessica S. Hower, "Under One (Inherited) Imperial Crown: The Tudor Origins of Britain and its Empire, 1603–1625," *Britain and the World*, 8, no. 2 (2015): 160–8.

7 John Prebble, *Darien: the Scottish Dream of Empire* (Edinburgh: Birlinn Ltd., 2000).

8 Lines 25–30. See, more generally, Philip Woodfine, *Britannia's Glories: The Walpole Ministry and the 1739 War with Spain* (Woodbridge: Royal Historical Society, 1998).

9 Carla Gardina Pestana, *The English Conquest of Jamaica: Cromwell's Bid for Empire* (Cambridge, MA: Belknap Press, 2017).

10 Andrew D. M. Beaumont, *Colonial America and the Earl of Halifax, 1748–1761* (Oxford: Oxford University Press, 2015).

11 For a different view, Brenda Simms, *Three Victories and a Defeat: The Rise and Fall of the First British Empire, 1714–1783* (London: Allen Lane, 2007).

12 Guy Arnold, *Held Fast for England: G.A. Henty, Imperialist Boys' Writer* (London: Hamish Hamilton, 1980).

13 Bernard Porter, *The Absent-Minded Imperialists: Empire, Society, and Culture in Britain* (Oxford: Oxford University Press, 2003); Catherine Hall and Sonya O. Rose, eds., *At Home With the Empire: Metropolitan Culture and the Imperial World* (Cambridge: Cambridge University Press, 2006); Brad Bevan, *Visions of Empire: Patriotism, Popular Culture and the City, 18709–1939* (Manchester: Manchester University Press, 2012).

14 *Julian Browning Autographs and Manuscripts*, catalogue 24 (2001), p. 7, item 55.

15 Paul Readman, "The Conservative Party, Patriotism and British Politics: The Case of the General Election of 1900," *Journal of British Studies* 40, no. 1 (2001): 107–45.

16 Andrew S. Thompson, *The Empire Strikes Back? The Impact of Imperialism on Britain from the Mid-Nineteenth Century* (Harlow: Routledge, 2005).

17 Dianne Lawrence, *Genteel Women: Empire and Domestic Material Culture, 1840–1970* (Manchester: Manchester University Press, 2012).

18 Christpher Frayling, *The Yellow Peril: Dr Fu Manchu and The Rise of Chinaphobia* (London: Thames and Hudson, 2014); Ruth Mayer, *Serial Fu Manchu: The Chinese Supervillain and the Spread of Yellow Peril Ideology* (Philadelphia: Temple University Press, 2014); Phil Baker and Anthony C. Clayton, eds., *Lord of Strange Deaths* (London, 2015).

19 Jesse Tumblin, "'Grey Dawn' in the British Pacific: Race, Security, and Colonial Sovereignty on the Eve of World War I," *Britain and the World* 9, no. 1 (2016): 32–54.

20 Erik Nielsen, *Sport and the British World, 1900–1930: Amateurism and National*

Identity in Australasia and Beyond (Basingstoke, UK: Palgrave Macmillan, 2014).

21 John M. MacKenzie, *Propaganda and Empire: the Manipulation of British Public Opinion, 1880–1960* (Manchester: Manchester University Press, 1984).

22 Andrekos Varnava, "European Subaltern War Asses: "Service" or "Employment" in the Cypriot Mule Corps During the Great War," *Britain and the World* 10, no. 1 (2017): 6–31.

23 Martin Thomas, *Empires of Intelligence: Security Services and Colonial Disorder after 1914* (Berkeley: University of California Press, 2008); Christopher Prior, *Exporting Empire: Africa, Colonial Officials and the Construction of the Imperial State, c. 1900–39* (Manchester: Manchester University Press, 2013); Robert S. G. Fletcher, *British Imperialism and the "Tribal Question": Desert Administration and Nomadic Societies in the Middle East, 1919–1936* (Oxford: Oxford University Press, 2015).

24 David Omissi, *Air Power and Colonial Control: The Royal Air Force, 1919–1939* (Manchester: Manchester University Press, 1990); Priya Satia, "The Defense of Inhumanity: Air Control in Iraq and the British Idea of Arabia," *American Historical Review* 111, no. 1 (2006): 16–51.

25 Antony Lentin, *The Last Political Law Lord: Lord Sumner, 1859–1934* (Cambridge: Cambridge University Press, 2009); and N. C. Fleming, "Diehard Conservatism, Mass Democracy, and Indian Constitutional Reform, c. 1918–35," *Parliamentary History* 32, no. 2 (2013): 33–60.

26 Jim English, "Empire Day in Britain, 1904–1948," *Historical Journal* 49 (2006): 247–76.

27 Gordon Pirie, *Cultures and Caricatures of British Imperial Aviation. Passengers, Pilots, Publicity* (Manchester: Manchester University Press, 2012).

28 John Griffiths, *Imperial Culture in Antipodean Cities, 1880–1939* (Basingstoke, UK: Palgrave Macmillan, 2014).

29 William Roger Louis, *In the Name of God, Go! Leo Amery and the British Empire in the Age of Churchill* (New York: W. W. Norton, 1992).

30 Kent Fedorowich, "Restocking the British World: Empire Migration and Anglo-Canadian Relations, 1919–30," *Britain and the World* 9, no. 2 (2016): 236–69.

31 Manolis Koumas, "Patterns of the Future? British Mediterranean Strategy and the Choice Between Alexandria and Cyprus 1935–8," *International History Review* 33, no. 3 (2011): 489–500.

32 Alayna Heinonen, "A Tonic to the Empire? The 1951 Festival of Britain and the Empire-Commonwealth," *Britain and the World* 8, no. 1 (2015): 76–99.

33 George Orwell, *Burmese Days* (London: 1934).

34 Reginald Coupland, ed., *The War Speeches of William Pitt the Younger* (Oxford, 1940).

35 Nicholas Owen, *The British Left and India: Metropolitan Anti-Imperialism 1885–1947* (Oxford: Oxford University Press, 2007).

36 Richard Toye, *Churchill's Empire: The World That Made Him and the World He Made* (New York: St. Martin's Press, 2010).

37 David Edgerton, *The Rise and Fall of the British Nation: A Twentieth-Century History* (London: Allen Lane, 2018), 187.

38 Steve Marsh, "Anglo-American Relations and the Labour Government's 'Scuttle' from Abadan: A 'Declaration of Dependence,'" *International History Review* 35, no. 4 (2013): 817–43.

39 Philip Ziegler, *Edward Heath* (London: HarperCollins, 2010), 107–8.

40 Leigh A. Gardner, *Taxing Colonial Africa: The Political Economy of British Imperialism* (Oxford: Oxford University Press, 2012).

41 Robert Holland, Susan Williams and Terry Barringer, eds., *The Iconography of Independence: 'Freedoms at Midnight'* (London: Routledge, 2010).

42 Mathias Haussler, "The Popular Press and Ideas of Europe: The *Daily Mirror*, the *Daily Express*, and Britain's First Application to Join the EEC, 1961–63," *Twentieth Century British History* 25, no. 1 (2014): 121; Robert Frank Dewey, *British National Identity and Opposition to Membership of Europe, 1961–63: The Anti-Marketeers* (Manchester: Manchester University Press, 2009).

43 Philip Williamson, "National Days of Prayer: The Churches, the State and Public Worship in Britain, 1899–1957," *English Historical Review* 128, no. 531 (2013): 363.

44 Udi Greenberg, "Protestants, Decolonization, and European Integration, 1885–1961," *Journal of Modern History* 89, no. 2 (2017): 314–54.

45 Judith M. Brown, "Epilogue," in *The Oxford History of the British Empire: Volume IV: The Twentieth Century*, eds. Judith M. Brown and WM. Roger Louis (Oxford: Oxford University Press, 1999), 707.

46 John Ramsden, *The Making of Conservative Party Policy* (New York: Longman, 1980), 177–8; Camilla Schofield, *Enoch Powell and the Making of Postcolonial Britain* (Cambridge: Cambridge University Press, 2013).

47 Julia Stapleton, *Sir Arthur Bryant and National History in Twentieth-Century Britain* (London: Lexington Books, 2005).

48 Jonathan Walker, *Aden Insurgency: The Savage War in South Arabia, 1962–67* (Staplehurst: Spellmount Publishers, 2005).

49 I have benefited from discussions with David Gladstone and Andrew Thorpe on this point.

50 Philip Murphy, *Monarchy and the End of Empire: The House of Windsor, the British Government, and the Postwar Commonwealth* (Oxford: Oxford University Press, 2013).

51 Robert Saunders, "The Many Lives of Margaret Thatcher," *English Historical Review* 132, no. 556 (2017): 657.

52 Andrew Novak, "Averting an African Boycott: British Prime Minister Edward Heath and Rhodesian Participation in the Munich Olympics," *Britain and the World* 6, no. 1 (2013): 30.

53 Richard Toye, "Churchill and the Empire," in *Winston Churchill: Politics, Strategy and Statecraft*, ed. Richard Toye (London: Bloomsbury Academic, 2017), p. 111.

54 Ian McEwan, *Solar* (London: Anchor Books, 2010; 2011 edn.), 110–11.

55 Ibid., 122.

56 Bill Schwarz, *The White Man's World* (Oxford: Oxford University Press, 2011), 264–6.

CHAPTER 10 — CONCLUSIONS

1   *Times*, April 15, 1905. See, more generally, Richard Toye, *Churchill's Empire: The World That Made Him and the World He Made* (London: Bloomsbury Academic, 2017).

2   James Beattie, Edward Melillo and Emily O'Gorman, eds., *Eco-Cultural Networks and the British Empire: New Views on Environmental History* (London: Bloomsbury Academic, 2015).

3   I have benefited from discussing this point with Dean Russell, who contested Luton North and Luton South in the 2015 and 2017 elections, respectively.

4   Jeremy Black, *English Nationalism: A Short History* (London: Hurst Publishers, 2018).

5   Anindta Ghosh, *Claiming the City: Protest, Crime, and Scandals in Colonial Calcutta, c. 1860–1920* (New York: Oxford University Press, 2016).

6   Israel Gershoni and James Jankowski, *Commemorating the Nation: Collective Memory, Public Commemoration, and National Identity in Twentieth-Century Egypt* (Chicago: Middle East Documentation Center, 2004).

7   Anon., *Observations on the Conduct of the Late Administration* (London, 1757), 13.

INDEX